2018

AF861878

103
Investment Planning

KAPLAN®

103 INVESTMENT PLANNING TEXTBOOK 2018

Published by Kaplan Financial Education

Printed in the United States of America.

ISBN: 978-1-4754-6302-6

Contents

Introduction

In this course, students consider the following broad concepts:

- Types of investment vehicles, including cash and cash equivalents, debt, and equities
- Alternative investments
- Derivatives
- Measures of investment risk and returns (quantitative investment concepts)
- Portfolio management theory
- Bond and stock valuation
- Asset allocation
- Investment strategies
- Portfolio development

LEARNING OBJECTIVES

Throughout this course you will see many learning objectives (LO) that emphasize the knowledge and application skills you will gain from this course. These specific statements, based on CFP Board's Principal Topics List, advise you what you should know and be able to do at the completion of this course.

On the following pages is a list of the CFP® Certification Principal Topics; eight of these topics are covered in this course. These eight topics are highlighted in the topic list. In the following pages you will also find a list of the CFP® Certification Job Task Domains. Each question on the CFP® Certification Examination will be associated with one of these domains.

CERTIFIED FINANCIAL PLANNER
BOARD OF STANDARDS, INC.

CFP® Certification Examination Principal Topics

The following Principal Topics are based on the results of CFP Board's 2009 Job Analysis Study and serve as a curricular framework.

General Principles of Financial Planning

- Financial planning process
- Financial statements
- Cash flow management
- Financing strategies
- Function, purpose, and regulation of financial institutions
- Education planning
- Financial planning for special circumstances
- Economic concepts
- Time value of money concepts and calculations
- Financial services regulations and requirements
- Business law
- Consumer protection laws

Insurance Planning

- Principles of risk and insurance
- Analysis and evaluation of risk exposures
- Health insurance and health care cost management (individual)
- Disability income insurance (individual)
- Long-term care insurance (individual)
- Annuities
- Life insurance (individual)
- Income taxation of life insurance
- Business uses of insurance
- Insurance needs analysis
- Insurance policy and company selection

Investment Planning

- Characteristics, uses and taxation of investment vehicles
- Types of investment risk
- Quantitative investment concepts
- Measures of investment returns
- Asset allocation and portfolio diversification
- Bond and stock valuation concepts
- Portfolio development and analysis
- Investment strategies

Income Tax Planning

- Income tax law fundamentals
- Tax compliance
- Income tax fundamentals and calculations
- Characteristics and income taxation of business entities
- Income taxation of trusts and estates
- Basis
- Tax consequences of the disposition of property
- Alternative minimum tax (AMT)
- Tax reduction/management techniques
- Passive activity and at-risk rules
- Tax implications of special circumstances
- Charitable contributions and deductions

2

Retirement Planning

- Retirement needs analysis
- Social Security (Old Age, Survivor, and Disability Insurance, OASDI)
- Types of retirement plans
- Qualified plan rules and options
- Other tax-advantaged retirement plans
- Regulatory considerations
- Key factors affecting plan selection for businesses
- Investment considerations for retirement plans
- Distribution rules, alternatives, and taxation

Estate Planning

- Characteristics and consequences of property titling
- Methods of property transfer at death
- Estate planning documents
- Gifting strategies
- Gift tax compliance and tax calculation
- Incapacity planning
- Estate tax compliance and tax calculation
- Sources for estate liquidity
- Powers of appointment
- Types, features, and taxation of trusts
- Qualified interest trusts
- Charitable transfers
- Use of life insurance in estate planning
- Marital deduction
- Intra-family and other business transfer techniques
- Deferral and minimization of estate taxes
- Generation-skipping transfer tax (GSTT)
- Fiduciaries
- Income in respect of a decedent (IRD)
- Postmortem estate planning techniques
- Estate planning for non-traditional relationships

Interpersonal Communication

- Client and planner attitudes, values, biases and behavioral characteristics and the impact on financial planning
- Principles of communication and counseling

Professional Conduct and Fiduciary Responsibility

- CFP Board's *Code of Ethics and Professional Responsibility* and *Rules of Conduct*
- CFP Board's *Financial Planning Practice Standards*
- CFP Board's *Disciplinary Rules and Procedures*

CERTIFIED FINANCIAL PLANNER
BOARD OF STANDARDS, INC.

CFP® Certification Examination
Job Task Domains

The following Job Task Domains are based on the results of CFP Board's 2009 Job Analysis Study and will serve as the blueprint for the March 2012 and later administrations of the CFP® Certification Examination. Each exam question will be linked to one of the following domains, in the approximate percentages indicated following the general headings.

Targeted First Test Administration: March 2012

8 Major Domains:

1. Establishing and Defining the Client-Planner Relationship (8%)
2. Gathering Information Necessary to Fulfill the Engagement (9%)
3. Analyzing and Evaluating the Client's Current Financial Status (25%)
4. Developing the Recommendation(s) (25%)
5. Communicating the Recommendation(s) (9%)
6. Implementing the Recommendation(s) (9%)
7. Monitoring the Recommendation(s) (5%)
8. Practicing within Professional and Regulatory Standards (10%)

2

Domain 1 - Establishing and Defining the Client-Planner Relationship (8%)

A. Identify the client (e.g., individual, family, business, organization)
B. Discuss financial planning needs and expectations of the client
C. Discuss the financial planning process with the client
D. Explain scope of services offered by the CFP® professional and his/her firm
E. Assess and communicate the CFP® professional's ability to meet the client's needs and expectations
F. Identify and resolve apparent and potential conflicts of interest in client relationships
G. Discuss the client's responsibilities and those of the CFP® professional
H. Define and document the scope of the engagement with the client
I. Provide client disclosures
  1. Regulatory disclosure
  2. Compensation arrangements and associated potential conflicts of interest

Domain 2 - Gathering Information Necessary to Fulfill the Engagement (9%)

A. Identify the client's values and attitudes
  1. Explore with the client their personal and financial needs, priorities and goals
  2. Explore the client's time horizon for each goal
  3. Assess the client's level of knowledge and experience with financial matters
  4. Assess the client's risk exposures (e.g., longevity, economic, liability, healthcare)
  5. Assess the client's risk tolerances (e.g., investment, economic, liability, healthcare)
B. Gather Data
  1. Summary of assets (e.g., cost basis information, beneficiary designations and titling)
  2. Summary of liabilities (e.g., balances, terms, interest rates). Summary of abilities (e.g., balances, terms, interest rates)
  3. Summary of income and expenses
  4. Estate planning documents
  5. Education plan and resources
  6. Retirement plan information
  7. Employee benefits
  8. Government benefits (e.g., Social Security, Medicare)
  9. Special circumstances (e.g., legal documents and agreements, family situations)
  10. Tax documents
  11. Investment statements
  12. Insurance policies and documents (e.g., life, health, disability, liability)
  13. Closely held business documents (e.g., shareholder agreements)
  14. Inheritances, windfalls, and other large lump sums
C. Recognize need for additional information

Domain 3 - Analyzing and Evaluating the Client's Current Financial Status (25%)

A. Evaluate and document the strengths and vulnerabilities of the client's current financial situation
  1. Financial status
    A. Statement of financial position/balance sheet
    B. Cash flow statement

3

C. Budget
D. Capital needs analysis (e.g., insurance, retirement, major purchases)

2. Risk management and insurance evaluation
   A. Insurance coverage
   B. Retained risks
   C. Asset protection (e.g., titling, trusts, business form)
   D. Client liquidity (e.g., emergency fund)
3. Benefits evaluation
   A. Government benefits (e.g., Social Security, Medicare)
   B. Employee benefits
4. Investment evaluation
   A. Asset allocation
   B. Investment strategies
   C. Investment types
5. Tax evaluation
   A. Current, deferred and future tax liabilities
   B. Income types
   C. Special situations (e.g., stock options, international tax issues)
6. Retirement evaluation
   A. Retirement plans and strategies (e.g., pension options, annuitization)
   B. Accumulation planning
   C. Distribution planning
7. Estate planning evaluation
   A. Estate documents
   B. Estate tax liabilities
   C. Ownership of assets
   D. Beneficiary designations
   E. Gifting strategies
8. Business ownership
   A. Business form
   B. Employer benefits
   C. Succession planning and exit strategy
   D. Risk management
9. Education planning evaluation
   A. Sources of financing
   B. Tax considerations
10. Other considerations
   A. Special circumstances (e.g., divorce, disabilities, family dynamics)
   B. Inheritances, windfalls, and other large lump sums
   C. Charitable planning
   D. Eldercare (e.g., CCRCs, LTC, Nursing Home)

B. Identify and use appropriate tools and techniques to conduct analyses (e.g., financial calculators, financial planning software, simulators, research services)

4

Domain 4 - Developing the Recommendation(s) (25%)

A. Synthesize findings from analysis of client's financial status
B. Consider alternatives to meet the client's goals and objectives
    1. Conduct scenario analysis (e.g., changing lifestyle variables)
    2. Conduct sensitivity analysis (e.g., changing assumptions such as inflation rate, rates of return, time horizon)
C. Consult with other professionals on technical issues outside of planner's expertise
D. Develop recommendations
    1. Considering client attitudes, values and beliefs
    2. Considering behavioral finance issues (e.g., anchoring, overconfidence, recency)
    3. Consider interrelationships among financial planning recommendations
E. Document recommendations

Domain 5 - Communicating the Recommendation(s) (9%)

A. Present financial plan to the client and provide education
    1. Client goals review
    2. Assumptions
    3. Observations and findings
    4. Alternatives
    5. Recommendations
B. Obtain feedback from the client and revise the recommendations as appropriate
C. Provide documentation of plan recommendations and any applicable product disclosures to client
D. Verify client acceptance of recommendations

Domain 6 - Implementing the Recommendation(s) (9%)

A. Create a prioritized implementation plan with timeline
B. Assign responsibilities (e.g., CFP® professional, client, other professional(s))
C. Support the client directly or indirectly with implementation of the recommendation(s)
D. Coordinate and share information, as authorized, with others
E. Define monitoring responsibilities with the client (e.g., explain what will be monitored, frequency of monitoring, communication method(s)

Domain 7 - Monitoring the Recommendation(s) (5%)

A. Discuss and evaluate changes in the client's personal circumstances (e.g., aging issues, change in employment)
B. Review the performance and progress of the plan with the client
C. Review and evaluate changes in the legal, tax and economic environments
D. Make recommendations to accommodate changed circumstances
E. Review scope of work and redefine engagement as appropriate
F. Provide client ongoing support (e.g., counseling, education)

5

Domain 8 - Practicing within Professional and Regulatory Standards (10%)

A. Adhere to CFP Board's *Code of Ethics and Professional Responsibility* and *Rules of Conduct*
B. Understand CFP Board's *Disciplinary Rules and Procedures*
C. Work within CFP Board's *Financial Planning Practice Standards*
D. Manage practice risk (e.g., documentation, monitor client noncompliance with recommendation(s)
E. Maintain awareness of and comply with regulatory and legal guidelines

CFP® Certification Examination Principal Topics E. Investment Planning

Principal Topic	Unit		Kaplan Schweser Learning Objective
E.33. Characteristics, Uses, and Taxation of Investment Vehicles	Unit 1	E.33.1	Describe the uses and taxation of cash and cash equivalents.
		E.33.2	Explain the characteristics of certificates of deposits, passbook savings accounts, and money market deposit accounts.
		E.33.3	Explain the features of a credit union.
		E.33.4	State the characteristics of a money market mutual fund.
		E.33.5	Explain the characteristics of U.S. Treasury bills.
		E.33.6	Describe the characteristics of commercial paper.
		E.33.7	Explain repurchase agreements and reverse repurchase agreements.
		E.33.8	Define banker's acceptances.
		E.33.9	Describe the attributes of eurodollars.
	Unit 2	E.33.10	Define the key terms and features of bonds.
		E.33.11	Define each bond type.
		E.33.12	Describe zero-coupon bonds.
		E.33.13	Discuss the types of U.S. government securities.
		E.33.14	Explain the types of U.S. government agency securities.
		E.33.15	Identify the advantages and disadvantages of municipal bonds.
		E.33.16	Discuss corporate and convertible bonds.
		E.33.17	List the risks associated with foreign bonds.
		E.33.18	Explain the characteristics of a promissory note.
	Unit 3	E.33.19	Discuss the differences between equity and debt securities.
		E.33.20	Discuss the characteristics and types of common stock and the payment of dividends.
		E.33.21	Explain the characteristics and primary purchasers of preferred stock.
		E.33.22	Analyze a stock dividend.
		E.33.23	Describe a rights offering.
		E.33.24	Discuss the use of warrants.
		E.33.25	Explain the benefits and methods of international investing.
		E.33.26	Describe the types, features, and taxation of open-end investment companies (mutual funds).
		E.33.27	Discuss the features of closed-end investment companies and how they differ from open-end investment companies.
		E.33.28	Explain the attributes of a unit investment trust (UIT) and provide reasons for purchasing this investment vehicle.
		E.33.29	Describe the characteristics and advantages of exchange-traded funds (ETFs).
		E.33.30	Identify the similarities and differences among the types of investment companies.
		E.33.31	Describe the benefits of a separately managed account.

	Unit 4	E.33.32	Define a guaranteed investment contract and identify its major purchasers.
		E.33.33	Discuss the types, valuation, and taxation of options.
	Unit 3	E.33.34	Explain how investors' tax obligations are impacted by capital gains and losses, dividends, and wash sales.
		E.33.35	Evaluate a stock split.
E.34. Types of Investment Risk	Unit 5	E.34.1	Discuss investment risk and diversification.
		E.34.2	Define and give examples of unsystematic and systematic risk.
	Unit 2	E.34.3	Explain the unique investment risks facing bondholders and how bond ratings affect bond yields.
E.35. Quantitative Investment Concepts	Unit 5	E.35.1	Explain how sensitivity analysis is used to evaluate an investment.
		E.35.2	Discuss the relationship between covariance and the correlation coefficient and their importance to portfolio construction and management.
		E.35.3	Explain the use of the coefficient of determination in portfolio evaluation.
	Unit 7	E.35.4	Explain the coefficient of variation and how it is used as a measure of total risk.
	Unit 5	E.35.5	Define and calculate the standard deviation of a single asset.
		E.35.6	Explain beta and weighted beta and how they are applied to the construction of an investment portfolio.
		E.35.7	Define the use of semivariance when addressing returns associated with an investment portfolio.
		E.35.8	Calculate the standard deviation of a two-asset portfolio.
		E.35.9	Evaluate and interpret probability distributions and statistical measures such as z-statistic, skewness, and kurtosis.
		E.35.10	Explain the use of stochastic modeling in projecting future portfolio performance.
		E.35.11	Explain and calculate expected return.
	Unit 7	E.35.12	Discuss capital market theory, the capital market line, the capital asset pricing model (CAPM), and the security market line.
		E.35.13	Explain the application of the arbitrage pricing theory.
E.36. Measures of Investment Returns	Unit 6	E.36.1	Contrast and calculate simple and compound rate of return.
		E.36.2	Explain arithmetic and geometric mean.
		E.36.3	Compare and contrast time-weighted and dollar-weighted returns.
		E.36.4	Calculate and interpret both the nominal and real rate of return for an investment asset.
		E.36.5	Define and calculate the various rates of returns dealing with stocks and mutual funds including total return, SEC yield, and holding period return.
		E.36.6	Define and calculate the returns dealing with bonds including current yield, yield to maturity, yield to call, and taxable equivalent yield.
		E.36.7	Calculate annual percentage rate and effective annual rate.

	Unit 7	E.36.8	Discuss, calculate, and evaluate the common types of performance measures including Jensen's alpha, the Sharpe ratio, the Treynor ratio, and the information ratio.
		E.36.9	Define and calculate risk-adjusted return.
E.37. Asset Allocation and Portfolio Diversification	Unit 7	E.37.1	Explain the assumptions of modern portfolio theory including the development of indifference curves and the efficient frontier.
		E.37.2	Define the efficient market hypothesis, discuss its three forms, and provide examples of anomalies.
	Unit 10	E.37.3	Explain how investors use strategic asset allocation to meet their investment objectives.
		E.37.4	Discuss the objectives of tactical asset allocation as an investment strategy.
		E.37.5	Discuss asset allocation and model portfolios.
E.38. Bond and Stock Valuation Concepts	Unit 8	E.38.1	Determine the intrinsic value of a bond.
		E.38.2	Explain the prevalent theories used to explain various yield curves.
		E.38.3	Describe the relationship between interest rates and bond prices.
	Unit 9	E.38.4	Define and interpret the discounted earnings method of stock valuation.
		E.38.5	Determine the intrinsic value of a stock using the constant growth dividend discount model, the multistage growth dividend discount model, the no-growth dividend discount model, and the discounted free cash flow model.
		E.38.6	Define, calculate, and analyze the price-to-earnings ratio, price-to-earnings divided by growth ratio, price-to-free-cash-flow ratio, and price-to-sales ratio to determine if a security warrants a purchase.
		E.38.7	Determine and analyze a company's book value.
		E.38.8	Explain the difference between a stock's par value, market value, and intrinsic value.
		E.38.9	Describe corporate/business accounting practices.
		E.38.10	Differentiate between fundamental and technical analysis.
E.39. Portfolio Development and Analysis	Unit 8	E.39.1	Define duration and explain its relationship to coupon rate, yield to maturity, and term of the bond.
		E.39.2	Explain convexity and its relationship to coupon rate, yield to maturity, and term of the bond.
		E.39.3	Calculate the estimated change in the price of a bond given its present value, duration, and change in yield to maturity.
	Unit 10	E.39.4	Discuss the importance of an investment policy statement as an integral part of the overall financial planning process.
	Unit 7	E.39.5	List the various security market indexes and averages and how they are used to compare actual investment performance to a benchmark.
		E.39.6	Explain the role of each of the security markets.
E.40. Investment Strategies	Unit 10	E.40.1	Differentiate between the types of orders investors use when either buying or selling securities.
	Unit 8	E.40.2	Discuss bond portfolio immunization.

	Unit 10	E.40.3	Explain and apply investment strategies such as market timing, indexing, buy-and-hold, and sector rotation.
		E.40.4	Evaluate the use of bond swaps.
		E.40.5	Discuss the types of formula investing including dollar cost averaging; share averaging/averaging down; dividend reinvestment plans; and bond ladders, barbells, and bullets.
		E.40.6	Explain the use of margin and when an investor would be subject to a margin call.
		E.40.7	Explain and apply short selling techniques.
	Unit 4	E.40.8	Describe hedging, protective puts, and zero-cost collars.
	Unit 10	E.40.9	Discuss the strategies investors use to manage a concentrated portfolio.
		E.40.10	Compare and contrast value and growth investing.
		E.40.11	Describe the core and satellite investment strategy.
E.41. Alternative Investments	Unit 3	E.41.1	Explain the distinguishing features of hedge funds and how they differ from investment company offerings.
		E.41.2	Cite the various uses of venture capital.
		E.41.3	Discuss why a company would use a private placement to generate capital.
		E.41.4	Discuss the advantages and disadvantages of limited partnerships.
	Unit 4	E.41.5	Explain the types, valuation, and taxation of real estate investments.
		E.41.6	Describe differences between real estate limited partnerships and real estate investment trusts.
		E.41.7	Define real estate mortgage investment conduits (REMICs) and collateralized mortgage obligations (CMOs).
		E.41.8	Describe the characteristics, uses, and taxation of futures.
		E.41.9	Describe the characteristics of tangible assets.
		E.41.10	Explain the characteristics of natural resources.

(The formula sheet below was current at press time. Please refer to **http://www.cfp.net/become-a-cfp-professional/cfp-certification-requirements/applications-resources** for any subsequent updates to the formula sheet.)

APPENDIX F: PROVIDED FORMULAS

Provided Formulas

These formulas are available to exam candidates when taking the CFP® Certification Examination:

$$V = \frac{D_1}{r-g}$$

$$r = \frac{D_1}{P} + g$$

$$COV_{ij} = \rho_{ij}\sigma_i\sigma_j$$

$$\sigma_p = \sqrt{W_i^2\sigma_i^2 + W_j^2\sigma_j^2 + 2W_iW_jCOV_{ij}}$$

$$\beta_i = \frac{COV_{im}}{\sigma_m^2} = \frac{\rho_{im}\sigma_i}{\sigma_m}$$

$$\sigma_r = \sqrt{\frac{\sum_{t=1}^{n}(r_t - \bar{r})^2}{n}}$$

$$S_r = \sqrt{\frac{\sum_{t=1}^{n}(r_t - \bar{r})^2}{n-1}}$$

$$r_i = r_f + (r_m - r_f)\beta_i$$

$$\alpha_p = \bar{r}_p - \left[\bar{r}_f + \left(\bar{r}_m - \bar{r}_f\right)\beta_p\right]$$

$$T_p = \frac{\bar{r}_p - \bar{r}_f}{\beta_p}$$

$$D = \frac{1+y}{y} - \frac{(1+y)+t(c-y)}{c\left[(1+y)^t - 1\right]+y}$$

$$\frac{\Delta P}{P} = -D\left[\frac{\Delta y}{1+y}\right]$$

$$IR = \frac{R_P - R_B}{\sigma_A}$$

$$EAR = (1 + \frac{i}{n})^n - 1$$

$$\text{TEY} = \text{r}/(1\text{-t})$$

$$AM = \frac{a_1 + a_2 + a_3 + \cdots + a_n}{n}$$

$$S_p = \frac{\bar{r}_p - \bar{r}_f}{\sigma_p}$$

$${}_1R_N = [(1+{}_1R_1)\,(1+E({}_2r_1))\ldots(1+E({}_Nr_1))]^{1/N} - 1$$

$$HPR = [(1+r_1) \text{ x } (1+r_2) \text{ x } \ldots(1+r_n)] - 1$$

$$\sqrt[n]{(1+r_1) \times (1+r_2) \times \ldots (1+r_n)} - 1$$

CFP Board Investment Formulas with Titles and Explanations

Constant Growth Dividend Discount Model (Gordon Model)

$$V = \frac{D_1}{r - g}$$

Expected Return Form of Dividend Discount Model

$$r = \frac{D_1}{P} + g$$

Covariance Between Two Sample Assets

$$COV_{ij} = \rho_{ij}\sigma_i\sigma_j$$

Standard Deviation of a Two-Asset Portfolio

$$\sigma_p = \sqrt{W_i^2\sigma_i^2 + W_j^2\sigma_j^2 + 2\,W_i\,W_j\,COV_{ij}}$$

Beta Coefficient of Sample Asset

$$\beta_i = \frac{COV_{im}}{\sigma_m^2} = \frac{\rho_{im}\sigma_i}{\sigma_m}$$

Population Standard Deviation of a Single Asset

$$\sigma_r = \sqrt{\frac{\sum_{t=1}^{n}\left(r_t - \bar{r}\right)^2}{n}}$$

Sample Standard Deviation of a Single Asset

$$S_r = \sqrt{\frac{\sum_{t=1}^{n}\left(r_t - \bar{r}\right)^2}{n-1}}$$

Arithmetic Mean

$$AM = \frac{a_1 + a_2 + a_3 + \ldots + a_n}{n}$$

Unbiased Expectations Theory

$${}_1R_N\left[(1 + {}_1R_1)(1 + E({}_2r_1))\ldots(1 + E({}_Nr_1))\right]^{1/N} - 1$$

Geometric Mean

$$\sqrt[n]{(1+r_1)\times(1+r_2)\times(1+r_3)\times\ldots(1+r_n)} - 1$$

Capital Asset Pricing Model

$$r_i = r_f + \left(r_m - r_f\right)\beta_i$$

Taxable Equivalent Yield

$$TEY = \frac{r}{(1-t)}$$

Sharpe Ratio

$$S_p = \frac{\bar{r}_p - \bar{r}_f}{\sigma_p}$$

Jensen's Alpha

$$\alpha_p = \bar{r}_p - \left[\bar{r}_f + \left(\bar{r}_m - \bar{r}_f\right)\beta_p\right]$$

Treynor Ratio

$$T_p = \frac{\bar{r}_p - \bar{r}_f}{\beta_p}$$

Effective Annual Rate of Return

$$EAR = (1 + \frac{i}{n})^n - 1$$

Macaulay Duration/Duration

$$D = \frac{1+y}{y} - \frac{(1+y) + t(c-y)}{c\left[(1+y)^t - 1\right] + y}$$

Estimated Change in Price of a Bond

$$\frac{\Delta P}{P} = -D\left[\frac{\Delta y}{1+y}\right]$$

Information Ratio

$$IR = \frac{R_P - R_B}{\sigma_A}$$

Holding Period Return

$$HPR = \left[(1+r_1)\times(1+r_2)\times\ldots(1+r_n)\right] - 1$$

Definitions of variables and symbols used in CFP Board formula page:

V = Intrinsic Value of Stock as used in Constant Growth Dividend Discount Model

D_1 = Next Year's Dividend payable by Stock in Constant Growth Dividend Discount Model

r = Required Rate of Return in Constant Growth Dividend Discount Model; also used to mean Expected Rate of Return in Expected Return Form of Dividend Discount Model

g = Growth Rate of Dividends in Constant Growth Dividend Discount Model

P = Purchase Price of Targeted Stock using Expected Return Form of Dividend Discount Model

COV_{ij} or COV_{im} = Covariance between Two Sample Assets ($_{ij}$) or Covariance between One Sample Asset and Market or Market Index ($_{im}$)

ρ_{ij} or ρ_{im} = Correlation Coefficient between Two Sample Assets ($_{ij}$) or Correlation Coefficient between One Sample Index and Market or Market Index ($_{im}$)

σ_i = Standard Deviation of First Sample Asset

σ_j = Standard Deviation of Second Sample Asset

σ_p = Standard Deviation of a Portfolio

W_i = Weighting Percentage of First Sample Asset in Standard Deviation of a Portfolio Formula

W_j = Weighting Percentage of Second Sample Asset in Standard Deviation of a Portfolio Formula

2 = Number of Sample Assets in Standard Deviation of a Portfolio Formula

r_m = Market Rate of Return in Capital Asset Pricing Model

β_i = Beta Coefficient of Sample Stock or Asset in Capital Asset Pricing Model

r_p = Portfolio Rate of Return in Capital Market Line Theory, Sharpe Ratio, Jensen's Alpha, and Treynor Ratio

S_p = Sharpe Ratio

α_p = Jensen's Alpha

β_p = Beta Coefficient of Sample Portfolio in Jensen's Alpha and Treynor Ratio

T_p = Treynor Ratio

D = Macaulay Duration

ΔP = Change in Bond Price given a respective change in market interest rates (Δy)

σ_m = Standard Deviation of Market or Market Line

σ_r = Population Standard Deviation of a Single Asset

Σ = Greek Sigma meaning multiple number (n) of actual returns

r = Average or Mean return among multiple number of actual returns (in standard deviation formulas)

s_r = Sample Standard Deviation of Single Asset

y = Yield to Maturity

t = Term to Maturity

c = Coupon Rate

r_i = Required Rate of Return in Capital Asset Pricing Model

r_f = Risk-Free Rate of Return in Capital Asset Pricing Model, Capital Market Line Theory, Sharpe Ratio, Jensen's Alpha, and Treynor Ratio

EAR = Effective Annual Return

TEY = Taxable Equivalent Yield

t = Tax Rate (as a decimal) in TEY Calculation

AM = Arithmetic Mean

a = Rate of Return for a Given Period

${}_1R_N$ = Rate of Return for Period N

N = Number of Periods

${}_1R_1$ = Interest Rate for Period 1

$E({}_1r_1)$ = Expected Interest Rate for Period 2

$E({}_Nr_1)$ = Expected Interest Rate for Given Period

HPR = Holding Period Return

Cash and Cash Equivalents

REFER TO

CFP Board Principal Knowledge Topics – E. Investment Planning, E.33. Characteristics, Uses, and Taxation of Investment Vehicles

INTRODUCTION

This unit presents cash and cash equivalents, which include certificates of deposit (CDs), U.S. Treasury bills, and commercial paper. All of the short-term investment vehicles discussed here are part of the money market (as opposed to the capital market) and are characterized by the short-term nature of the investor's time horizon and relative liquidity of these particular investments. The level of liquidity also provides some understanding of the risk of the investment; generally, the more liquid an investment, the less its investment risk. Cash, of course, is the most liquid investment in the money market.

LEARNING OBJECTIVES

After completing this unit, you should be able to achieve the following learning objectives:

CFP® Board Principal Knowledge Topics – E. Investment Planning

E.33. Characteristics, Uses, and Taxation of Investment Vehicles

- LO E.33.1 Describe the uses and taxation of cash and cash equivalents.
- LO E.33.2 Explain the characteristics of certificates of deposits, passbook savings accounts, and money market deposit accounts.
- LO E.33.3 Explain the features of a credit union.
- LO E.33.4 State the characteristics of a money market mutual fund.
- LO E.33.5 Explain the characteristics of U.S. Treasury bills.
- LO E.33.6 Describe the characteristics of commercial paper.
- LO E.33.7 Explain repurchase agreements and reverse repurchase agreements.
- LO E.33.8 Define banker's acceptances.
- LO E.33.9 Describe the attributes of eurodollars.

KEY TERMS

Banker's acceptances
Cash
Certificates of deposit (CDs)
Commercial paper
Credit unions
Eurodollars
Eurodolllar CD
Liquidity
Marketability
Money market deposit accounts (MMDAs)
Money market mutual funds
Negotiable CDs
Passbook savings account
Repo rate
Repurchase agreements
Reverse repurchase agreements
U.S. Treasury bills

A. CASH AND CASH EQUIVALENTS

LO E.33.1 Describe the uses and taxation of cash and cash equivalents.

Most individuals believe that they have a clear understanding of what is meant by the term *cash*. In financial planning, **cash** has a very specific meaning and refers to cash equivalents and bank instruments of deposit that have a high level of liquidity. **Liquidity** is the ability to sell or redeem an investment quickly and at a known price, without a significant loss of principal. Liquidity may be compared with **marketability**, which is the ability to sell an investment quickly in a readily identifiable market (i.e., no consideration of whether a corresponding loss of principal occurs at the time of sale). Cash and cash equivalents are generally characterized by both their relative liquidity and marketability; however, just because a cash equivalent is liquid does not necessarily mean it is marketable. For example, a money market deposit account is liquid, but not marketable. Rather, such an account is only redeemable—that is, there is no market beyond the issuer of the obligation, which is the bank in this case. Alternatively, a U.S. Treasury bill is both liquid and marketable. Accordingly, whenever cash and cash equivalents (and investments generally) are discussed in the financial planning process, the financial planner should understand the difference between liquidity and marketability and that one does not necessarily lead to the other.

All individuals need some cash and cash equivalents, if for no other reason than to pay for current expenses. However, some individuals tend to have too much cash, which leads them to incur a great deal of purchasing power risk. One of the financial mistakes that retirees make is to position too much of their investment portfolios in cash and cash equivalents, only to find a few years later, their ability to buy life's necessities has been eroded by inflation. Indeed, the financial planner should remember that one of the biggest risks to a senior's income is not the loss of an investment's principal but, rather, the loss of an investment's purchasing power.

The income taxation of cash and cash equivalents essentially follows the normal rule that taxation on disposition of these assets is eligible for capital gains treatment (and the limitation on capital losses), whereas interest paid is taxed as ordinary income. However, because these investments are usually held short term (and primarily for income-generating purposes), the capital gains element is not often triggered.

PRACTICE QUESTION

Choose the best answer for the question below.
The answer can be found at the end of this unit.

1. Which of the following assets are liquid but NOT marketable?
- A. Personal residence
- B. Personal checking account
- C. U.S. Treasury bills
- D. Stock in a privately owned corporation

B. BANK OBLIGATIONS

LO E.33.2 Explain the characteristics of certificates of deposits, passbook savings accounts, and money market deposit accounts.

Certificates of Deposit (CDs)

Certificates of deposit (CDs), also known as time deposits, are deposits made with a bank or savings and loan for a specified period, commonly one month to five years. CDs have traditionally been used to provide an income stream to retirees. Interest is subject to ordinary income tax in the year earned. The financial institution usually pays a fixed rate of interest for the term of the certificate, with rates increasing as the term gets longer. Usually, an investor who wants to redeem (i.e., liquidate) the CD before its stated maturity date must pay a penalty in the form of either a one-time fee or a lower overall interest rate and this penalty is deductible as an above-the-line deduction on the taxpayer's IRS Form 1040. Investors with relatively large amounts of money to invest should purchase multiple certificates with varying terms to maturity. This strategy, known as *laddering*, enables investors to more effectively manage the interest rate risk associated with a fixed income cash equivalent, such as a CD. CDs are FDIC insured, which is often a reason for investors' interest in purchasing CDs. The basic FDIC-insured amount is $250,000 per ownership category.

Negotiable CDs are deposits of $100,000 or more placed with commercial banks at a specified interest rate for a term of up to one year. Because of their large denominations, negotiable CDs are bought most often by institutional investors, including money market mutual funds. Unlike regular CDs, which are redeemable by the issuing bank, negotiable CDs are bought and sold in the secondary market at a market-determined price (i.e., an amount that is potentially different from the original principal invested).

PRACTICE QUESTION

Choose the best answer for the question below.
The answer can be found at the end of this unit.

2. Which of the following is a primary purchaser of negotiable CDs?

A. Institutional investor
B. Individual of modest means
C. Hedge fund
D. Highly risk-tolerant investor

Passbook Savings Account

A **passbook savings account** is established with a commercial bank or savings and loan and is a redeemable investment. The account usually has no minimum balance and features a penalty-free withdrawal of funds at any time. However, the account does not typically include a check-writing privilege and pays a relatively low rate of interest.

Money Market Deposit Accounts (MMDAs)

Some banks and savings and loans offer **money market deposit accounts (MMDAs)**. These accounts should not be confused with money market mutual funds, which are offered by open-end investment companies and are not federally insured. Rather, MMDAs are bank obligations and are federally insured, subject to the $250,000 per ownership category limit. As a result, MMDAs are very safe and highly liquid. In addition, although MMDAs require a minimum balance to be maintained, they offer limited check-writing privileges. Typically, six preauthorized withdrawals are permitted from the MMDA each month, up to three of which may be by personal check. Investors may use MMDAs as a temporary place to store money for future investments.

C. CREDIT UNIONS

LO E.33.3 Explain the features of a credit union.

Like banks, **credit unions** sponsor a number of financial products. Members of such institutions are provided with a convenient place to save and borrow, although membership may be restricted on the basis of employer or other association affiliation. Similar to bank loans, loans from credit unions are permitted for a number of purposes, including some commercial loans.

The National Credit Union Share Insurance Fund (NCUSIF), an agency of the federal government, regulates credit unions unless the institution is chartered by a state where separate regulation is provided. Like bank deposits, deposits in a credit union are insured up to $250,000 per qualifying account. Administered by the National Credit Union Administration, the NCUSIF is backed by the full faith and credit of the U.S. government. However, no federal tax dollars have been deposited into the fund. The NCUSIF is approximately 1.30% of federally insured credit union deposits.

D. MONEY MARKET MUTUAL FUNDS

LO E.33.4 State the characteristics of a money market mutual fund.

Open-end investment companies offer both taxable and tax-exempt **money market mutual funds**. These funds typically invest in high-quality, short-term investments, such as U.S. Treasury bills, commercial paper, and negotiable CDs. The investments within the fund usually mature within one year and have an average maturity of less than 60 days. The typical minimum investment is $1,000, and funds may be withdrawn from the account at any time without penalty by writing a check on the account (usually for a minimum amount). The rate of return on the fund is highly sensitive to changes in short-term interest rates, particularly the federal funds rate, or the overnight lending rate between banks that are members of the Federal Reserve System.

Money market mutual funds are used by investors as part of their emergency fund because the funds are extremely liquid. In addition, such funds serve as a short-term depository for investors in a managed (wrap) account who are waiting for a more appropriate time to invest in other securities.

PRACTICE QUESTION

Choose the best answer for the question below.
The answer can be found at the end of this unit.

3. Which of the following statements best describes money market mutual funds?

A. They allow up to six withdrawals per month and are insured by the FDIC.
B. They are an asset that provides a modest rate of return, diversification, and liquidity.
C. They are used primarily to finance imports and exports.
D. The average maturity date of the investments within these types of funds is 270 days.

E. U.S. TREASURY BILLS

LO E.33.5 Explain the characteristics of U.S. Treasury bills.

U.S. Treasury bills are short-term government securities. The U.S. Treasury regularly issues, by way of weekly auction (52-week T-bills are auctioned every four weeks), 4-, 13-, 26-, and 52-week Treasury bills (T-bills) in $100 increments with a $100 minimum purchase. Another type of Treasury bill, the cash management bill, is issued in variable terms, usually of only a matter of days. Cash management bills are not auctioned on a regular schedule. T-bills are purchased at a discount, which means they are sold at a price less than their par or face value. However, because T-bills have a maturity date of no more than one year, they are not subject to the original issue discount taxation rules that apply to other bonds. Interest income from the bill, which is not taxable until the bill matures, is taxed at ordinary federal income tax rates, but is not subject to state or local income tax. An investor holding the bill as of the date of maturity includes the amount of the discount as ordinary income. If an investor sells a T-bill before it reaches maturity, the difference between the sales price and the investor's original purchase price is taxable. Investors may use T-bills to diversify their portfolios and to participate in a secure, short-term investment.

Because of their lack of default risk and high degree of marketability, T-bills are often used as the proxy for a risk-free investment, an asset having the lowest level of risk among all available assets, in modern portfolio management theory (see Unit 7 of this course). Specifically, the 13-week (90-day) T-bill is cited as the risk-free rate (r_f) in various asset pricing models and performance measures because it is not sensitive to interest rates and inflation changes. The risk-free rate is used as a benchmark to measure the return of other assets. This rate represents the lowest level of return an investor expects to receive.

PRACTICE QUESTION

Choose the best answer for the question below.
The answer can be found at the end of this unit.

4. U.S. Treasury bills would be most appropriate for which of the following investors?

A. John, age 25, single, no dependents, aggressive risk tolerance, need for growth and speculation

B. Mary and Ed, ages 43 and 41, moderate risk takers, need for college funding in 8 years for their 10-year-old daughter, Megan

C. Jack and Krissy, ages 65 and 63, conservative risk tolerance, need for liquidity and safety of principal

D. Lucy, age 54, divorced, moderate to aggressive risk tolerance, need for retirement funding in 11 years, provides some financial support for her 78-year-old mother

F. COMMERCIAL PAPER (CORPORATE SHORT-TERM DEBT)

LO E.33.6 Describe the characteristics of commercial paper.

Commercial paper is a negotiable, short-term, unsecured promissory note issued by a large corporation to finance accounts receivable and inventories. This type of debt is usually issued in denominations of $100,000 or more and is a substitute for short-term bank financing. Money market mutual funds are the primary purchasers of commercial paper.

Commercial paper is normally sold at a discount and is rated by a rating service (such as Standard & Poor's) as to quality. The term to maturity is no more than 270 days, and is often backed by lines of credit from banks. Compared to Treasury bills, commercial paper is slightly less liquid and has a higher risk of default; therefore, it has a nominally higher yield. Commercial paper is taxed in a fashion similar to that used for other money market securities. The income is taxed to the investor at ordinary income rates when earned.

PRACTICE QUESTION

Choose the best answer for the question below.
The answer can be found at the end of this unit.

5. Why would an institutional investor choose to purchase commercial paper for a portfolio?

A. Commercial paper provides higher yields than U.S. Treasury bills.
B. Commercial paper offers tax-free interest payments.
C. Commercial paper is generally not rated as to quality.
D. Commercial paper is usually offered in denominations below $50,000.

G. REPURCHASE AGREEMENTS

LO E.33.7 Explain repurchase agreements and reverse repurchase agreements.

Dealers in government securities use **repurchase agreements**, or repos. To satisfy short-term liquidity needs, dealers will sell some of those securities to another dealer with an agreement to buy them back at a later date at an agreed-upon price. The buyer of the repurchase agreement then receives the equivalent of a fixed yield or return on the investment. Although it is legally a sale and subsequent purchase of securities, a repurchase agreement is essentially a collateralized loan, where the difference between the sale and repurchase prices is the interest on the loan. The rate of interest on the repo is called the **repo rate**. Similar to commercial paper, repurchase agreements are frequently found in money market mutual funds because they have an extremely short maturity and very low risk.

The opposite of the repo is the **reverse repurchase agreement** (or reverse repo). In a reverse repo, the dealer buys government securities from another dealer and then sells them back later at a higher price. Many central banks use repurchase agreements and reverse repurchase agreements in government debt as part of their open market operations.

PRACTICE QUESTION

Choose the best answer for the question below.
The answer can be found at the end of this unit.

6. In a repurchase agreement, the percentage difference between the repurchase price and the amount borrowed is most accurately described as

A. the haircut
B. the repo rate
C. the repo margin
D. the federal funds rate

H. BANKER'S ACCEPTANCES

LO E.33.8 Define banker's acceptances.

Banker's acceptances are short-term drafts drawn by a private company on a major bank used to finance imports and exports. They are typically traded at a discount from their face value in the secondary market. Companies that are too small to issue commercial paper sometimes use banker's acceptances to finance their short-term debt needs.

When using a banker's acceptance, the bank usually acts as an intermediary between the American company and the foreign company (i.e., the company furnishing or receiving the goods). For example, an American importer may request acceptance financing from its bank when the foreign company will not provide credit. As a result, the importer's bank agrees to pay the foreign supplier on behalf of the importer. The importer is then contractually obligated to repay the bank within three to six months. In turn, the importer's bank may sell the obligation at a discount to obtain immediate cash.

Banker's acceptances are analogous to a personal line of credit issued to a borrower by a financial institution. However, in the case of banker's acceptances, an unsecured line of credit is provided to a corporate or small business customer. They are taxable as ordinary income for federal and state income tax purposes.

PRACTICE QUESTION

Choose the best answer for the question below.
The answer can be found at the end of this unit.

7. Which of the following is the best reason that an import company would use banker's acceptances?
   A. When the company is seeking the use of a secured line of credit
   B. When the company is looking to raise long-term capital for a new product line
   C. When the company needs to finance international purchases
   D. When the company needs to provide collateral for a bond issue

I. EURODOLLARS

LO E.33.9 Describe the attributes of eurodollars.

Eurodollars are U.S. dollar-denominated deposits at banks outside the United States used to settle international transactions. The average deposit is very large (in the millions) and has a maturity of less than six months. Interest income is taxable to the owner as ordinary income when earned. A variation on the eurodollar time deposit is the **eurodollar CD** (or euro CD). This type of CD shares the same characteristics as its domestic counterpart except that the obligation is the liability of a non-U.S. bank. Accordingly, euro CDs are less liquid and, therefore, offer a slightly higher yield than domestic CDs. Generally, only the largest financial institutions invest in the eurodollar market. Individual investors may participate in the eurodollar market indirectly through the use of money market mutual funds.

PRACTICE QUESTION

Choose the best answer for the question below.
The answer can be found at the end of this unit.

8. Which of the following is NOT a characteristic of Eurodollars?
A. They are used to settle international transactions.
B. The average deposit is in the millions.
C. They have a maturity of greater than one year.
D. Interest income is taxable as ordinary income when earned.

103 UNIT 1 ANSWERS TO PRACTICE QUESTIONS

1. B. A personal checking account cannot be traded or sold and, therefore, is not marketable. The account can be turned into cash quickly without penalty. A personal residence and stock in a privately owned corporation are illiquid but marketable. U.S. Treasury bills are both liquid and marketable.

2. A. A large institutional investor is likely the primary purchaser of a negotiable CD. With a minimum denomination of $100,000, an individual of modest means probably could not afford its purchase, and a highly risk-tolerant investor or hedge fund is more interested in growth and a greater return on investment than that afforded by a negotiable CD.

3. B. A money market mutual fund is an asset that provides a modest rate of return, diversification, and liquidity. Unlike an MMDA, the fund is not insured by the FDIC. The average maturity date of the investments in the fund is usually less than 60 days. Banker's acceptances are used primarily to finance imports and exports.

4. C. Investors seeking diversification, liquidity, and safety of principal are the best candidates for U.S. Treasury bills. In this case, the best choice is Jack and Krissy.

5. A. Compared to U.S. Treasury bills, commercial paper is slightly less liquid and has a higher risk of default; therefore, it has a nominally higher yield. The interest paid on commercial paper is subject to income tax in the year earned. Commercial paper is rated by independent rating services as to quality and is offered in denominations generally in excess of $100,000.

6. B. The repo rate is the percentage difference between the repurchase price and the amount borrowed. The repo margin or haircut is the percentage difference between the amount borrowed and the value of the collateral.

7. C. Importers may turn to banker's acceptances to finance their international purchases. Banker's acceptances are similar to unsecured lines of credit and are not used as collateral for other loans or new product development.

8. C. Eurodollars have a maturity of less than six months.

103 UNIT 1 POST-STUDY CHECKLIST

- ☐ Can I explain the uses, taxation, and types of cash and cash equivalents?
- ☐ Am I able to describe the features of a credit union?
- ☐ Can I describe the characteristics of a money market mutual fund?
- ☐ Do I understand the characteristics of U.S. Treasury bills?
- ☐ Can I explain banker's acceptances?
- ☐ Can I describe the characteristics of commercial paper?
- ☐ Can I explain the uses of repurchase agreements and reverse repurchase agreements?
- ☐ Do I understand the attributes of eurodollars?

Am I able to define and understand the application of the following terms as they relate to investment planning?

- ☐ Banker's acceptances
- ☐ Cash
- ☐ Certificates of deposit (CDs)
- ☐ Commercial paper
- ☐ Credit unions
- ☐ Eurodollars
- ☐ Eurodollar CD
- ☐ Liquidity
- ☐ Marketability
- ☐ Money market deposit accounts (MMDAs)
- ☐ Money market mutual funds
- ☐ Negotiable CDs
- ☐ Passbook savings account
- ☐ Repo rate
- ☐ Repurchase agreements
- ☐ Reverse repurchase agreements
- ☐ U.S. Treasury bills

UNIT 2

Debt Investments

REFER TO

CFP Board Principal Knowledge Topics – E. Investment Planning, E.33. Characteristics, Uses, and Taxation of Investment Vehicles

CFP Board Principal Knowledge Topics – E. Investment Planning, E.34. Types of Investment Risk

INTRODUCTION

This unit considers the broad topic of debt obligations including corporate and individual debt. Bonds can be further categorized according to the issuer of the debt obligation. Specifically, these categories include:

- U.S. government or Treasury securities (e.g., Treasury notes and Treasury bonds);
- municipal obligations (e.g., general obligation bonds); and
- corporate debt (e.g., debentures).

In addition, government agencies issue debt obligations, some of which are directly backed (or guaranteed) by the U.S. government. Some of these agency obligations, particularly those involving mortgages, are also pooled, or collateralized, and made into asset-backed securities.

LEARNING OBJECTIVES

After completing this unit, you should be able to achieve the following learning objectives:

CFP® Board Principal Knowledge Topics – E. Investment Planning

E.33. Characteristics, Uses, and Taxation of Investment Vehicles

LO E.33.10 Define the key terms and features of bonds.

LO E.33.11 Define each bond type.

LO E.33.12 Describe zero-coupon bonds.

LO E.33.13 Discuss the types of U.S. government securities.

LO E.33.14 Explain the types of U.S. government agency securities.

LO E.33.15 Identify the advantages and disadvantages of municipal bonds.

LO E.33.16 Discuss corporate and convertible bonds.

LO E.33.17 List the risks associated with foreign bonds.

LO E.33.18 Explain the characteristics of a promissory note.

E.34. Types of Investment Risk

LO E.34.3 Explain the unique investment risks facing bondholders and how bond ratings affect bond yields.

KEY TERMS

After-tax yield
Basis point
Bond
Call provision
Collateral trust bond
Conversion price
Conversion ratio
Convertible bonds
Corporate bonds
Coupon rate
Currency risk
Debenture
Discount
Eurodollar bonds
Exchange rate risk
Federal Home Loan Mortgage Corporation (FHLMC)
Market discount bond
Market premium bond
Mortgage bond
Municipal bonds
Nominal yield
Original issue discount (OID)
Par value
Phantom income
Premium
Private activity (private purpose) bond
Promissory note
Qualified private activity bonds
Revenue bonds
Savings bonds
Secured bond
Subordinated debentures
Taxable equivalent yield (TEY)

Federal National Mortgage Association (FNMA)
General obligation bonds
Government National Mortgage Association (GNMA)
High-yield bond
Indenture
Investment grade bond
Treasury inflation-protected securities (TIPS)
Treasury STRIPS (Separate Trading of Registered Interest and Principal of Securities)
U.S. Treasury bonds
U.S. Treasury notes
Yankee bonds
Zero-coupon bonds

A. BOND TERMINOLOGY

LO E.33.10 Define the key terms and features of bonds.

A **bond** is a debt security, similar to an IOU, obligating the issuer (i.e., the federal government, a municipality, or a corporation) to make periodic interest (coupon) payments and to repay the principal at the time of maturity. Generally, a bond can be issued in one of three ways: registered form, bearer form, and book-entry form. If the bond is issued in registered form, payments will be made to the owner of record. If the bond is issued in bearer form, payments will be made to whoever holds or possesses the bond. Lastly, a bond held in book-entry form has its record of ownership held electronically in a central depository, allowing for greater efficiency in bond transactions.

The bond **indenture** is the formal agreement, or contract, between the issuer and the bondholder. The provisions in the bond indenture are known as the covenants and include both prohibitions on the borrower and actions the borrower promises to perform. Sometimes the indenture will include a *sinking fund*, which is a separate fund established and funded each year by the bond issuer designed to accumulate an amount required to pay off the debt at maturity. Such a fund is included to reduce the default risk associated with some bonds.

The **par value** (face value) of the bond is the amount of principal that the bond owner or holder will receive at time of maturity. For CFP® Exam purposes, this par value is assumed to be $1,000 unless stated otherwise.

The **coupon rate** or **nominal yield** of the bond is the stated annual interest rate that will be paid each period for the term of the bond and is stated as a percentage of the par value of the bond. For example, a $1,000 par value bond with a coupon rate of 4% will return an interest payment of $40 annually or $20 semiannually. For CFP® Exam purposes, coupon payments are made semiannually unless otherwise specified. Understand that the coupon rate of the bond never changes although the current yield of the bond will fluctuate on the basis of the direction and amount of change in market interest rates. A **basis point** is a measurement of bond's yield and is equal to 1/100 of 1% of yield. For example, a bond that increases in yield by 2% is said to increase by 200 basis points.

A bond is selling at a **discount** when its price in the secondary market is less than the bond's par value. Also, a bond can also be issued at a discount. This type of bond is known as an original issue discount (OID) bond. A bond is selling at a **premium** when its price in the secondary market is greater than the bond's par value.

A **call provision** included in the bond indenture allows the issuer to pay off the bond principal after a specified period, usually at a stipulated price higher than par value. The issuer is most likely to call the bond if market interest rates have declined, thereby making it possible for the issuer to refinance the bond issue with one that is paying a lower coupon rate.

B. BOND TYPES

LO E.33.11 Define each bond type.

A **secured bond**, such as a **mortgage bond** or **collateral trust bond**, pledges specific assets (e.g., real property or equipment) that may be sold by the bond purchaser in the event that the bond issuer defaults in paying either the interest or principal on the bond.

A **debenture** is a bond that promises payments of interest and principal but pledges no specific assets. In other words, a debenture is an unsecured bond. To account for the greater default risk, a debenture will have a higher yield than a secured bond issued for the same term by the same issuer.

An **investment grade bond** is a bond that is rated BBB– or higher by the Standard & Poor's rating service; generally, it is a high quality bond with little risk of default by the issuer.

A **high-yield bond** (sometimes referred to as a junk bond) is a bond that is rated BB+ or lower by the Standard & Poor's rating service; generally, a lower quality bond with a higher risk of default by the issuer.

PRACTICE QUESTION

Choose the best answer for the question below.
The answer can be found at the end of this unit.

1. Which type of bond is typically collateralized by the issuer?
   A. High-yield
   B. Mortgage
   C. Zero-coupon
   D. Debenture

C. BOND RISKS AND RATINGS

LO E.34.3 Explain the unique investment risks facing bondholders and how bond ratings affect bond yields.

The primary risks bonds are subject to include:

- interest rate risk;
- purchasing power risk;
- reinvestment rate risk (for exam purposes, zero-coupon bonds are not subject to reinvestment rate risk); and
- default (credit) risk.

Bonds also may be evaluated on the basis of their quality. Bond rating agencies, such as Standard & Poor's and Moody's, analyze the financial information of thousands of bond issuers (corporations) to determine a credit rating for their various debt issues. Essentially, all bonds are then categorized as investment-grade bonds or noninvestment-grade bonds (also known as high-yield or junk bonds). Because noninvestment-grade bonds carry higher default risk than investment-grade bonds, their yields are generally higher.

Bond ratings are summarized below.

	Standard & Poor's	Moody's
Investment Grade		
High Grade	AAA–AA	Aaa–Aa
Medium Grade	A–BBB-	A–Baa
Noninvestment Grade		
Speculative	BB+–B	Ba–B
Default	CCC–D	Caa–C
Overall Ratings	AAA–D	Aaa–C

You should observe that the first four ratings indicate that the bond is investment-grade. However, anything below BBB– (Standard & Poor's) and Baa (Moody's) is considered a non-investment grade (junk) bond.

The effect of rating changes on bond yields can be defined as:

- an upward revision (e.g., from AA to AAA) will cause the market yield on the bond to decline, reflecting the bond's improved quality; or
- a downward revision (e.g., from AAA to AA) will cause the market yield on the bond to increase, reflecting the bond's decline in quality.

D. U.S. GOVERNMENT SECURITIES

LO E.33.13 Discuss the types of U.S. government securities.

U.S. Treasury Notes and Bonds

U.S. Treasury notes and bonds are identical except for their terms of maturity. Specifically, **U.S. Treasury notes** are issued with maturity dates of 2, 3, 5, 7, and 10 years, whereas **U.S. Treasury bonds** have a maturity of 30 years. These investments may be used to diversify a portfolio, fund college education expenses, and supplement retirement income.

Unlike Treasury bills, both Treasury notes and bonds are issued at their stated par value and provide semiannual coupon payments. They are sold in increments of $100 with a minimum purchase of $100. The actual price of a newly issued note or bond is determined at auction. Bidders present competitive and noncompetitive yield bids. From the competitive yield bids, the Treasury determines the highest yield it must offer to achieve its sales goals. This yield determines the price at which the note or bond will be sold to investors.

Treasury notes and bonds are considered default risk free and are exempt from income taxation at both the state and local levels. For federal income tax purposes, all interest from either obligation is taxable at ordinary income tax rates in the year earned. Finally, both obligations trade in the secondary market, and prices are quoted as percentages of par value in a bid-ask manner rather than as final closing prices as with stocks. However, the bid-ask is from the standpoint of the seller, so that the ask price (i.e., the price that the seller wants for the bond) is higher than the bid price (i.e., the price the buyer is willing to pay for the bond), to allow for transaction costs.

Taxation of Treasury Notes and Treasury Bonds

If the bond or note was originally issued at a discount after July 1, 1982, any investor who did not pay more than the face value of the obligation must include in income each year a calculated share of this **original issue discount (OID)**. This calculation is complex, but note that the investor is paying tax on income that has not yet been received in cash (i.e., phantom income). The investor's basis is then increased by the amount of OID included in income each year. If a note or bond is sold before its maturity date, proceeds from the sale must then be separated into the following components.

- An amount equal to the investor's adjusted basis in the note or bond is recovered tax free; this amount is usually the purchase price of the obligation plus the addition of any accrued OID.
- If the sale occurs before an interest date, the seller usually receives from the buyer an amount separately stating interest accrued but not yet due; this is reported by the seller as interest income.
- The excess of proceeds received over basis and interest is treated as capital gain (or loss).

PRACTICE QUESTION

Choose the best answer for the question below.
The answer can be found at the end of this unit.

2. John and Mary are planning to send their daughter, Rachel, to college in 15 years. They are conservative risk takers and do not feel comfortable with volatility. They wish to invest in a low-risk asset to help them begin planning for Rachel's future expenses. They tell you that they have $5,000 to invest at this time. Based on this information, which of the following would be best choice for the couple?

A. Money market mutual fund
B. U.S. Treasury bonds maturing in 15 years
C. Eurodollars
D. Passbook savings account

Treasury STRIPS

Treasury STRIPS (Separate Trading of Registered Interest and Principal of Securities) are zero-coupon bonds created by separating the semiannual coupon payments and the principal repayment portions of a U.S. Treasury note or bond.

EXAMPLE A five-year 4% Treasury note, face value of $10,000, can be separated into 11 zero-coupon bonds. The first payment creates a $200 par value six-month zero-coupon bond; the second payment creates a $200 par value 12-month zero-coupon bond, and so forth. The principal repayment would create a $10,000 par value five-year zero-coupon bond. The price of each zero-coupon bond would be determined by the appropriate market interest rate on the basis of maturity. Thus, if the five-year market interest rate is 3%, the principal unit would sell for $8,626.09 (FV = 10,000; I/YR = 3; N = 5; solve for PV).

STRIPS are purchased through financial institutions and government securities brokers and dealers; they cannot be purchased directly from the U.S. Treasury. STRIPS are issued at a deep discount. Due to their relatively short time to maturity, STRIPS that are closest to maturity trade at higher prices. However, as with any zero-coupon bond, STRIP prices are extremely sensitive to interest rate changes because the investor receives all the proceeds from the investment at maturity. STRIPS may be used by investors who want to receive a known payment on a specific future date. STRIPS are not subject to call risk and have virtually no liquidity risk or default risk.

The interest on STRIPS is taxed as ordinary income as it accrues, even though no actual interest is paid until the bond matures (or is sold). For this reason, Treasury STRIPS (or any zero-coupon bond) are best positioned in a tax-deferred account.

PRACTICE QUESTION

Choose the best answer for the question below.
The answer can be found at the end of this unit.

3. Which of the following applies to U.S. Treasury STRIPS?

A. No taxable income is associated with these investments.
B. These obligations do not subject purchasers to interest rate risk.
C. Their price volatility is much less than that of coupon bonds of similar maturity.
D. STRIPS are purchased through financial institutions and government securities brokers and dealers.

Treasury Inflation-Protected Securities (TIPS)

Treasury inflation-protected securities (TIPS) are marketable securities whose principal is adjusted by changes in the Consumer Price Index (CPI). They are issued in terms of 5, 10, and 30 years. They are sold in increments of $100 with a minimum purchase of $100. The principal value of the bond is adjusted for changes in the CPI, and the semiannual interest payments received by the investor are determined by multiplying the inflation-adjusted principal value by one-half of the fixed interest rate (because the interest payments are payable semiannually). Therefore, the coupon rate remains the same for the life of the security, but the amount of the coupon payment changes on the basis of the inflation-adjusted principal or par value. At maturity, an investor will receive the greater of the original principal or the adjusted principal.

EXAMPLE Assume a TIPS has a 4.5% coupon rate, and the annual inflation rate is 4%. On January 1, an investor purchases $100,000 of par value of the issue. The semiannual inflation rate is 4% ÷ 2 = 2%.

The inflation-adjusted principal at the end of the six-month period is calculated by multiplying the original par value by the semiannual inflation rate as follows: $100,000 × 1.02 = $102,000.

This new inflation-adjusted principal is then used as the basis for computing the coupon interest rate for the first six months as follows: The six-month coupon rate is 4.5% ÷ 2 = 2.25% giving a coupon payment of $2,295 ($102,000 × 2.25%). If the semiannual inflation rate for the next six months is 1.5%, the inflation-adjusted principal will be $103,530 ($102,000 × 1.015), and the coupon payment would be $2,329.43 ($103,530 × 2.25%).

For federal income tax purposes (remember, as a U.S. Treasury security, the obligation is free of income taxes at both the state and local levels), all interest received from TIPS is taxable at ordinary income tax rates in the year earned. Also, during any year when the principal value of TIPS increases as a result of the inflation-adjustment, the increase in principal is also taxed as ordinary income for that year. The tax basis of TIPS is also adjusted upward to account for this increase in principal. For example, Sally purchases an 8%, 10-year TIPS. In year 1, the inflation adjustment increases the principal from $980 to $1,010. Sally's taxable income will include any interest payments received on the TIPS as well as the $30 increase in principal. If Sally sells the bond for $1,015 immediately after the principal increase, she will recognize a gain on the sale of $5 (not $35) for income tax purposes.

Savings Bonds

Savings bonds, a part of the federal government debt structure, include Series E, EE, H, HH, and I bonds. Historically purchased for patriotic reasons, these bonds may be purchased and used for funding education costs and gifting.

The Series E bond was replaced in July 1980 with the Series EE bond. The electronic EE bond is sold at 100% of face value in any denomination from $25 to $10,000 and is eligible to earn interest for up to 30 years. Since May 2005, the interest rate applied to the EE bond is fixed for the life of the bond (with the rate for new issues adjusted semiannually). Series EE bonds must be held for a minimum of 12 months, and a 3-month interest penalty is assessed if the bond is redeemed within 5 years of issue.

The Series H bond was replaced in January 1980 with the Series HH bond. Unlike E or EE bonds that could be purchased with cash, Series HH bonds could be obtained only by exchanging Series E/EE bonds that were at least six months old. Until September 2004 (when Series H/HH bonds were no longer issued by the Treasury), the exchange of E/EE bonds for HH bonds was a popular way of continuing the income tax deferral on the accrued interest portion of the E/EE bonds. Beginning September 1, 2004, this deferral was no longer available, and investors must separately redeem E/EE bonds and pay the income tax due on the accrued interest at the time of redemption. Unlike Series E/EE bonds, Series H/HH bonds pay semiannual interest for up to 20 years in cash, and there is no penalty for early redemption.

The Series I savings bond is an inflation-indexed, or inflation-protected, debt security that is purchased electronically in any denomination from $25 to $10,000. The interest rate is a combination of two separate rates: (1) a fixed rate of return that remains the same for the life of the bond and (2) a semiannual inflation rate based on changes in the Consumer Price Index during the previous six-month period. The semiannual inflation rate is then combined with the fixed rate of return to determine the Series I bond's interest rate for the next six months. Like Series E/EE bonds, Series I bonds may be redeemed any time 12 months after the issue date for the principal plus interest accrued to that date. However, if redeemed within the first 5 years, there is a 3-month interest penalty.

The interest on Series EE and Series I bonds may be completely excluded from income tax if the bond proceeds are used to pay for qualified higher education costs. However, a phaseout applies to both types of bonds if the taxpayer's adjusted gross income is above a certain limit at the time of the bond's redemption. The interest accrued or received on Series E/EE, H/HH, and I bonds is exempt from income taxation by states and other municipalities regardless of the use of the bond's proceeds.

PRACTICE QUESTION

Choose the best answer for the question below.
The answer can be found at the end of this unit.

4. Which one of the following statements with respect to the features of U.S. savings bonds is CORRECT?

A. Series EE and Series I bonds are sold at a discount and accrue interest annually.
B. Series EE and Series HH bonds may be used in payment of qualified higher education costs free of income tax.
C. Series I bonds feature a combination fixed and inflation-adjusted interest rate.
D. Series HH bonds may be obtained only by using cash and not with a tax-free exchange of Series EE bonds.

E. U.S. GOVERNMENT AGENCY SECURITIES

LO E.33.14 Explain the types of U.S. government agency securities.

Congress authorizes the following agencies of the federal government to issue debt securities:

- Farm Credit Administration—provides American agriculture with a source of credit.
- Government National Mortgage Association (GNMA, or Ginnie Mae)—guarantees investors the timely payment of principal and interest on mortgage-backed securities backed by federally insured loans.

Accordingly, any securities issued by these agencies (the most prominent of which is GNMA) has the direct backing and guarantee of the U.S. government.

In addition, securities are issued by private corporations and have an indirect backing and guarantee of the U.S. government. These include the following:

- Federal Home Loan Mortgage Corporation (FHLMC, or Freddie Mac)—purchases mortgage loans and mortgage-related securities for investment and issues guaranteed mortgage-related securities.
- Federal National Mortgage Association (FNMA, or Fannie Mae)—keeps funds flowing to the mortgage market, helps distressed homeowners, and encourages sustainable lending.
- Student Loan Marketing Association (SLMA, or Sallie Mae)—offers solutions that help families save, plan, and finance college expenses.

Because these agency issues have only the indirect backing and guarantee of the federal government, they tend to have a slightly higher coupon rate than do direct issues. However, unlike U.S. Treasury securities (bills, notes, and bonds), all agency issues are generally taxable at both the state and local levels and for federal income tax purposes.

NOTE: In 2008, the Federal Housing Finance Agency (FHFA) became the conservator of Fannie Mae and Freddie Mac. As conservator, the FHFA has taken over the assets and assumed all the powers of the shareholders, directors, and officers and may take any necessary action to restore the firms to a sound and solvent condition.

Government National Mortgage Association (GNMA)

The **Government National Mortgage Association (GNMA)** (Ginnie Mae) buys Federal Housing Administration and Department of Veterans Affairs mortgages and auctions them to private lenders, which pool the mortgages to create pass-through certificates for sale to investors. The minimum size of a GNMA certificate sold to an individual investor is $25,000. However, because few mortgages last the full term (they are refinanced and paid off as market interest rates fall), yield quotes are based only on a 12-year prepayment assumption. GNMA certificates trade over the counter.

Federal Home Loan Mortgage Corporation (FHLMC)

The **Federal Home Loan Mortgage Corporation (FHLMC)** (Freddie Mac) was created to promote the development of a nationwide secondary market in mortgages by purchasing conventional mortgages from financial institutions and packaging them into mortgage-backed securities for sale to investors. Like GMNA, FHLMC creates pass-through certificates as a mechanism to pass homebuyers' interest and principal payments from the mortgage holder to the investor. Also like GNMA, Freddie Mac pass-through certificates carry significant reinvestment rate risk to a potential purchaser because of the risk of prepayment of these mortgages by the owner.

Federal National Mortgage Association (FNMA)

The **Federal National Mortgage Association (FNMA)** (Fannie Mae) competes with FHLMC for investor money in the secondary marketplace. Like FHLMC, FNMA is a publicly held corporation that purchases conventional mortgages from financial institutions and repackages them into mortgage-backed securities for sale to investors. However, unlike FHLMC, FNMA is a government-sponsored corporation that is owned entirely by private stockholders. The securities it creates are backed by FNMA's general credit, not by the U.S. government, and they consist of debt securities and mortgage-backed securities.

PRACTICE QUESTION

Choose the best answer for the question below.
The answer can be found at the end of this unit.

5. Historically, which of the following government agencies has been directly backed by the U.S. government?

A. Fannie Mae
B. Freddie Mac
C. Ginnie Mae
D. Sallie Mae

F. MUNICIPAL BONDS

LO E.33.15 Identify the advantages and disadvantages of municipal bonds.

Municipalities include states, counties, parishes, cities, and towns. They frequently issue debt obligations, known as **municipal bonds**, to finance various projects. The two basic types of municipal bonds are general obligation bonds and revenue bonds. The interest income earned on these investments is excluded from the recipient's taxable income for regular income tax purposes, usually both for federal and state income tax purposes, if the bondholder is also a resident of the state or municipality issuing the bond.

General Obligation Bonds (GOs)

General obligation bonds (GOs) are municipal bonds that are issued to finance capital improvements benefiting the community. Typically, these improvements do not produce revenues, so the principal and interest on the obligation must be paid by the revenues of the municipal issuer. Because of this backing, GOs are often referred to as *full faith and credit* bonds. In turn, because taxes back most GOs, most municipalities require a taxpayer vote to approve new issues. The amount of debt a municipal government may incur may be limited by state or local statutes, to protect taxpayers from excessive taxes, making GOs less risky for investors.

Revenue Bonds

Revenue bonds may be used to finance any municipal facility (e.g., community airport) that generates sufficient income to satisfy the ongoing debt obligation. These types of bonds are more risky than GOs and, therefore, offer higher yields for similar maturities.

Depending on the type of project, revenue bonds may be categorized a number of different ways including:

- industrial development revenue bonds (issued by governments to assist companies with specific projects);
- special assessment bonds (financed by those directly benefiting from the project);
- special tax bonds (used for specific projects and repaid by special assessments, ad valorem taxes, or excise taxes); and
- new housing authority (or Section 8) bonds (used to finance rehabilitation or construction of affordable housing).

Private Activity (Private Purpose) Bonds

Generally, a **private activity (private purpose) bond** is part of a state or local government bond issue for which more than 10% of the proceeds of the issue are to be used for a private business use (such as the financing of a sports stadium). More than 10% of the payment of the principal and interest is secured by an interest in the property (of payments for the property) or derived from payments for property (or borrowed money). Examples of private activity bonds include exempt facility bonds, qualified mortgage bonds, and qualified veterans' mortgage bonds.

Qualified private activity bonds are tax-exempt bonds issued by a local or state government, the proceeds of which are used for a defined qualified purpose by an entity other than the government issuing the bonds. For a bond to be tax exempt, 95% or more of the net bond proceeds must be used for one of several qualified purposes as described in the Internal Revenue Code. These bonds qualify for tax-exempt treatment of the interest. Certain types of state or local government bonds are considered to be nonexempt private activity bonds, and interest received on those bonds is not exempt from federal income tax. The stated interest rate on tax-exempt bonds is typically lower than the rate on taxable bonds. However, for individuals in high income tax brackets, their after-tax return may be greater than that received from a fully taxable corporate bond after the applicable taxes are taken into account.

Insured Municipal Bonds

Some municipal bonds may be insured against default, thereby reducing the credit risk associated with the bond. A municipality may insure its debt issue in hopes of increasing the bond rating, which, in turn, will allow the municipality to lower the coupon rate on the issue. Lowering the coupon rate on the bond will help the municipality lower the cost of borrowing.

PRACTICE QUESTION

Choose the best answer for the question below.
The answer can be found at the end of this unit.

6. John is interested in selling one of the municipal bonds in his portfolio. He is generally risk averse and wants to sell the bond with the most default or credit risk. Of the following four types of municipal bonds in his portfolio, which one do you recommend he sell?

A. A general obligation bond
B. A revenue bond
C. An insured utility revenue bond
D. A private activity bond

Tax Characteristics of Municipal Bond Issues

Generally, a municipal bond of any type is exempt from regular federal income tax but is subject to state and local taxes, unless the bond is purchased by a resident of the issuing state and the bond indenture agreement allows for that exclusion. Therefore, to compare the advisability of investing in municipal, tax-exempt issues to taxable, corporate issues, we need to determine the **taxable equivalent yield (TEY)** of the municipal issue. The coupon rate for corporate issues is, by nature, stated as a taxable yield because the payments from these bonds are taxable to the holder. Therefore, no adjustment needs to be made to the coupon rate for sake of comparison. Use the following formula to make this comparison:

$$\text{TEY} = \frac{\text{tax-exempt yield}}{1 - \text{marginal tax rate}}$$

EXAMPLE Kate owns a municipal bond with a coupon rate of 6%. She is in the 33% federal marginal income tax bracket. Therefore, to achieve the same yield on a taxable corporate bond, the corporate bond must have a coupon rate of at least 8.96% (rounded), calculated as follows:

$$\text{TEY} = \frac{6.00}{1 - 0.33} = 8.9552\text{, or } 8.96\%$$

However, if Kate were in a 15% federal marginal income tax bracket, she would need to obtain only a taxable equivalent yield of 7.06% for it to be preferable to invest in the taxable corporate issue, calculated as follows: 6.00 ÷ (1 – 0.15, or 0.85) = 7.0588, or 7.06%. This illustrates the point that the higher the investor's marginal income tax bracket, the greater the advantage to the investor of investing in an asset that returns federally tax-exempt income.

Another formula, the **after-tax yield** computation, may be used to compare the advisability of investing in taxable issues with that of investing in municipal tax-exempt issues. In this case, an adjustment is made to the coupon rate of the corporate bond without making any adjustment to the coupon rate of the municipal issue. This formula is as follows:

$$\text{after-tax yield} = \text{pretax return} \times (1 - \text{marginal tax rate})$$

EXAMPLE Investors are concerned with after-tax returns. For an investor in the 35% marginal tax bracket, 35 cents of every additional dollar of taxable interest income must be paid in taxes. For a taxable corporate bond that yields 4.35%, the after-tax yield to an investor with a 35% marginal tax rate is:

After-tax yield = 4.35% × (1 – 0.35) = 4.35% × 0.65 = 2.8275, or 2.83%

PRACTICE QUESTIONS

Choose the best answer for each of the questions below.
Answers can be found at the end of this unit.

7. Cheryl is in a 28% federal marginal income tax bracket and resides in a state with a flat 5% state income tax rate. She has $50,000 to invest and wants to invest the entire sum in a single bond issue. Which bond should Cheryl choose?

A. Taxable corporate bond, with a rate of 6%
B. Another state's municipal bond, with a rate of 5%
C. Her city's municipal bond, with a rate of 3%
D. Her state's municipal bond, with a rate of 4%

8. Brian owns a taxable corporate bond with a coupon rate of 5%. He pays taxes at a marginal rate of 28%. What is the after-tax yield he will receive on this investment?

A. 6.40%
B. 3.60%
C. 4.72%
D. 1.40%

G. CORPORATE BONDS

LO E.33.16 Discuss corporate and convertible bonds.

Corporate bonds are debt securities issued by public and private companies to raise capital. Essentially, a bond is a loan made to the corporation by an investor for a specific period of time at a fixed annual interest rate. Most corporate bonds issued today are issued in the form of debentures or unsecured, corporate debt obligations. Unsecured debt securities are backed only by the reputation, credit record, and financial stability of the corporation. Furthermore, most bonds issued in this form are subordinated in security or safety to all other corporate creditors, including general corporate creditors. Because of the greater risk associated with **subordinated debentures**, they feature higher coupon (interest) rates than corporate secured bonds, municipal bonds, or other U.S. Treasury securities. However, even when they are subordinated, debentures still carry less risk than the common stock of the corporation, which is last on the payment ladder in the event of corporate default or bankruptcy.

Corporate bonds may be issued in either callable or noncallable forms. Callable bonds can be redeemed or paid off by the issuer prior to the bonds' maturity date. When an issuer calls its bonds, it pays investors the call price together with accrued interest to date. Callable bonds are usually less attractive to a potential investor than noncallable bonds. Callable bond investors may be confronted with reinvesting the bond's proceeds at a lower, less attractive market interest rate than that available at the time of the original investment. Therefore, to protect investors who expect and rely on long-term steady income, call provisions included in the bond indenture specify that the bond may not be called before a certain number of years have passed, generally at least 10 years.

Convertible Bonds

Convertible bonds are corporate bonds that may be exchanged for a fixed number of shares of the issuing company's common stock. The conversion privilege is exercised at the discretion of the investor. The bond indenture normally tells the investor the number of shares into which the bond is convertible. Because they are convertible into common stock, convertible bonds pay lower interest rates (i.e., they have lower coupon rates) than do nonconvertible bonds. However, because they are bonds with fixed and promised interest payments, as well as a known maturity date, the price of convertible bonds is less volatile than that of common stock. In addition, because convertible bonds generally have a relatively low correlation with nonconvertible (or regular) corporate bonds and only a moderate correlation to common stock, convertible bonds are usually a good diversifier within an investor's portfolio.

The **conversion price** is the stock price at which a convertible bond can be exchanged for shares of the issuer's common stock. The **conversion ratio**, also known as the conversion rate, expresses the number of shares of stock into which a bond may be converted. The conversion ratio formula is as follows:

$$\text{conversion ratio} = \frac{\text{par value of convertible security}}{\text{conversion price}}$$

EXAMPLE Assume that a convertible bond has a conversion price of $40 per share. If the par value of the bond is $1,000, the conversion ratio is 25, or $1,000 ÷ $40.

You should also note that although the conversion ratio of a bond is always stated on the bond certificate, it is not stated directly in the number of common shares that may be obtained, but instead is stated in terms of the price at which a conversion can occur ($40 in this example).

Once the conversion ratio of the convertible bond has been determined, the conversion value of the bond may be easily calculated. The conversion value represents the value of the bond if it were converted on the basis of current market conditions and is determined by the following formula:

$$\text{conversion value} = \text{conversion ratio} \times \text{market price of common stock}$$

EXAMPLE If we continue with our previous example but now add a market price of $50 for the common stock, we find a conversion value of $1,250 for the convertible bond, or 25 (conversion ratio) × $50. In turn, this means that if the current market price of the bond were less than $1,250, bond investors would buy the bond because its conversion value is greater than its current market price. Accordingly, a convertible bond will always sell for no less than the greater of its straight value or its conversion value.

Note: A bond's straight value is the price a convertible security would sell for in the secondary market if the bond did not contain the convertible option.

PRACTICE QUESTION

Choose the best answer for the question below.
The answer can be found at the end of this unit.

9. ABC Company common stock is currently trading at $75 per share. Joe owns a $1,000 par value bond convertible into ABC common stock with a conversion ratio of 15. What is the conversion value of Joe's bond?

A. $875
B. $1,000
C. $1,125
D. $1,500

Taxation of Corporate Bonds

Bond prices fluctuate as interest rates change and as the borrower's bond rating varies. Therefore, a bond can be bought at a discount because of a decline in the value of the obligation after issue. A bond acquired at a discount is called a **market discount bond**. Students should distinguish between a bond selling at a market discount and a bond issued at an original issue discount. We have already discussed the taxable consequences of an OID bond in the context of a Treasury note or bond; this consequence is the same for a corporate OID bond. However, the amount attributable to a market discount generally is not includable in income until sale or disposition of the bond, and then it is treated as interest income. Although an election may be made by the investor to include this market discount as it accrues each year, as a practical matter, this election is not often chosen. In general, deferring the tax on a market discount until disposition of the bond is preferable. On sale or disposition of the bond, only gain in excess of the accrued market discount is treated as capital gain income.

Finally, what about a bond that is purchased at premium, **market premium bond**, in the marketplace (i.e., above its stated face value)? Investors are willing to pay premiums for bonds when the interest paid is greater than that of the current market on bonds of similar quality and risk. However, the premium creates an unfavorable tax-timing issue. Specifically, investors are taxed at ordinary income tax rates (federal and state) as bond interest is paid, but they have to wait until they dispose of the bond to recover their premium. As a result of this generally adverse tax treatment with respect to a bond premium, the tax law permits investors to make an election to amortize the premium over the remaining life of the bond. If this election is made, investors then apply the part of the premium attributable to a given year to reduce the basis in the bond. This is the case for all bonds except a municipal bond where the amortization is handled differently (because the bond returns tax-free interest). The amortization of the premium must reduce the investors' basis annually but is not a tax-deductible event.

PRACTICE QUESTION

Choose the best answer for the question below.
The answer can be found at the end of this unit.

10. Which of the following statements regarding the taxation of corporate bonds is NOT correct?

A. The amount attributable to a market discount is generally not includable in income until disposition of the bond.
B. At disposition, the market discount is treated as interest income.
C. Upon sale, only gain in excess of the accrued market discount is treated as capital gain income.
D. When a market premium bond is purchased, the tax law does not permit the taxpayer to elect to amortize the premium over the remaining life of the bond.

H. ZERO-COUPON BONDS

LO E.33.12 Describe zero-coupon bonds.

In addition to the U.S. Treasury, corporations and municipalities also issue **zero-coupon bonds**. These bonds are sold at a deep discount to their face value and are referred to as original issue discount (OID) bonds. Investors receive the difference in value at the bond's maturity date rather than in the form of periodic interest payments, which eliminates the opportunity to reinvest such proceeds at a higher interest rate. For example, John purchases a two-year coupon bond, and Louisa purchases a two-year zero-coupon bond of similar credit quality. If market rates increase 50 basis points (0.50%) during the two-year period, John will have the opportunity to reinvest his coupon payments at a higher interest rate. Louisa, on the other hand, will not be able to take advantage of the higher interest rate because she will not receive any return until maturity.

Because zero-coupon bonds do not pay interest until maturity, their prices are more volatile than other bonds of similar quality and they are not subject to reinvestment rate risk. Zero-coupon bonds are issued in taxable form by corporations, meaning that the investor must include the accrued interest in his taxable income annually, even though no cash is received until the bond matures, is sold, or is called. This accrued interest is sometimes referred to as **phantom income**. This leads to the conclusion that taxable zero-coupon bonds are usually most appropriate if they are positioned within a retirement plan or other tax-deferred account.

Corporations may favor zero-coupon bonds because they have an extended period to use the money that has been raised without making periodic interest payments. Many zero-coupon bonds do not mature for 10 or more years. Thus, they can be an effective cash management tool for a corporation. Investors favor zero-coupon bonds because the heavily discounted bond price means they can purchase more bonds with the same amount of investment dollars and can time the maturity of the bonds to coincide with anticipated expenses (e.g., college education costs).

PRACTICE QUESTION

Choose the best answer for the question below.
The answer can be found at the end of this unit.

11. For which of the following investors would zero-coupon bonds be most appropriate?

A. Nancy, age 67, recently retired, conservative risk tolerance, has a need for immediate income
B. Jim, age 26, aggressive risk tolerance, modest income, has a need for an emergency fund
C. Ralph and Gina, ages 42 and 40, have a 13-year-old daughter, need $25,000 for college funding in 5 years
D. Marvin and Juanita, ages 56 and 50, moderate to aggressive risk takers, both employed, high net worth, wish to retire in 13 years

I. FOREIGN BONDS

LO E.33.17 List the risks associated with foreign bonds.

The two major types of foreign bonds are: (1) those payable in U.S. dollars and (2) those payable in foreign currency. The investor who invests in the second type of foreign bond (i.e., a foreign-pay bond denominated in foreign currency) may see the return reduced by the risk inherent in exchanging currencies. This is known as **exchange rate risk**, or **currency risk**, and is a potential disadvantage of investing in a bond that is denominated in a currency that may weaken against the U.S. dollar. Simply defined, currency risk is the potential for loss due to fluctuations in currency exchange rates. Accordingly, this risk may turn a profit on a foreign investment into a loss or vice-versa.

Yankee bonds are foreign bonds payable in U.S. dollars. As such, Yankee bonds are not subject to exchange rate risk and may be effective diversification tools within a portfolio. Such bonds are issued by foreign governments, banks, or corporations but are traded in the United States in the secondary market and are generally of very high quality. **Eurodollar bonds** are a second type of U.S. pay bond, but unlike Yankee bonds, they do not have to be registered with the Securities and Exchange Commission because they are issued and traded outside the United States.

EXAMPLE Sharon, a U.S. citizen, purchases a 1,000 UK pound par value bond with a 5% coupon rate. At the time that she made the investment, the currency exchange rate was 1.50 U.S. dollars to 1.00 UK pounds. This means that Sharon paid $1,500 in U.S. currency for the UK bond. Several years later, the bond matured and Sharon was issued a check for 1,000 UK pounds (the par value of the foreign bond). Unfortunately, when she goes to convert the pounds to U.S. dollars, Sharon finds that the currency exchange rate has adjusted to 1.40 U.S. dollars to 1.00 UK pounds (or the dollar has "strengthened" against the pound). As a result, Sharon incurs a loss of $100 due entirely to the currency fluctuation (that is, she only receives $1,400 for a bond that she purchased for $1,500).

Of course, an investor can *profit* from currency risk. If the dollar had "weakened" against the pound (e.g., the exchange rate adjusted to 1.80 U.S. dollars to 1.00 UK pounds), Sharon would have received $1,800, or $300 more than she had paid for the foreign bond.

PRACTICE QUESTION

Choose the best answer for the question below.
The answer can be found at the end of this unit.

12. What type of risk is generally eliminated with the purchase of a Yankee bond?

A. Currency risk
B. Interest rate risk
C. Credit risk
D. Insurance risk

J. PROMISSORY NOTES

LO E.33.18 Explain the characteristics of a promissory note.

A **promissory note** is a promise to pay a certain sum of money or make a series of payments to others, usually individuals. Because the structure of a promissory note is similar to that of a bond (i.e., it generally involves a fixed amount and time of payment), many of the same investment considerations that apply to a bond are also relevant to a promissory note. The present value of a promissory note is found using time value of money principles and discounting back future cash flows from the note at a specified discount rate over the stipulated time period of the note.

All of the interest from a promissory note (whether imputed under the below-market interest tax rules or stated under the terms of the note) is taxable to the investor at ordinary income rates in the year earned.

103 UNIT 2 ANSWERS TO PRACTICE QUESTIONS

1. B. High-yield, zero-coupon, and debenture bonds are generally not collateralized by the issuer. Alternatively, a mortgage bond or secured bond is collateralized with (typically) either real property or equipment of the issuer.

2. B. The best choice for John and Mary is the U.S. Treasury bonds. This investment offers a modest rate of return with low risk. In addition, the bonds will mature in 15 years, equaling the time when the money is needed for the college planning goal.

3. D. The income from STRIPS is taxable annually as accrued interest to the purchaser. STRIPS' prices are more volatile than those of coupon bonds of similar maturities, and STRIPS carry substantial interest rate risk for the purchaser.

4. C. The Series I bond interest rate is a combination of a fixed rate of return and a semiannual, inflation-adjusted interest rate. Like a Series EE bond, a Series I bond may also be used for the payment of higher education costs free of income tax so long as the taxpayer's adjusted gross income is not above the phaseout limit. However, Series HH bonds may not be used for this purpose.

5. C. Before 2008, only the Government National Mortgage Association (GNMA, or Ginnie Mae) was directly backed by the U.S. government.

6. D. The bond with the most amount of credit risk is the private activity bond; therefore, if John is generally risk averse, he should sell the private activity bond.

7. B. The other state's municipal bond will generate the highest after-tax yield of 4.75% for Cheryl, calculated as follows: 5% × (1 – 0.05) = 5% × 0.95 = 4.75%. The after-tax yield for the taxable corporate bond is only 4.02%, or 6% × (1 – 0.33).

8. B. Brian will earn an after-tax yield of 3.60%, or 5% × (1 – 0.28).

9. C. The conversion value of Joe's bond is $1,125, or 15 × $75 per share. This is the minimum value for which the convertible bond will sell in the secondary market.

10. D. The tax law does permit an investor to make an election to amortize the premium over the remaining life of the bond.

11. C. Ralph and Gina would be the best choice to invest in zero-coupon bonds. Their need is clearly defined in terms of amount and time frame. Zero-coupon bonds could be purchased to provide the necessary funds at the desired time.

12. A. The purchase of a Yankee bond generally eliminates currency risk because the proceeds are payable in U.S. dollars. As a fixed-income security, such a bond still has interest rate risk, and although the credit risk may be minimal, it is not completely eliminated.

103 UNIT 2 POST-STUDY CHECKLIST

- ☐ Can I explain the unique investment risks facing bondholders and how bond ratings affect bond yields?
- ☐ Am I able to describe the key terms, types, and features of bonds?
- ☐ Do I understand the types of U.S. government securities?
- ☐ Do I understand the types of U.S. government agency securities?
- ☐ Can I explain the advantages and disadvantages of municipal bonds?
- ☐ Am I able to explain corporate and convertible bonds?
- ☐ Can I describe zero-coupon bonds?
- ☐ Do I understand the risks associated with foreign bonds?
- ☐ Can I explain the characteristics of a promissory note?

Am I able to define and understand the application of the following terms as they relate to investment planning?

- ☐ After-tax yield
- ☐ Basis point
- ☐ Bond
- ☐ Call provision
- ☐ Collateral trust bond
- ☐ Conversion price
- ☐ Conversion ratio
- ☐ Convertible bonds
- ☐ Corporate bonds
- ☐ Coupon rate
- ☐ Currency risk
- ☐ Debenture
- ☐ Discount
- ☐ Eurodollar bonds
- ☐ Exchange rate risk
- ☐ Federal Home Loan Mortgage Corporation (FHLMC)
- ☐ Federal National Mortgage Association (FNMA)
- ☐ General obligation bonds
- ☐ Government National Mortgage Association (GNMA)
- ☐ High-yield bond
- ☐ Indenture
- ☐ Investment grade bond
- ☐ Market discount bond
- ☐ Market premium bond
- ☐ Mortgage bond
- ☐ Municipal bonds
- ☐ Nominal yield
- ☐ Original issue discount (OID)
- ☐ Par value
- ☐ Phantom income
- ☐ Premium
- ☐ Private activity (private purpose) bond
- ☐ Promissory note
- ☐ Qualified private activity bonds
- ☐ Revenue bonds
- ☐ Savings bonds
- ☐ Secured bond
- ☐ Subordinated debentures
- ☐ Taxable equivalent yield (TEY)
- ☐ Treasury inflation-protected securities (TIPS)
- ☐ Treasury STRIPS (Separate Trading of Registered Interest and Principal of Securities)
- ☐ U.S. Treasury bonds
- ☐ U.S. Treasury notes
- ☐ Yankee bonds
- ☐ Zero-coupon bonds

UNIT 3

Equity Investments and Managed Assets

REFER TO

CFP Board Principal Knowledge Topics – E. Investment Planning, E.33. Characteristics, Uses, and Taxation of Investment Vehicles

CFP Board Principal Knowledge Topics – E. Investment Planning, E.41. Alternative Investments

INTRODUCTION

Equity investments are the third class of traditional assets included in a diversified portfolio. In addition, stocks are what most investors think of when they consider financial assets that may generate a significant return. The two basic types of stock are common and preferred. In addition, this unit will discuss various stock attributes including dividends.

The subject of managed investment assets is broad and complex. Investment assets that are professionally managed include open-end investment companies (mutual funds), closed-end funds, exchange-traded funds (ETFs), unit investment trusts, and hedge funds. Limited partnerships are another form of managed or pooled assets; however, because of the significant income tax implications of this type of investment, they will also be addressed in *104 Tax Planning*.

Finally, some financial planners are managing investor funds in a separately managed account. This unit will consider the characteristics of these types of advisory accounts, in which the planner is paid an advisory fee based on a percentage of the assets under management.

LEARNING OBJECTIVES

After completing this unit, you should be able to achieve the following learning objectives:

CFP® Board Principal Knowledge Topics – E. Investment Planning

E.33. Characteristics, Uses, and Taxation of Investment Vehicles

LO E.33.19 Discuss the differences between equity and debt securities.

LO E.33.20 Discuss the characteristics and types of common stock and the payment of dividends.

LO E.33.21 Explain the characteristics and primary purchasers of preferred stock.

LO E.33.22 Analyze a stock dividend.

LO E.33.23 Describe a rights offering.

LO E.33.24 Discuss the use of warrants.

LO E.33.25 Explain the benefits and methods of international investing.

LO E.33.26 Describe the types, features, and taxation of open-end investment companies (mutual funds).

LO E.33.27 Discuss the features of closed-end investment companies and how they differ from open-end investment companies.

LO E.33.28 Explain the attributes of a unit investment trust (UIT) and provide reasons for purchasing this investment vehicle.

LO E.33.29 Describe the characteristics and advantages of exchange-traded funds (ETFs).

LO E.33.30 Identify the similarities and differences among the types of investment companies.

LO E.33.31 Describe the benefits of a separately managed account.

LO E.33.34 Explain how investors' tax obligations are impacted by capital gains and losses, dividends, and wash sales.

LO E.33.35 Evaluate a stock split.

E.41. Alternative Investments

LO E.41.1 Explain the distinguishing features of hedge funds and how they differ from investment company offerings.

LO E.41.2 Cite the various uses of venture capital.

LO E.41.3 Discuss why a company would use a private placement to generate capital.

LO E.41.4 Discuss the advantages and disadvantages of limited partnerships.

KEY TERMS

- American depositary receipts (ADRs)
- Average cost method
- Blue-chip stocks
- Closed-end investment company
- Common stock
- Country risk
- Cyclical stocks
- Defensive stocks
- Developed markets
- Emerging markets
- Equity
- Exchange-traded fund (ETF)
- Ex-dividend date
- First in, first out (FIFO)
- Global mutual fund
- Growth stocks
- Hedge fund
- Income stocks
- International mutual fund
- Limited partnerships
- Net asset value (NAV)
- Open-end investment company (mutual fund)
- Perpetuity
- Preferred stock
- Private placements
- Reverse stock split
- Record date
- Rights
- Separately managed account
- Shareholder of record
- Specific identification method
- Stock dividend
- Stock split
- Unit investment trust (UIT)
- Value stocks
- Venture capital
- Warrants
- Wash sale

A. EQUITY VS. DEBT

LO E.33.19 Discuss the differences between equity and debt securities.

In the investment marketplace, stock is frequently referred to as **equity**. The equity owner (commonly called a stockholder) is entitled to a proportionate share of the assets and earnings of the corporation. In contrast, with a debt obligation (such as a bond), the bondholder is entitled to a fixed rate of payment and a return of principal but does not have an ownership interest in the corporation. Bondholders do have a right, above that of stockholders, to the corporation's assets in the event of default or liquidation.

Equity has one major corporate advantage over debt—it does not require fixed payments to investors, which could deplete much needed cash for operations. However, from the standpoint of the issuing corporation, equity also has a major disadvantage—specifically, dividends are not tax deductible for income-tax purposes, but bond interest is tax deductible. Equity investors generally demand a higher return on their investment than do bondholders because equities lack a fixed rate of return and payment schedule. Dividends received by the shareholder are taxable as ordinary income (unless qualified), leading to a double taxation effect on distributions of corporate profits.

Historically, stock returns tend to have low positive correlation with bond returns. That is, what is good for the stock market is not so good for the bond market because they both compete for investor money. Conversely, as bond yields improve (i.e., the price of bonds declines), money may shift into bonds and out of stocks.

PRACTICE QUESTION

Choose the best answer for the question below.
The answer can be found at the end of this unit.

1. Which of following are reasons why an investor would choose stocks over bonds?

1. A stockholder is not entitled to share in the earnings of the company.
2. Bondholders do not have an ownership interest in the company.
3. A stockholder has the right above a bondholder to assets of the corporation in case of liquidation.
4. A stockholder is entitled to a proportionate share of the assets of the company.

A. 1 and 3
B. 2 and 4
C. 1, 2, and 4
D. 2, 3, and 4

B. COMMON STOCK

LO E.33.20 Discuss the characteristics and types of common stock and the payment of dividends.

Common stock represents units of ownership in a publicly traded corporation. Owners are entitled to vote (usually by proxy) on the selection of the board of directors of the corporation and on other important matters, as well as to receive any dividends that are declared by the corporation. Investors purchase stock for capital appreciation and dividend payments. Companies issue stock to raise capital to pay off debts, develop new products, and expand business operations.

As mentioned previously, a dividend has to be declared on common (or preferred) stock by the board of directors of the corporation before the shareholder may realize any income. This is a major difference from bonds—the interest payment due on bonds (absent default by the issuer) is a guaranteed payment from the corporation, but this is not the case with a dividend payment on stock. In addition, not all shareholders will receive a dividend; rather, only shareholders of record are entitled to the dividend. A **shareholder of record** is any owner who is listed as such on the record date. The **record date** for the corporation is the first business day after the ex-dividend date. On the record date, trades are settled and reflected on the corporation's books. Accordingly, to be listed as a shareholder of record, the investor must purchase stock before the ex-dividend date. The **ex-dividend date** is the first date on which a security is traded that a buyer is not entitled to receive a previously declared dividend.

> **EXAMPLE** If Friday, October 5, 2018, is the record date for ABC Corporation, when must an investor have purchased the stock in order to be entitled to receive a declared dividend? The answer is determined as follows: Count back one business day from October 5 to determine the ex-dividend date, or Thursday, October 4, 2018. As a result, the investor must have purchased the stock no later than Wednesday, October 3, 2018, to be entitled to receive the dividend (whether that dividend was declared payable in cash or in additional stock of ABC Company).

Individual common stock may be directly owned in two ways.

- An investor is issued a certificate (certificate form) of ownership by the corporation indicating the number of shares owned.
- Investors may use a brokerage firm to hold stock in a brokerage account on their behalf (street name).

Types of Common Stock

Investors may choose from a wide variety of types of common stock depending on their investment objectives.

- **Blue-chip stocks** are stocks issued by highly regarded, usually well-capitalized companies that have historically paid dividends regardless of the condition of the broader economy.
- **Growth stocks** are stocks issued by companies that usually have sales and earnings growth rates exceeding those of the average company in their industry. Growth stocks typically do not pay dividends; instead, they invest their earnings back into the company.
- **Income stocks** are stocks issued by companies that pay regular, consistent dividends and provide current income for investors. Stock issued by a utility is an example of an income stock.
- **Value stocks** are stocks currently trading at prices that are low, given the issuing company's historical earnings and asset values.
- **Cyclical stocks** are stocks issued by companies that tend to prosper in a growing economy and tend to do poorly during declining economic conditions.
- **Defensive stocks** are stocks issued by companies that are relatively unaffected by the business cycle.

PRACTICE QUESTION

Choose the best answer for the question below.
The answer can be found at the end of this unit.

2. Karl and Wendy, ages 35 and 34, respectively, have provided their financial planner with the following information:

Salary (Wendy)	$100,000
Salary (Karl)	$55,000
Investment portfolio[1]	$150,000
Personal debt	$5,000
Personal residence	$250,000
Mortgage	$188,000
Checking account	$12,000

[1]100% of the assets are invested in stocks.

They have communicated that they are aggressive risk-takers and wish to reposition $3,000 from their checking account to their investments. They prefer a risky investment to add to their mostly blue-chip stock portfolio. Which of the following stocks would be most appropriate for the couple to add to their portfolio?

A. International airline stock
B. Grocery stock
C. Pharmaceutical stock
D. Utility stock

C. PREFERRED STOCK

LO E.33.21 Explain the characteristics and primary purchasers of preferred stock.

Preferred stock has characteristics of both a bond and common stock. Like a bond, shareholders of preferred stock receive dividends each year equal to a stated percentage of the par value of the stock (e.g., a 6% dividend on a $100 par value of preferred stock). However, like common stock, a shareholder of preferred stock is not guaranteed the payment of the dividend; in other words, a dividend still needs to be declared by the board of directors of the corporation. However, if a dividend is declared, the corporation must pay the dividend to the preferred shareholder before paying a dividend to the common shareholder. Furthermore, if the preferred stock is cumulative, the corporation is also required to first pay any unpaid preferred dividends from prior years to the preferred shareholder before paying any current dividends.

The primary purchasers of preferred stock include the following:

- Investors looking for a potential yield (in the form of dividend income) higher than that available from the company's common stock
- Investors wanting a fixed, relatively steady cash flow

In the case of a corporation, there will be allowed as a deduction an amount equal to 70% of the amount received as dividends from a domestic corporation. You should note that large corporations are the most prominent purchasers of preferred stock because of favorable tax treatment and not necessarily the investment potential of the stock issue.

Finally, preferred stock is a **perpetuity**, which means that it has no specified maturity date. Accordingly, to recover their initial investment, investors must sell their preferred shares. Because of the perpetual time frame of the security, the prices of preferred stock are sensitive to changes in market interest rates.

PRACTICE QUESTION

Choose the best answer for the question below.
The answer can be found at the end of this unit.

3. Shelley is contemplating buying 100 shares of ABC corporation's preferred stock for $42 per share. She knows the dividend is a fixed amount, paid quarterly, and is determined by taking a percentage of which of the following?

A. Market value
B. Book value
C. Par value
D. Intrinsic value

D. TAX OBLIGATIONS

LO E.33.34 Explain how investors' tax obligations are impacted by capital gains and losses, dividends, and wash sales.

Wash Sales

A **wash sale** occurs if the taxpayer sells or exchanges stock or securities for a loss and, within 30 days before or after the date of the sale or exchange, acquires similar securities. If this event occurs, the basis of the new stock or securities will include the unrecovered portion of the basis of the formerly held stock or securities. Usually, an investor wants to take advantage of a capital loss and then turn around and repurchase the same shares immediately thereafter. The wash sale rule is designed to prevent this technique. The wash sale rules are easily avoided in the case of fixed-income securities by substituting a bond with the same or similar characteristics (i.e., coupon, term, and quality), as long as it is issued by a different company.

EXAMPLE Caroline purchased 100 shares of Ace Corporation stock for $28,000 on January 1 of last year. In the current tax year, she sold 30 shares of the 100 shares purchased on January 1 of last year for $8,000. Twenty-nine days earlier, she purchased 30 shares for $7,500. Caroline's recognized loss is $0, calculated as follows:

Amount realized	$8,000
Adjusted basis (30 × $280)	(8,400)
Realized loss	(400)
Recognized loss	$0

(Loss postponed because the wash sale rule applies)

Her basis in the new shares is $7,900:

Basis in new shares	$7,500
Add postponed loss	400
Basis in new shares	$7,900

Taxation of Dividends

Qualifying (qualified) dividend income may be treated at favorable long-term capital gain rates (0%, 15%, or 20%) if it meets the following criteria.

- The dividend is received from a domestic corporation or a qualified foreign corporation.
- The stock must be held for more than 61 days during the 121-day period beginning 60 days before the ex-dividend date.
- Regular dividends from real estate investment trusts will not qualify for a reduced rate, but long-term distribution dividends will be taxed at a reduced rate.
- Dividends from a regulated investment company will qualify for the reduced rate to the extent they resulted from a long-term capital gain. Also, the long-term gain on the sale of the shares will qualify.

Most dividends declared by a corporate board of directors of a domestic corporation are considered qualifying dividends and are permitted preferential tax treatment. Dividends from a qualified foreign corporation also qualify for preferential tax treatment. Corporations whose stock of American depositary receipts is readily tradable on an established U.S. securities market also qualify. Nonqualified dividends are taxed at the ordinary income tax rate.

Taxation of Stock Sales

When an investor sells individual shares of stock, a capital gain or loss is recognized. Whether that gain or loss is long term (and thus qualifying for preferential tax treatment) or short term depends on how long the investor has owned the shares. When shares of stock are sold, the amount of gain or loss is the difference between the net sales price and the shareholder's basis in the shares. If these shares were a one-time purchase, the shareholder should have little difficulty in establishing the cost basis. However, basis determination becomes more problematic when shares were acquired at different times and prices. In this instance, the shareholder will need to specifically identify (specific identification method) the lot (100-share increments) from which the taxpayer acquired the shares or rely on the first in, first out (FIFO) method and attribute the basis of the shares to the earliest of lots purchased or acquired.

PRACTICE QUESTION

Choose the best answer for the question below.
The answer can be found at the end of this unit.

4. Greg has come to his financial planner with questions about dividends he received on some of his stock this year. He has received $1,000 in qualified dividends paid in cash. He also has received stock dividends of $4,000 but without a cash-dividend option. How much will Greg have to report as dividend income for the current year?

A. $0
B. $1,000
C. $4,000
D. $5,000

E. STOCK DIVIDENDS

LO E.33.22 Analyze a stock dividend.

A **stock dividend** is a dividend paid to shareholders of record in the form of additional shares of company stock, rather than in cash. Because all common shareholders receive their proportionate share of the dividend, the market value of the company is, theoretically, unchanged. However, when a stock dividend is declared and paid by the company, the value of each common stockholder's shares is reduced proportionally. As a result, the market price of each share of stock should decrease on a basis relative to the stock dividend.

EXAMPLE If a company worth $11 million with 1 million shares outstanding issues a 10% stock dividend, the market price should decline from $11 to $10 per share. The company's market value, theoretically, is not affected by the payment of the stock dividend.

Unless the stockholder has the right to receive the dividend in cash rather than in stock (which would trigger the constructive receipt doctrine of income taxation), receipt of the stock dividend is generally not taxable for federal income tax purposes. However, the stockholder's basis per share of stock is adjusted downward to reflect the stock dividend.

F. STOCK SPLITS

LO E.33.35 Evaluate a stock split.

In a **stock split**, the par value of each share of stock is reduced, and the number of shares is increased proportionately. Companies will typically split their stock to reduce the stock's market price per share, thereby making a purchase of the stock more attractive to the smaller investor. As a result, the company increases the total number of shares outstanding.

> **EXAMPLE** ABC stock is currently selling for $120 per share on the New York Stock Exchange. ABC declares a 2-for-1 stock split. Accordingly, the market price of its shares is now $60 per share, or $120 ÷ 2. In addition, ABC now has twice as many shares outstanding.

Many unsophisticated investors believe they own more of the corporation for the same amount of investment dollars. However, you should note that the investor still owns exactly the same total percentage of the company as before, but each share now represents a correspondingly smaller percentage. As a result, stock splits are never income taxable to the shareholders. Like a stock dividend, the shareholder's basis per share of stock is adjusted downward.

In a **reverse stock split**, the company reduces the total number of shares outstanding. Companies typically do this to increase the price of the outstanding shares, thereby making the company less likely to be delisted by an exchange and more attractive to potential investors.

> **EXAMPLE** John owns 100 shares of ABC stock with a current market price of $5 per share. If the stock should reverse split 4 for 1, he would own 25 shares with a new market price of $20 per share.

PRACTICE QUESTION

Choose the best answer for the question below.
The answer can be found at the end of this unit.

5. Patricia owns 100 shares of Blue stock, which has a current market price of $150. She also owns 300 shares of Red stock, which has a current market price of $5. If Blue Corporation undergoes a 2-for-1 stock split and Red Corporation undergoes a 1-for-3 reverse split, which row would correctly identify Patricia's holdings?

	Blue		Red	
	# shares	Value of shares	# shares	Value of shares
A.	100	$7,500	300	$3,000
B.	200	$15,000	100	$1,500
C.	200	$15,000	900	$1,500
D.	50	$7,500	900	$4,500

G. RIGHTS

LO E.33.23 Describe a rights offering.

Rights, sometimes referred to as *subscription rights*, are issued by a corporation that plans to raise funds by issuing new stock to the public. Normally, each current shareholder is given one right for each share of stock. These rights give the shareholder a short-term opportunity to buy new shares of the new stock issue, thereby maintaining the shareholder's respective overall percentage ownership of the corporation. Similar to a warrant, a right gives the owner the right to purchase common shares. However, in contrast to the warrant, the life of a stock right is very short, usually for only a few weeks, and, thus, equates to a short-term call option. Because the time until expiration is generally very small, a right typically has little or no speculative premium like other options. Stockholders who are offered rights may purchase the company's common stock *below* the current market price. Rights are valued separately from the stock and trade in the secondary market during a prescribed subscription period. Shareholders may exercise their rights, may sell them for cash, or let them expire.

H. WARRANTS

LO E.33.24 Discuss the use of warrants.

Warrants are essentially long-term, customized call options used to purchase the stock of the underlying corporation. Warrants guarantee, for a small premium, the opportunity to buy stock at a fixed price during a particular period of time. In essence, they are a bet that the future price of the issuer's stock is going to increase. Thus, investors buy warrants if they are optimistic or bullish regarding the prospects for the stock. Like call options, warrants give the owner the right to purchase a specified number of common stock shares for a specified period of time at a specified price, normally *higher* than the current market price, as of the date of the issue of the warrant. However, unlike a call option, for which the owner has only the right to purchase a round lot of common shares (i.e., 100 shares), warrants generally do not give the owner the right to purchase 100 shares. In addition, warrants also differ from call options (a call) in the following ways.

- A warrant is issued by a corporation, whereas a call is written by an individual.
- A warrant is customized to fit the needs of the issuing corporation and owner, whereas a call includes standardized terms required by the Options Clearing Corporation.
- A warrant typically has a maturity date of several years (up to five years or more), whereas a call normally expires within nine months.

EXAMPLE David purchases a warrant for $1 per share that gives him the right to buy 50 shares of KRF stock at $10 per share for a period of five years from date of purchase. Assume that KRF stock goes up to $14 per share after three years and David exercises the warrant. Accordingly, he makes a profit of $150 on the 50 shares.

Profit = (Gain on stock – Cost of warrant) × Number of shares

Profit = ($4/share – $1/share) × 50 shares = $150

If the price of the warrant is below the specified price when the warrant expires, the warrant is worthless. However, because little money has been expended for the warrant (in the previous example, only $50), and because it has a longer right of exercise than a regular option, warrants are actively traded in the secondary market.

If corporations issue warrants, they usually do so in conjunction with new bond issues or preferred stock issues. These warrants give the bond or stock purchaser a sweetener or equity kicker, making the particular issue more attractive to buyers. In addition, issuing the bonds or preferred stock with a warrant will typically permit the issuer to lower the coupon or dividend rate necessary to entice investors to make the investment. These lower rates will reduce the overall cost of capital for the issuer.

Rights	Warrants
Short term	Long term
On issuance, exercise price below market price	On issuance, exercise price higher than market price
May trade with or separate from the common stock	May trade with or separate from the units
Offered to existing stakeholders with preemptive rights	Offered as a sweetened for another security

PRACTICE QUESTION

Choose the best answer for the question below.
The answer can be found at the end of this unit.

6. All of the following are reasons for a corporation to issue a warrant EXCEPT
- A. as an incentive for investors to purchase preferred stock
- B. to allow for standardization of terms among all potential investors
- C. to lower the cost of capital necessary to float an issue
- D. as an incentive for investors to purchase corporate debentures

I. INTERNATIONAL INVESTING

LO E.33.25 Explain the benefits and methods of international investing.

International investing offers an investor the benefits of diversification and potential higher returns. Although foreign securities offer investors the potential for substantial gains, they bear a variety of risks that are not present with domestic investments. An investor will be subject to the additional risks of exchange rate risk (currency risk) and country risk. **Country risk** is a composite of all the risks of investing in a particular country. These may include political risks, such as revolutions or military coups, and structural risks, such as confiscatory policies toward profits, capital gains, and dividends. Economic policies, interest rates, and inflation are also elements of risk of investing in emerging countries.

Emerging Markets

Emerging markets are markets in lesser developed countries. They are generally associated with:

- low levels of income, as measured by the country's gross domestic product (GDP);
- low levels of equity capitalization;
- questionable market liquidity;
- potential restrictions on currency conversion;
- high volatility;
- prospects for economic growth and development;
- stabilizing political and social institutions;
- high taxes and commission costs for foreign investor;
- restrictions on foreign ownership and on foreign currency conversion; and
- lower regulatory standards resulting in a lack of transparency.

Despite primitive market infrastructures, many emerging markets have rapid growth rates that make their securities attractive to foreign investors whose local markets experience more modest growth.

Developed Markets

Developed markets are those associated with countries that have highly developed economies with stable political and social institutions. These are characterized by:

- large levels of equity capitalization;
- low commission rates;
- few, if any, currency conversion restrictions;
- highly liquid markets with many brokerage institutions and market makers;
- many large capitalization securities; and
- well-defined regulatory schemes leading to transparency similar to that enjoyed by those investing in U.S. securities.

In summation, why would a planner include foreign securities in a client's portfolio?

- The planner has expanded the potential investment universe leading to greater diversification.
- Foreign securities sometimes outperform domestic ones.
- Foreign securities are usually not highly correlated with domestic ones and, as a result, the overall risk of the portfolio is reduced.

An investor may use one or more of the following ways to invest internationally:

- Purchase shares of a foreign mutual fund or exchange-traded fund
- Purchase shares of a foreign closed-end fund
- Direct purchase of foreign shares on a foreign stock exchange
- Purchase American depositary receipts (ADRs)

American Depositary Receipts (ADRs)

American depositary receipts (ADRs) are trust receipts issued by a U.S. bank for shares of a foreign company purchased and held by a foreign branch of the bank. They are an alternative to direct investing in foreign companies or mutual funds and provide several benefits.

- ADRs are denominated and pay dividends in U.S. dollars, not foreign currencies, thus saving the investor transaction costs with respect to converting currencies. Such dividends, however, are declared in the local currency and converted into U.S. dollars. Therefore, exchange rate risk is not completely eliminated.
- Information about the foreign company is often more easily attainable with ADRs because the U.S. bank (or its foreign branch) holding the security generally has ready access to that information.
- Because ADRs are traded on exchanges, they are relatively liquid and marketable investments. An ADR's price corresponds to the foreign stock's price in its home market.

Dividends paid by ADRs are taxed to the investor as ordinary income in the year earned. However, corporations whose stock of American depositary receipts is readily tradable on an established U.S. securities market qualify for the same 0%/15%/20% rates as are long-term capital gains. Before dividends are passed through to the shareholder on ADRs, the entity may withhold foreign taxes due. These foreign taxes paid may then be eligible for the foreign tax credit on the U.S. investor's income tax return (IRS Form 1040), or alternatively, the foreign taxes paid may be taken as an itemized deduction on that return.

PRACTICE QUESTION

Choose the best answer for the question below.
The answer can be found at the end of this unit.

7. Which of the following risks would be of greatest concern to a holder of ADRs?

1. Currency
2. Liquidity
3. Market
4. Purchasing power

A. 1 and 2
B. 1 and 3
C. 2 and 4
D. 3 and 4

J. OPEN-END INVESTMENT COMPANIES (MUTUAL FUNDS)

LO E.33.26 Describe the types, features, and taxation of open-end investment companies (mutual funds).

An **open-end investment company (mutual fund)** is the most popular form of investment asset for the small or individual investor. Mutual funds pool capital from many investors and invest in stocks, bonds, money-market instruments, and other securities according to a specific investment objective outlined in the prospectus. This investment provides both the advantage of diversification as well as access to professional money management. The investment company is categorized as open end because an unlimited number of shares may be sold to investors. In addition, the ownership of shares is constantly changing because some investors are purchasing shares in the fund while others are selling (redeeming) shares. The open-end investment company can raise an unlimited amount of capital by continuously issuing new shares. Mutual fund shares are purchased and redeemed only through the fund; they are not traded on exchanges. The shares of the fund are always priced at net asset value at the end of the trading day. **Net asset value (NAV)** is defined as the fair market value of the securities within the portfolio, less any outstanding liabilities, divided by the number of shares outstanding.

Mutual funds offer investors a wide variety of investment objectives and may be classified according to the types of securities in which they invest. Normally, funds are first categorized by the type of major investment (i.e., stocks, bonds, or money market securities) and second categorized by their investment objective (e.g., growth, income, and balanced).

- Stock funds
  - *Growth*: Invested in stocks of companies that are growing rapidly, these funds are focused on stocks that generate capital gains rather than income and are oftentimes further categorized as large cap, mid cap, aggressive, or small cap (*cap* stands for capitalization and references the market size of the company's outstanding stock issues).
  - *Income*: An income fund emphasizes current income over growth. The fund's objectives are accomplished by investing in the stocks of companies with long histories of dividend payments, such as utility companies or blue-chip stocks.
  - *Growth and income*: These funds invest in securities offering potentially increasing value. They are primarily interested in so-called *value stocks* or stocks that are underpriced relative to a stock that exhibits similar risk and return characteristics.
  - *Index*: These funds invest in securities designed to mirror a selected market index, such as the Standard & Poor's 500 Index. They track the selected index's performance and buy and sell securities in a manner that mirrors its composition.
  - *Sector*: A fund that restricts its investments to a particular sector of the market, such as energy or health care. Such fund tends to be more risky than a more diversified fund or portfolio.

- Bond funds
  - *Corporate bond funds*: These funds seek a high level of income by investing two-thirds or more of their portfolios in corporate bonds and have no explicit restrictions on average maturity.
  - *U.S. government bond funds*: These funds purchase securities issued by the U.S. Treasury or an agency of the U.S. government. Investors in these funds seek current income and maximum safety.
- Hybrid funds
  - *Asset allocation funds*: These funds focus on providing a diversified portfolio by investing across various asset classes including equities, bonds, and money markets.
  - *Balanced funds*: These funds invest in fixed percentages of equity, bond, and money market securities.

Investors may also consider international or global mutual funds for purposes of diversification. An **international mutual fund** invests in securities of companies that are located outside the United States, whereas a **global mutual fund** invests in securities that are traded worldwide, including U.S. issues. These funds attempt to reduce exchange rate risk.

Suitability

In determining suitability of mutual funds, the first step is to determine the client's primary investment objective. In general, the following rules apply.

- Investors seeking growth should invest in stock funds.
- Investors seeking income should invest in bond funds.
- Investors who are concerned about safety of principal should invest in government bond funds.
- Investors who are concerned with immediate liquidity should invest in money market funds.

Additional objectives must also be taken into consideration. Some possibilities are listed below.

- Investors seeking aggressive growth should invest in technology stock funds or stock funds invested in new companies. Aggressive funds or small-cap funds are usually most suitable for investors who have high risk tolerance, a long time horizon, or both.
- Investors who are seeking growth but are more conservative should consider balanced funds, which are likely to be large-cap funds. These funds are not as speculative as smaller-cap and aggressive funds.
- Investors seeking higher income who can assume moderate risk should invest in a corporate bond fund.
- Investors with a very high risk tolerance can maximize current income through investing in a high-yield (junk) bond fund.
- High tax bracket investors seeking income should invest in a municipal bond fund.
- Investors seeking income-producing stock should select a large-cap stock fund (a large-cap stock is a large company stock that has a consistently strong performance history and regularly pays dividends), a preferred stock fund, or a utility stock fund (utility stocks historically pay high, consistent dividends).

Taxation

Investors in a mutual fund typically receive annual income in one of three forms: (1) ordinary taxable dividends, (2) exempt interest dividends (e.g., from a municipal bond fund), and (3) capital gain distributions. Shareholders who receive the latter do not report the distributions as ordinary income dividends but—typically—as long-term capital gains. Occasionally, shareholders will also receive a distribution from the mutual fund that is a tax-free return of capital from a sale of shares; these will be considered nontaxable distributions. Finally, mutual fund investors often have an automatic reinvestment option under which dividend income and capital gain distributions are used to purchase additional shares for the investor's account. Although no actual cash payments are received, an investor is considered in constructive receipt of the dividends (and distributions) that are subsequently reinvested and must pay tax on these payments.

Note that although dividends paid from a tax-exempt fund (such as a municipal bond fund) are nontaxable annually, a sale or exchange of shares from such a fund does result in a taxable event. However, to the taxpayer's benefit, the original cost basis of tax-exempt fund shares is increased by the amount of any reinvested dividends. This rule applies even though the distribution is considered an exempt interest dividend and not otherwise reportable as income.

Taxable distributions are one of the largest drawbacks to investing in mutual funds (compared to owning stocks directly). When an investor buys a stock, no taxes are owed (except for those on dividends) until the shares are sold. Therefore, the investor controls the timing of the taxable event. This is not the case with mutual funds. The law requires that cash from the year's net gains—those left after taking offsetting losses—must be distributed by December 31. However, generally the taxpayer is at the mercy of the mutual fund manager in the timing and implementation of these distributions. This means the taxpayer's best strategy is to find out about potentially taxable distributions before they take place. An investor may wish to choose funds with a lower turnover ratio, potentially minimizing taxable distributions.

If an investor sells shares of a mutual fund, there is a tax owed on any gain. This gain is measured by the net sales price received for the shares (after deducting any expenses of sale) less the investor's basis (or adjusted cost) in the shares. The calculation of shareholder's basis may be quite complicated, particularly if (as is often the case) these shares have been accumulated at different times over different years. In this instance, there are three methods the investor may use to calculate basis: (1) the **specific identification method**; (2) the **average cost method**; and (3) **first in, first out (FIFO)**. Of the three methods, the specific identification method will generally be the most favorable for the investor (i.e., result in the highest cost basis and least tax due), but it requires the investor to keep detailed records and identify to the IRS the exact shares sold.

Generally, FIFO is the least favorable method and is the method used by the IRS in the event that the investor-taxpayer cannot identify the specific shares or use the average cost method. Of course, this is the case only in a rising market where the price of earlier mutual fund shares purchased is less than those involving later purchases. Finally, the average cost method is the most frequently used means of calculating shareholder basis. In this method, the investor pools all of the purchased shares into one account and then divides the total cost by the number of shares held. In this case, all shares will have the same unit cost or basis. Many mutual funds will provide the average cost basis of shares to their investors as part of the fund's shareholder services.

PRACTICE QUESTIONS

Choose the best answer for each of the questions below.
Answers can be found at the end of this unit.

8. In a rising stock market, which of the following methods of establishing basis in mutual fund shares is the most favorable to the taxpayer-owner?

A. Average cost method
B. FIFO
C. Specific identification
D. Amortized cost method

9. Janine's investment portfolio is 50% growth stocks, 10% foreign stocks, and 40% blue-chip stocks. Janine is interested in further diversification. Which mutual fund would best meet her goal?

A. Emerging market fund
B. Global equity fund
C. Bond fund
D. Aggressive growth fund

10. Mary and Ed, ages 62 and 68 respectively, would like to add a new mutual fund investment to their portfolio. They are seeking income along with a preservation of capital. Which of the following would be the best alternative based on their investment objective?

A. High-Yield Bond Fund
B. Asset Allocation Fund
C. Russell 2000 Index Fund
D. U.S. Government Bond Fund

K. CLOSED-END INVESTMENT COMPANIES (CLOSED-END FUNDS)

LO E.33.27 Discuss the features of closed-end investment companies and how they differ from open-end investment companies.

A **closed-end investment company** is a type of company whose shares trade in the same manner that publicly traded stocks trade in the secondary market. Shares of the closed-end fund are traded on a stock exchange or over the counter. Because shares are subject to supply and demand, they will generally sell at a discount or premium relative to NAV. This is a major difference between a closed-end fund and an open-end (mutual) fund. Most closed-end investment companies publish their actual NAV after each trading day so investors can determine if their shares are currently trading at a premium or discount to NAV.

After the initial public offering, a closed-end fund will generally not issue additional shares. Therefore, unlike a mutual fund, the capitalization of the closed-end fund is considered fixed, which has both advantages and disadvantages. The manager does not have to worry about cash redemptions (as with a mutual fund), which in turn, may permit the manager to invest in less-liquid securities. On the other hand, the fund does not have readily available additional sources of funds because its capitalization is fixed at the time the fund is first offered to potential shareholders. Some closed-end investment companies use leverage or borrow funds to help increase the current yield within the portfolios. This also increases the risk dramatically.

Financial planners who use closed-end funds should encourage their clients to read the prospectus of each fund they plan on using and understand the level of risk each portfolio manager is permitted to take. Closed-end funds may have varying investment objectives, strategies, and investment portfolios. Also, the fund may be subject to varying risks, volatility, and fees and expenses.

PRACTICE QUESTION

Choose the best answer for the question below.
The answer can be found at the end of this unit.

11. A pooled investment with a share price significantly different from its net asset value (NAV) per share is most likely:

A. a closed-end fund
B. an open-end fund
C. an exchange-traded fund
D. a unit-investment trust

L. UNIT INVESTMENT TRUSTS (UITs)

LO E.33.28 Explain the attributes of a unit investment trust (UIT) and provide reasons for purchasing this investment vehicle.

A **unit investment trust (UIT)** is a type of investment company whose units are sold in the secondary market but not on the major exchanges. UIT investors generally purchase units (instead of shares), which are sold at NAV plus a broker's commission. As income is earned and securities mature, investors receive both income and principal from the trust.

UITs are generally known as unmanaged, or passively managed, funds because professional managers initially select the securities to be included in the portfolio and then hold those securities (usually bonds) until they mature. UITs do not have corporate officers, a board of directors, or an investment adviser to provide advice during the term of the trust. At the maturity date of the portfolio, the securities are generally liquidated, and the proceeds are distributed to the investors or trust beneficiaries. During the term of the trust, the unit holders are taxed like shareholders of a mutual fund, with capital gains, interest, and dividends earned by the trust passed through and taxed to the unit holders.

PRACTICE QUESTION

Choose the best answer for the question below.
The answer can be found at the end of this unit.

12. Which of the following statements regarding unit investment trusts is NOT correct?

A. They do not have a board of directors.
B. They do not employ an investment adviser.
C. They do not actively manage their own portfolios.
D. Unit holders are not taxed on capital gains, interest, or dividends until they dispose of their units or the trust terminates.

M. EXCHANGE-TRADED FUNDS (ETFs)

LO E.33.29 Describe the characteristics and advantages of exchange-traded funds (ETFs).

An **exchange-traded fund (ETF)** is an index fund that, unlike a mutual fund, can be bought and sold in market transactions by investors throughout the trading day. Some investors, such as large broker/dealers, may purchase and redeem shares directly from the ETF; usually in large blocks (e.g., 50,000 ETF shares). Because they mimic indexes, ETFs typically have lower annual expenses than mutual funds. They also have lower turnover of assets than mutual funds and are, as a result, more tax efficient. A shareholder in an ETF may also request an in-kind redemption, which occurs when the investor redeems some of the shares in the fund for a distribution of some of the fund's underlying stock. As a result, the investor does not receive a cash distribution and is not taxed on the transaction.

An ETF is usually passively managed and attempts to track a specific index (e.g., S&P 500 Index) or sector within the index. The price of the fund shares is based on the value of the underlying securities; thus, this price may or may not be equal to the NAV, which is calculated every business day, of the fund because of supply and demand for the shares. An actively managed ETF is more expensive than the average passive exchange-traded fund. The investment manager makes investment decisions on a daily basis and may invest beyond the benchmark index.

An investment in ETFs may be advantageous for investors who:

- seek to invest in an industry sector or index but who do not want to have to consider a multitude of actively managed securities;
- are interested in a low-cost, tax-efficient portfolio; and
- are interested in a security that may be bought on margin and can be sold short.

PRACTICE QUESTION

Choose the best answer for the question below.
The answer can be found at the end of this unit.

13. Stewart, age 29, is seeking an investment that offers the potential for long-term growth based on a broad market index representative of the largest domestic and international non-financial companies. He considers himself a moderate to aggressive risk-taker and is interested in a low-cost, tax-efficient portfolio. Which of the following would be the best investment for Stewart?

A. Long-Term Corporate Bond ETF
B. Green Energy Mutual Fund
C. NASDAQ 100 ETF
D. Pacific Rim Growth ETF

N. INVESTMENT COMPANY COMPARISON

LO E.33.30 Identify the similarities and differences among the types of investment companies.

All investment companies are subject to SEC registration and regulations, which are designed to protect investors. In summary, you should be able to identify the similarities and differences among the types of investment companies.

	Open-End	Closed-End	UIT	ETF
Capitalization	Unlimited	Fixed	Fixed	Varies
Trading	Fund company	Exchange	Exchange	Exchange*
Pricing	NAV + sales charge (if applicable)	Current market value	NAV + commission	NAV + commission**
Management	Active	Active	Passive	Passive / Active

*May accept in-kind redemptions.
**ETFs generally trade close to NAV; however, supply and demand may cause the price to fluctuate.

O. HEDGE FUNDS

LO E.41.1 Explain the distinguishing features of hedge funds and how they differ from investment company offerings.

A **hedge fund** is generally an unregistered, privately offered, managed pool of capital for wealthy, financially sophisticated investors. Hedge funds invest in a broad range of investments, from shares, debt, and commodities to works of art. Each fund will have its own unique portfolio strategy. This type of fund is usually structured as a partnership, with the general partner acting as the investment manager and investors constituting the limited partners. The fund typically implements a wide array of investment strategies, including heavy borrowing and short selling, in an attempt to achieve a superior return for investors. A hedge fund strives to capture market inefficiencies and, unlike most ETFs, uses active management techniques. Finally, unlike mutual fund managers, whose compensation depends on the amount of assets under management, hedge fund managers are paid on the basis of fund performance and commonly own a significant percentage of the fund's shares.

A speculative investor of considerable means who is most interested in managing the risk of possible loss from an investment is the most likely type of investor in a hedge fund. In addition, an investor who is very concerned about the skill and expertise of the portfolio manager should strongly consider contributing to a hedge fund. Conversely, such a fund is usually beyond the financial means of the smaller investor who is looking for capital growth or current income, the two primary investment objectives of mutual fund shareholders.

Risks associated with hedge funds include:

- Leverage—a hedge fund will typically borrow money, with certain funds borrowing amounts exponentially greater than the initial investment
- Short selling—due to the nature of short selling, the losses that can be incurred are potentially unlimited
- Higher risk investments—by their nature, hedge funds are more likely than other types of funds to take on underlying investments that carry high degrees of risk, such as debt obligations based on sub-prime mortgages
- Lack of transparency—hedge funds have few public disclosure requirements

PRACTICE QUESTION

Choose the best answer for the question below.
The answer can be found at the end of this unit.

14. Which of the following clients would be the best candidate for a hedge fund?
- A. Marcy, age 23, recent college graduate, student debt, low net worth, entry-level position at a local law firm
- B. Bob and Carol, mid 30s, two young kids, homeowner, $50,000 net worth, long-term investment perspective
- C. Howard, age 78, widowed, conservative risk taker, $250,000 net worth, lives on a fixed income
- D. Drew and Fran, late 50s, no dependents, semi-retired, $5 million net worth, moderate risk takers, diversified holdings

P. SEPARATELY MANAGED ACCOUNTS

LO E.33.31 Describe the benefits of a separately managed account.

A **separately managed account** is an account comprising a diversified portfolio of individual securities managed by a professional money manager. Similar to a mutual fund, the account manager will develop a model portfolio specializing in a particular aspect of the market (e.g., large-cap, small-cap, or value). Many of these accounts have a minimum investment requirement of $50,000 or more. In this type of account, the investor owns 100% of the securities in the account, and the investment decisions are made by the money manager. However, investors may have the ability to exclude specific investments based on personal preferences. The account differs from a mutual fund in that the professional manager purchases the securities in the portfolio on behalf of the investor, not on behalf of the fund. A major advantage of the account is that it gives the investor the ability to maintain an individual cost basis in the securities within the portfolio, thereby making it easier for prudent income tax management. This advantage is not available to a mutual fund shareholder, who owns only a percentage of the total pooled assets.

PRACTICE QUESTION

Choose the best answer for the question below.
The answer can be found at the end of this unit.

15. An investor in a separately managed account versus a mutual fund has the advantage of
- A. maintaining an individual cost basis in the securities within the portfolio, thereby making it easier to income tax plan
- B. the investment manager purchasing securities for the benefit of the fund
- C. owning a set proportion of the securities in the account
- D. owning a percentage of the total pooled assets of the fund

Q. VENTURE CAPITAL

LO E.41.2 Cite the various uses of venture capital.

Venture capital is financing for privately held companies (e.g., start-ups) typically in the form of convertible preferred stock and is characterized by high risk with the potential for high return. Venture capitalists are willing to take significant risks, and lose their entire investment in several ventures, in hopes of cashing in on a few highly profitable ventures. These investments are characterized by high risk, high return, lack of liquidity, and a low correlation with equities. Venture capital can be used for the early stages of financing, such as start-up financing (funding for product development and marketing) and expansion financing (funding for the expansion of an existing company). Other uses of venture capital include turnarounds (companies losing market share and close to bankruptcy) and leveraged buyouts (use of the company's assets as collateral in a sale).

PRACTICE QUESTION

Choose the best answer for the question below.
The answer can be found at the end of this unit.

16. Which of the following statements regarding venture capital are CORRECT?

1. Venture capitalists have a high risk tolerance.
2. They offer investors the potential for high rates of return.
3. Investors are willing to lose their entire principal.
4. Venture capital investments exhibit a high level of liquidity.

A. 1 and 2
B. 3 and 4
C. 1, 2, and 3
D. 1, 2, 3, and 4

R. PRIVATE PLACEMENTS

LO E.41.3 Discuss why a company would use a private placement to generate capital.

Instead of incurring the time and expense of an IPO, some businesses choose to sell their securities privately in order to meet their capital formation needs. Companies may use **private placements** to sell an issue, most commonly bonds, to a small group of institutions or sophisticated individual investors. Private placements avoid the SEC registration requirements of an IPO and a company's information is not accessible by the general public. Private placements are limited to 35 unaccredited investors, but are available to an unlimited number of accredited investors [individuals with more than $200,000 of annual income (or $300,000 jointly with a spouse) or net worth of $1 million or more]. Also, officers and directors of the issuer are considered accredited investors.

PRACTICE QUESTION

Choose the best answer for the question below.
The answer can be found at the end of this unit.

17. John, age 47, is considering diversifying his large portfolio. He has contacted his broker to discuss the merits of investing in a private placement. Which of the following are considerations to determine the suitability of a private placement for John?

1. How much information regarding the company is available to John?
2. How and when might he be able to liquidate the investment?
3. What are the risk factors?
4. How does this investment mix with his current holdings?

A. 1 only
B. 3 and 4
C. 2, 3, and 4
D. 1, 2, 3, and 4

S. LIMITED PARTNERSHIPS

LO E.41.4 Discuss the advantages and disadvantages of limited partnerships.

Limited partnerships are characterized by a partnership entity that consists of a general partner and limited partners. The general partner controls the business activities of the partnership, determines when distributions are made to the limited partners, and has unlimited liability. The limited partners do not participate in the management of the partnership and have limited liability. Advantages for limited partners include: business venture participation with limited liability; start-up financing shared with other partners, whereby, one individual is not responsible for all the start-up costs; and receipt of periodic income payments. The disadvantages of limited partnerships include: they are generally riskier investments than bonds or exchange-traded equities; they are usually illiquid; limited partners cannot participate in the management of the partnership; and the sale of partnership interest may be restricted.

Limited partnership investments tend to be relatively risky and generally *unsuitable* for the average investor. Mutual funds or exchange-traded funds (ETFs) offer investors many of the same advantages of limited partnerships, including diversification and professional management, but without as much marketability or liquidity risk.

PRACTICE QUESTION

Choose the best answer for the question below.
The answer can be found at the end of this unit.

18. Kim owns a Marina Limited Partnership worth $25,000. She is interested in selling her interest in order to raise money for a down payment on a new rental property. Which of the following are NOT characteristics of her investment in the limited partnership?

A. Kim's investment is managed by someone other than herself.
B. Tax-free income is provided by the partnership to Kim.
C. Her interest may be subject to liquidity and marketability risk.
D. The sale of her interest may be restricted.

T. SUMMARY OF TAXATION OF INVESTMENT TRANSACTIONS

	Income*	Sale at Capital Gain**	Sale at Loss	Adjusted Tax Basis
Stocks	Taxable	Capital gain	Capital loss	Generally cost
Bonds—corporate or Treasury	Taxable	Capital gain	Capital loss	Generally cost
Municipal bonds	Not taxable	Capital gain	Capital loss	Generally cost
OID bonds—corporate or Treasury	Taxable	Capital gain	Capital loss	Generally cost
Mutual funds	Taxable	Capital gain	Capital loss	Cost + income reinvested

*Income refers to proceeds from the investment after acquisition.
**Capital gains are long term or short term, depending on the holding period.

103 UNIT 3 ANSWERS TO PRACTICE QUESTIONS

1. B. Only 2 and 4 are correct. A stockholder is entitled to share in the earnings of the company. A bondholder has the right above a stockholder to assets of the corporation in case of liquidation.

2. C. The best choice for the couple is the pharmaceutical stock. This type of stock is generally riskier and may provide a higher rate of return than the other choices. Grocery stock is considered a defensive stock. Utility stock is an example of an income stock. An international airline stock is a cyclical stock.

3. C. Shareholders of preferred stock receive dividends each year equal to a stated percentage of the par value of the stock (e.g., a 4% dividend on a $100 par value of preferred stock).

4. B. Only the dividends paid in cash to Greg are reported as income. The stock dividends did not have a cash-dividend option and are not taxable.

5. B. Stock splits and reverse splits do not change the total value of shares. Thus, Patricia will own 100 × $150 = $15,000 of Blue stock and 300 × $5 = $1,500 of Red stock. In a 2-for-1 stock split, the number of shares doubles, so Patricia will own 200 shares of Blue stock. In a 1-for-3 reverse split, the number of shares is divided by 3, so Patricia will own 100 shares of Red stock.

6. B. Warrants are essentially customized (not standardized) call options issued to meet the needs of both the issuing corporation and the investor.

7. B. ADRs represent ownership in a foreign security that subjects the holder to currency risk. Since most ADRs are traded on the exchanges, they are subject to little liquidity risk, and, because they represent equity, they are usually a good hedge against inflation.

8. C. In a stock market where prices are rising, specific identification of mutual fund shares sold will generally prove most favorable to the taxpayer. (FIFO is least favorable.) However, most taxpayers do not keep good financial records, and therefore, the average cost method of determining basis in mutual fund shares is the most common.

9. C. Janine's portfolio contains foreign equities and growth stocks. She does not own fixed-income securities.

10. D. With an investment objective of income and capital preservation, they should choose the U.S. Government Bond Fund. This type of fund is designed to offer an investor income. Also, the securities within this type of portfolio should provide the investor with principal stability.

11. A. Closed-end funds' share prices can differ significantly from their NAVs. Open-end fund shares can be purchased and redeemed at their NAVs. Market forces keep exchange-traded fund share prices close to their NAVs because arbitrageurs can profit by trading when there are differences. UIT investors purchase units, which are sold at NAV plus a broker's commission.

12. D. During the term of the trust, capital gains, interest, and dividends earned by the trust and passed through to the unit holders are subject to taxation.

13. C. Based on his investment objectives and risk tolerance, the NASDAQ 100 ETF is the best choice for Stewart. The Long-Term Corporate Bond ETF does not meet his need for a long-term growth investment. The Pacific Rim Growth ETF and the Green Energy Mutual Fund would be too concentrated in one market segment.

14. D. The best choice for a hedge fund is Drew and Fran. They have no dependents, have high net worth (diversified), and exhibit a moderate risk tolerance. A hedge fund is generally an unregistered, privately offered, managed pool of capital for wealthy, financially sophisticated investors. The other three clients would generally not be considered candidates for a hedge fund based on net worth and investment objectives.

15. A. The investment manager purchases securities for the benefit of the investor, not the fund. The investor owns 100% of the securities in the account, while a mutual fund owner only owns a percentage of the total pooled assets of the fund.

16. C. Only statement 4 is incorrect. Venture capital investments exhibit a lack of liquidity.

17. D. All of these are considerations for an investor when deciding on the purchase of a private placement.

18. B. The income from limited partnerships is not tax exempt. An investor, however, may use a tax loss from a partnership to offset the income from another passive investment.

103 UNIT 3 POST-STUDY CHECKLIST

- ☐ Do I understand the differences between equity and debt securities?
- ☐ Am I able to describe the characteristics and types of common stock?
- ☐ Can I describe how dividends are paid and taxed to shareholders?
- ☐ Do I understand the characteristics and primary purchasers of preferred stock?
- ☐ Can I describe a stock dividend and a stock split?
- ☐ Do I understand the use of rights?
- ☐ Can I explain how corporations use warrants?
- ☐ Am I able to explain the benefits and methods of international investing?
- ☐ Am I able to describe the types, features, and taxation of open-end investment companies?
- ☐ Can I explain the features of closed-end investment companies and how they differ from open-end investment companies?
- ☐ Do I understand the attributes of unit investment trusts?
- ☐ Can I describe the characteristics and advantages of exchange-traded funds?
- ☐ Am I able to explain the distinguishing features of hedge funds and how they differ from investment company offerings?
- ☐ Can I describe the benefits of a separately managed account?
- ☐ Do I understand the uses of venture capital?
- ☐ Can I summarize why a company would use a private placement?
- ☐ Do I understand the advantages and disadvantages of limited partnerships?
- ☐ Can I explain how investors' tax obligations are impacted by capital gains and losses, dividends, and wash sales?

Am I able to define and understand the application of the following terms as they relate to investment planning?

- ☐ American depositary receipts (ADRs)
- ☐ Average cost method
- ☐ Blue-chip stocks
- ☐ Closed-end investment company
- ☐ Common stock
- ☐ Country risk
- ☐ Cyclical stocks
- ☐ Defensive stocks
- ☐ Developed markets
- ☐ Emerging markets
- ☐ Equity
- ☐ Exchange-traded fund (ETF)
- ☐ Ex-dividend date
- ☐ First in, first out (FIFO)
- ☐ Global mutual fund
- ☐ Growth stocks
- ☐ Hedge fund
- ☐ Income stocks
- ☐ International mutual fund
- ☐ Limited partnerships
- ☐ Net asset value (NAV)
- ☐ Open-end investment company (mutual fund)
- ☐ Perpetuity
- ☐ Preferred stock
- ☐ Private placements
- ☐ Reverse stock split
- ☐ Record date
- ☐ Rights
- ☐ Separately managed account
- ☐ Shareholder of record
- ☐ Specific identification method
- ☐ Stock dividend
- ☐ Stock split
- ☐ Unit investment trust (UIT)
- ☐ Value stocks
- ☐ Venture capital
- ☐ Warrants
- ☐ Wash sale

UNIT 4

Alternative Investments and Derivatives

REFER TO

CFP Board Principal Knowledge Topics – E. Investment Planning, E.33. Characteristics, Uses, and Taxation of Investment Vehicles

CFP Board Principal Knowledge Topics – E. Investment Planning, E.40. Investment Strategies

CFP Board Principal Knowledge Topics – E. Investment Planning, E.41. Alternative Investments

INTRODUCTION

Alternative investments differ from traditional investments (e.g., publicly traded stocks, bonds, cash) both in the types of assets and securities included in this asset class and in the structure of the investment vehicles in which these assets are held. The primary motivation for holding alternative investments is their historically low correlation of returns with those of traditional investments, which can reduce an investor's overall portfolio risk. However, the risk measures used for traditional assets may not be adequate to capture the risk characteristics of alternative investments. Asset allocation is improved with the addition of alternative investments. Investors can improve their risk-adjusted performance with alternatives. Also, they can reduce risk for a given return or increase return for a given risk. As a result, investors, especially those that are high net worth, should consider alternative investments for their portfolios.

LEARNING OBJECTIVES

After completing this unit, you should be able to achieve the following learning objectives:

CFP® Board Principal Knowledge Topics – E. Investment Planning

E.33. Characteristics, Uses, and Taxation of Investment Vehicles

LO E.33.32 Define a guaranteed investment contract and identify its major purchasers.

LO E.33.33 Discuss the types, valuation, and taxation of options.

E.40. Investment Strategies

LO E.40.8 Describe hedging, protective puts, and zero-cost collars.

E.41. Alternative Investments

LO E.41.5 Explain the types, valuation, and taxation of real estate investments.

LO E.41.6 Describe differences between real estate limited partnerships and real estate investment trusts.

LO E.41.7 Define real estate mortgage investment conduits (REMICs) and collateralized mortgage obligations (CMOs).

LO E.41.8 Describe the characteristics, uses, and taxation of futures.

LO E.41.9 Describe the characteristics of tangible assets.

LO E.41.10 Explain the characteristics of natural resources.

KEY TERMS

At-the-money
Binomial option pricing model
Black-Scholes option valuation model
Call option
Collateralized mortgage obligation (CMO)
Derivatives
Futures contract
Guaranteed investment contract (GIC)
Hedging
In-the-money
Intrinsic value
Long-term equity anticipation securities (LEAPS)
Natural resources
Net operating income (NOI)
Options
Out-of-the-money
Portfolio insurance
Protective put
Put-call parity
Put option
Real estate investment trust (REIT)
Real estate limited partnership (RELP)
Real estate mortgage investment conduit (REMIC)
Tangible assets
Time value
Tranches
Undeveloped land
Zero-cost collar

A. REAL ESTATE INVESTMENTS

LO E.41.5 Explain the types, valuation, and taxation of real estate investments.

Many individuals own what they consider to be an investment in real estate: their personal residence. However, more appropriately, one's personal residence should be considered a personal use asset; as we know, that is how a residence is shown when a financial planner prepares the statement of financial position. Real estate investing provides many benefits including leverage and tax deductions. Leverage permits an investor to use a high percentage of debt financing in the acquisition of the property. In addition, tax deductions are available to investors including mortgage interest, property taxes, and depreciation.

> **EXAMPLE** If a $100,000 building is purchased with a $10,000 down payment and a mortgage of $90,000, any appreciation will be magnified 10 times. If the building is sold for $110,000, the investor will have realized a 100% return on invested capital [($110,000 – $100,000) ÷ $10,000].

Undeveloped Land

Undeveloped land is a passive investment and produces negative cash flows (in the form of ongoing expenses), while generating no income. Therefore, this asset is held by an investor strictly for the possibility of significant capital appreciation. When sold, undeveloped land is permitted capital gains treatment, as long as the owner is not considered to be a dealer in such land. Dealer tax treatment, in which the land is considered to be inventory, will result in the gain being taxed at ordinary income tax rates.

The risks associated with undeveloped land include the following.

- The land may be adversely rezoned; for example, property bought for residential development purposes may be rezoned as commercial use only.
- The investor may not be able to obtain permits to build on the land.
- Access to the investor's land may be restricted by adjacent landowners.
- The population growth anticipated by the investor may not occur.

As a result, an investment in undeveloped land is extremely risky; therefore, the investor should expect a significant, future capital return or the investment will likely not be made.

Undeveloped land does not usually produce significant income or cash flow to the owner; accordingly, current taxation is of little consequence. The primary tax advantage to the owner is that appreciation in the value of the land is not recognized as income until the owner disposes of the land in a taxable transaction; at such time, the appreciation is taxed as capital gain income unless the owner is treated as a dealer in real estate by the IRS, in which case ordinary income treatment will result. In addition, the real estate taxes are normally tax deductible by the owner of the undeveloped land during the entire period of ownership.

Commercial or Residential Rental Property

Certainly, only more experienced investors participate in the commercial rental property market. As such, in evaluating whether to purchase this type of real estate, an investor will usually employ the services of a professional appraiser. The appraiser will typically use several methods to determine the proper, or intrinsic, fair market value of the property, but among them will likely be a value based on **net operating income (NOI)**.

NOI is computed using the following steps:

Gross rental receipts from the property
\+ Nonrental or other income (e.g., laundry receipts)
= Potential gross income (PGI)
– Vacancy and collection losses
= Effective gross income (EGI)
– Operating expenses (excluding interest and depreciation)
= Net operating income (NOI)

You should note several important provisions with respect to this computation.

- Operating expenses include only cash expenses. Depreciation is not a cash expense, but rather a tax adjustment only and does not affect the actual cash flow from the property.
- Also not included among operating expenses is debt service, such as interest expense incurred by the investor in buying or financing the property. The focus of the NOI computation is the property's cash flow, not the investor's cash flow.

Once the NOI from the real property is calculated, we can then determine the intrinsic value of the property. Technically, intrinsic value is the discounted present value of the real property based on its future cash flows, but for most investors, it simply serves as the benchmark amount above which the property is not a prudent investment. To determine the intrinsic value of the real property, divide its NOI by an estimated capitalization (discount) rate for the market and location of the property. This capitalization (cap) rate is not easy to determine, which is why the investor will likely employ the services of a qualified appraiser.

EXAMPLE Assume that the annual NOI from real property is $92,250 and that the appraiser has determined a cap rate of 10% is appropriate for the market and location of the property. Accordingly, the intrinsic value of the property is $922,500 ($92,250 ÷ .10). If the property is listed for a sales price of $1 million, all other factors being equal, the property is currently overvalued, and the investor will likely choose not to purchase the property. However, if the appraiser determines a cap rate of 9% is appropriate, the investor would be willing to pay an intrinsic value of $1,025,000 ($92,250 ÷ .09) and, therefore, would consider the property to be currently undervalued.

NOI may also be used to decide whether to invest in residential real property, although that market tends to be dominated by less-experienced investors, and other nonfinancial pressures may, therefore, be more important. For example, many times an investment in residential real property is made because the investor falls in love with the property and makes the purchase for personal satisfaction. As a financial planner, you should emphasize the financial aspects of any real property purchase and minimize any other emotional or nonfinancial attachment that the investor may have for the property.

Unlike undeveloped land, current income from rental real estate is received in the form of rents. These rents are taxable as ordinary income to the owner, and net profit (that is, after deductible expenses) is reported by the owner on Schedule E of Form 1040. Because an annual depreciation deduction is afforded the owner who invests in rental real estate, recovery of some of the investment dollars expended through the claiming of such a deduction may occur. Note, however, that the depreciation allowance is only a tax benefit and does not affect the cash flow generated from the rental real estate to its owner.

PRACTICE QUESTIONS

Choose the best answer for each of the questions below.
Answers can be found at the end of this unit.

1. Roger is interested in purchasing a commercial real property investment currently offered for $2 million. He will finance the investment by taking out a $1.5 million loan, on which the debt service will be $9,000 per month. The real property will be depreciated using the straight-line depreciation method at $6,000 per month. Roger has determined that the gross rental receipts from the property will be $25,000 per month and that the vacancy and collection losses will be estimated at 5% of potential gross income. Operating expenses will be $12,000 per month. What is the monthly NOI of Roger's potential investment?

A. $2,750
B. $8,750
C. $11,750
D. $13,000

2. Brandon is considering selling a piece of residential real estate that he has owned for 12 years. The apartment complex consists of 100 units with an average rental rate of $400 per month. Laundry and parking gross potential income is $20,000 per year. The vacancy rate is 7%, and operating expenses are 30% of potential gross income. Brandon takes $40,000 of depreciation each year, and his mortgage costs $6,000 per month. If the capitalization rate for comparable properties is 9%, what should be the selling price for Brandon's property?

A. $3,500,000
B. $3,472,000
C. $3,056,000
D. $2,256,000

B. INDIRECT OWNERSHIP OF REAL ESTATE (RELPs AND REITs)

LO E.41.6 Describe differences between real estate limited partnerships and real estate investment trusts.

Real Estate Limited Partnerships (RELPs)

A popular form of indirect ownership of real estate is to invest as a limited partner, usually through a non-publicly traded **real estate limited partnership (RELP)** or syndication. A syndicated limited partnership consists of two owners: one is the syndicator or promoter of the partnership, who usually also serves as the general partner, and the second is the investor or limited partner. The syndicator will typically acquire a tract or tracts of real property and then attempt to sell it (or them) to the limited partner investors. In addition to charging fees for management of the real property tracts, the syndicator will retain an ownership interest and will be liable for all acts of the partnership. Investors will have no management responsibilities, and their liability will be limited to the extent of investment. RELPs may provide capital growth through appreciation of property. They may also distribute income, which can be sheltered from taxes by deductions of mortgage interest and depreciation.

Real estate syndications are usually adopted as much for tax reasons as for economic reasons. Accordingly, since the 1986 Tax Reform Act, minimum participation rules were included in the Internal Revenue Code to ensure that a partner is actually participating in the economic activity of the syndication. These rules are likely impossible for a limited partner to meet; thus, he is treated as only a passive investor with respect to the real property. As a result, the ability to deduct losses from the property is restricted under tax law. This is a major disadvantage of the limited partnership form of real estate investment and, in turn, limits the marketability of the limited partner's interest for sale to other potential investors.

Real Estate Investment Trusts (REITs)

A **real estate investment trust (REIT)** serves as a source of long-term financing for real estate projects by investing in real estate, short-term construction loans, and mortgages. A REIT pools capital in a manner similar to an investment company. Some REITs are publicly traded on the exchanges and may sell at a premium or discount to net asset value (NAV). As a result, the REIT investor achieves diversification and marketability that is generally lacking with the real estate limited partnership (RELP) form.

A REIT entity is not subject to federal income taxation as long as it distributes at least 90% of its net annual earnings to shareholders each year. Another requirement is that at least 75% of an entity's gross income must be derived from real estate. For the shareholders, income received is considered investment (not passive) income. This means that losses from the REIT are considered capital losses and are not restricted by the passive income activity rules that apply to RELPs. Dividends received from a REIT are taxed as ordinary income. However, they may be classified as qualified dividends for purposes of the 0%/15%/20% capital gain tax rates.

The types of REITs include the following.

- *Equity REITs* acquire real estate for the purpose of renting the space to other companies. Income is generated from the rents and sales of the real estate properties.
- *Mortgage REITs* are in the business of financing real estate ventures. Generally, mortgage REITs make loans to develop property or finance construction.
- *Hybrid REITs* have characteristics of both equity and mortgage REITs, as they rent properties and make construction loans.

Investors generally invest in REITs either for purposes of portfolio diversification or current income.

RELPs vs. REITs

- *Liquidity:* REITs are generally liquid and actively traded on national and regional stock exchanges, as well as over the counter. RELPs, with the exception of a small number of publicly traded partnerships, are generally not readily marketable and illiquid. In addition, a REIT shareholder may sell as few or as many shares as she deems appropriate, whereas a RELP investor must generally sell the entire interest.

- *Organizational Structure*: A REIT (as a corporation) is managed by a board of directors, whereas a RELP is managed by a general partner. Further, upon the death of a REIT shareholder, the organizational structure does not automatically terminate.
- *Risk*: The major risk associated with a REIT is usually the loss of potential purchasing power, although this may be mitigated with certain underlying investments. A RELP (as a limited partnership) suffers from extreme liquidity and marketability risk.

PRACTICE QUESTION

Choose the best answer for the question below.
The answer can be found at the end of this unit.

3. Which of the following statements describing the difference between a RELP and a REIT is CORRECT?

A. A RELP is actively traded on a stock exchange.
B. A REIT is a portfolio investment and generates investment income.
C. A RELP is not subject to the passive income taxation rules.
D. A REIT is managed by a general partner.

C. REAL ESTATE MORTGAGE INVESTMENT CONDUITS (REMICs)

LO E.41.7 Define real estate mortgage investment conduits (REMICs) and collateralized mortgage obligations (CMOs).

A **real estate mortgage investment conduit (REMIC)** is a self-liquidating, flow-through entity (similar to a partnership) that invests exclusively in real estate mortgages or mortgage-backed securities and terminates when the mortgages that constitute the investment of the REMIC are repaid. Typically, a REMIC issues debt securities to investors in the form of publicly traded REMIC bonds. However, some issue residual interests, which are privately placed and not available to the general public. Most newly issued CMOs and REMICs provide for monthly payments to the investor and are offered in denominations ranging from $1,000 to $25,000, depending on the issuer.

Investors who own either a REMIC bond or residual interest receive a specified cash flow from the underlying pool of mortgages. REMICs often are structured to offer classes of bonds that mature over a period of 3–30 years. Accordingly, investors may invest in a bond class that matches their investment time horizon, thereby, avoiding the uncertainty of bond principal repayment. As evident from the word conduit in its name, a REMIC is a pass through entity that is wholly exempt from federal income tax. Thus, it acts as a conduit, and holders of REMIC bonds (not the entity itself) must report any taxable income from the underlying mortgages.

One of the most common forms of REMIC is the **collateralized mortgage obligation (CMO)**. CMOs, which are mortgage derivatives created by private investment firms, are similar to mortgage-backed securities in that they are both backed by large pools of mortgages. However, CMOs, also referred to as multiclass securities, differ from mortgage-backed securities in that the cash flows associated with the pool of underlying mortgages are divided into repayment periods known as **tranches**. In the traditional mortgage-backed pass-through certificate, each investor receives a pro rata share of principal and interest each month, no matter the repayment period. This is not the case with CMOs; instead, each of the tranches receives regular interest payments, with the investors of the first tranche (Tranche A) receiving all principal payments until they are completely repaid. Once all of the obligations of Tranche A are satisfied, all principal payments are made to the second tranche (Tranche B) and so on until all of the tranches are repaid. As a result, the holders of Tranche A have less interest rate risk than do the holders of all the other tranches, because the maturity date (or repayment period) of the mortgage principal obligation is the shortest.

Tranche Z, on the other hand, has the longest repayment period, subjecting its investors to the most interest rate risk. Tranche Z bondholders do not receive any interest or principal payments until all other tranches are repaid. The interest due on Tranche Z bonds accrues in a similar fashion to that of zero-coupon bonds and is taxable in the year earned.

PRACTICE QUESTION

Choose the best answer for the question below.
The answer can be found at the end of this unit.

4. Which tranche of a collateralized mortgage obligation (CMO) carries the greatest amount of interest rate risk?

A. Tranche A
B. Tranche B
C. Tranche C
D. Tranche Z

D. GUARANTEED INVESTMENT CONTRACTS (GICs)

LO E.33.32 Define a guaranteed investment contract and identify its major purchasers.

Guaranteed investment contracts (GICs) are similar to certificates of deposit (CDs) but are issued by insurance companies, not commercial banks. They are called guaranteed investment contracts because the rate of return is guaranteed by the insurance company for a fixed period (e.g., five years). However, unlike CDs, GICs are not federally insured; therefore, despite the inclusion of the word *guaranteed* in the title, GICs carry slightly more investment risk than CDs. The proceeds are generally invested in commercial mortgages and investment-grade corporate and government bonds.

The major purchasers of GICs are institutions, specifically employers, who find such vehicles attractive as an investment option in a Section 401(k) or pension plan for vested employees. Employers typically choose between either a participating or a nonparticipating insurance contract. A participating GIC provides the employer with a variable rate of return based on interest rate changes. Alternatively, a nonparticipating GIC earns a fixed rate of return. If the employer believes that market interest rates are likely to increase over the term of the contract, the purchase of a participating GIC is likely prudent, whereas a nonparticipating GIC is a better choice if market interest rates are expected to decline.

PRACTICE QUESTION

Choose the best answer for the question below.
The answer can be found at the end of this unit.

5. The risk level of a typical guaranteed investment contract (GIC) with an insurance company is best described as
   A. conservative
   B. aggressive
   C. extremely risky
   D. default risk free

E. OPTIONS

LO E.33.33 Discuss the types, valuation, and taxation of options.

Derivatives are investment vehicles whose value is based on that of another security, such as a listed stock. The most common of these are options and futures contracts. For each of these investments, an investor may take a long position (i.e., buying or owning the underlying security or commodity) or a short position (i.e., selling or wanting to own the underlying security or commodity). Institutional investors have historically used derivatives to increase portfolio return or to limit portfolio risk. However, individual investors also use derivatives to generate income from an otherwise flat or extremely volatile stock market.

Options

An option contract is a two-party contract that allows the holder the right, but not the obligation, to buy (call) or sell (put) shares of an underlying security at a specified price on or before the expiration date. The two parties to the contract are the buyer, or holder, and the seller, or writer, of the option. The buyer pays a premium for the right to exercise the option. In turn, the seller receives the premium from the buyer and has an obligation to buy or sell the underlying security if the option is exercised by the buyer. Option contracts are typically issued with expiration dates no longer than nine months. The exception to this is a special type of option, known as **long-term equity anticipation securities (LEAPS)**, which can have expiration dates extending beyond two years. **Options** trade on all major exchanges and generally have standardized exercise prices, also known as strike prices, and expiration dates. The Options Clearing Corporation acts as a clearing house and guarantor for options contracts. Each option contract represents 100 shares of the underlying stock.

There are two primary types of options:

- A **call option**, which gives the buyer the right to purchase the underlying security for a specified price within a specified period
- A **put option**, which gives the buyer the right to sell the underlying security for a specified price within a specified period

There are four option positions:

- Purchasing (or being long) a call
- Writing (or going short) a call

- Purchasing (or being long) a put
- Writing (or going short) a put

Generally, the position that the buyer or writer will assume depends on his view of the future direction of market prices and the underlying security on which the option was written. If the investor is bullish (i.e., thinks that market prices will increase), he will either purchase a call or write a put. If the investor is bearish (i.e., thinks that market prices will decline), he will either write a call or purchase a put. A summary of the maximum economic gain and loss with respect to the basic option positions is shown in the following table.

Option Position	Maximum Gain	Maximum Loss
Buy Call	Unlimited	Amount of premium paid
Write Call	Amount of premium received	Unlimited (if naked)
Buy Put	Exercise price less amount of premium paid	Amount of premium paid
Write Put	Amount of premium received	Exercise price less amount of premium received

Characteristics and Definitions

Options and option transactions have their own language and terminology.

- The **intrinsic value** of an option is the minimum price at which the option will trade on an exchange. The trading value of the option consists of two parts: the intrinsic value of the option and the time value of the option. These two parts make up the option premium. An option never has a negative intrinsic value.
  - The *intrinsic value of a call* option is the greater of zero and the market price less the exercise price of the underlying stock. For example, stock ABC is trading at $45. A call option on ABC with an exercise price of $40 would have an intrinsic value of $5. If ABC was trading at $35, the call option would have an intrinsic value of $0. An investor would not exercise the call option in this case, because he could purchase the stock for less.
  - The *intrinsic value of a put* option is the greater of zero and the exercise price less the market price of the underlying stock. For example, stock XYZ is trading at $50. A put option on XYZ with an exercise price of $48 would have an intrinsic value of $0. The investor could sell his XYZ stock at $50 in the market and thus would not exercise his put option. However, if XYZ was trading at $42, the intrinsic value of the put option would be $6.
- The **time value** of the option is the amount by which the trading value of the option exceeds its intrinsic value. For example, MNO stock is trading at $80. An MNO $76 call is trading at $5. The intrinsic value of the call option is $4, and the time value is $1.
- An option is **in-the-money** when its intrinsic value is positive.
- An option is **out-of-the-money** when its intrinsic value is zero and the exercise price does not equal the market price of the underlying security.
- An option is **at-the-money** when the exercise price of the option equals the market price of the underlying stock.

- A call option is *covered* when it is written on a security that is already owned by the writer. An investor would write a covered call to earn premium income for a portfolio, which is a popular strategy in a flat market.
- A call option is *naked* when it is written on a security that is not owned by the writer. This is the most risky form of option transactions, because the writer is subject to an unlimited potential loss.

EXAMPLE Assume the market price of ABC stock is $50 per share and the investor owns a call option on ABC stock with an exercise price of $45 per share. Therefore, the call option is $5 in-the-money ($50 less $45) and will likely be exercised. The option also has an intrinsic value of $5. Alternatively, if the market price of ABC stock had declined to $30 per share and the investor is still holding the same call option, the option is $15 out-of-the-money ($30 less $45). Thus, the option will go unexercised and currently has an intrinsic value of zero.

Taxation of Options

An option contract that is purchased as an investment is a capital expenditure and is eligible for capital gains tax treatment. Furthermore, the tax consequence depends on whether:

- the option is a call or put;
- the investor is in the buyer (holder) or seller (writer) position; and
- the option is exercised, expires unexercised, or is sold by the holder.

A summary of taxation of a call option is shown below.

When a call:	If investor is holder:	If investor is writer:
Is exercised	Add premium on call to basis in stock purchased	Increase amount realized on sale of stock by call premium
Expires	Premium is capital loss on date of expiration	Premium is short-term capital gain on same date
Is sold by the holder	Difference between call premium paid and amount received for same is a capital gain or loss	Does not affect the writer

A summary of taxation of a put option is shown below.

When a put:	If investor is holder:	If investor is writer:
Is exercised	Reduce amount realized on sale of stock by put premium	Reduce basis in the stock purchased by premium received for put
Expires	Premium is capital loss on date of expiration	Premium is short-term capital gain on same date
Is sold by the holder	Difference between put premium paid and amount received for same is a capital gain or loss	Does not affect the writer

Binomial Option Pricing Model

The **binomial option pricing model** attempts to estimate the price of a call option. This model assumes the price of the option will change in discrete increments (up or down) on the basis of movements in the price of the underlying stock. Therefore, the model is sometimes referred to as the two-state option pricing model because the underlying security's price may always be simplified to either an up or down movement. The model also assumes that the call option being valued has an exercise price of $100.

The computation of the estimated price of the option under the binomial model is much too complex to be reproduced. Rather, you need to know only the assumptions upon which the model is based and that the analysis leads to the more popular method of valuing options, the Black-Scholes option valuation model.

Black-Scholes Option Valuation Model

The **Black-Scholes option valuation model** is designed to determine the estimated price of a European call option. However, unlike the binomial model, Black-Scholes assumes that the price of the option will change constantly (i.e., geometric Brownian motion) because the market price of the underlying security also changes constantly. Ultimately, this process is summarized by a volatility factor ascribed to the underlying security represented by the Greek symbol s, like the reference in the standard deviation formula.

Functionally, Black-Scholes holds that the value of the option is dependent on five factors:

- The current underlying stock price on which the option is written
- The option's exercise price
- The time to expiration of the option
- The risk-free rate of return
- The volatility (standard deviation) of the security's returns

All of these factors are directly related to the price of the option (i.e., the price of the option will move in the same direction as the numerical factor) except the option's exercise price, which moves inversely to that of the value of the option.

Factor	Call Option Price Increases if Factor
Market price	↑
Exercise price	↓
Time to expiration	↑
Volatility	↑
Risk-free rate	↑

For CFP® Exam purposes, you will not be required to calculate the estimated price of the option using Black-Scholes. Instead, you should:

- understand the difference in assumptions used for Black-Scholes versus the binomial model; and
- understand that, for any call option, an increase in the option's exercise price leads to a decrease in the value of the option because the price of the underlying stock has to increase further before the option has intrinsic value.

If the holder of an American option elected to exercise the option before its expiration, the time value associated with the option would not be realized. Therefore, an investor should sell the American option on the secondary market, capturing both the time value and the intrinsic value, than to exercise the option early. This is why option-pricing models are based on European options, although variations of these models also apply to both European and American options.

Put-Call Parity

Put-call parity is based on the premise that the premium of a call option implies a certain fair price for the corresponding put option having the same exercise price and expiration date, and vice versa. Put and call option pricing must be in parity to prevent arbitrage opportunities. An arbitrage opportunity is the ability to earn a riskless return without any investment of personal funds. Put-call parity is the difference between the call price and the put price and equals the difference between the market price of the stock and the present value of the exercise price continuously discounted at the risk-free rate.

PRACTICE QUESTIONS

Choose the best answer for each of the questions below.
Answers can be found at the end of this unit.

6. All of the following are factors used in determining the price of a call option under the Black-Scholes option valuation model EXCEPT

A. time to expiration
B. risk-free rate
C. call money rate
D. exercise price

7. Which of the following subjects the investor to the greatest possible loss?

A. Selling a naked call option
B. Selling a covered call
C. Buying a put option
D. Buying a call option

8. Baylor stock is currently selling for $63 per share. A call option for this stock with an exercise price of $65 per share may be purchased for a premium of $4. The option expires in 3 months. Which of the following terms best describes this option?

A. In-the-money
B. At-the-money
C. Out-of-the-money
D. By-the-money

9. An investor sells (writes) a call option with an exercise price of $45 on KRF stock for $2.50. The option expires when the stock is trading at $44.50. What is the investor's gain or loss?

A. $50 gain
B. $50 loss
C. $250 gain
D. $250 loss

F. OPTIONS STRATEGIES

LO E.40.8 Describe hedging, protective puts, and zero-cost collars.

Hedging

Hedging is considered any transaction involving derivatives (including options) in which the investor attempts to minimize investment risk. As such, combining different types of option contracts allows the investor to create a new risk/return relationship for derivatives. Generally, these combinations may be categorized under the techniques of straddles and spreads.

Protective Put

Most investors have a bullish outlook with respect to the overall market and, therefore, will take a long position (i.e., a buy position) with respect to their portfolios. However, for investors concerned about a decline in the market, purchasing a put option will protect them against possible loss. Specifically, because the put will increase in value as the stock portfolio decreases in value, the portfolio is protected and the investor's loss on the option is limited to the amount of the premium paid for the put. This is commonly known as a **protective put** (or, sometimes, **portfolio insurance**) and is commonly used by sophisticated investors to hedge their amount of investment risk.

Zero-Cost Collar

A **zero-cost collar** is a strategy used to protect a gain in a long position of a stock. This strategy consists of:

- a long (or buy) position in the underlying stock;
- a long put option; and
- a short (or writing of a) call option.

Specifically, the investor purchases a put option to protect against a decline in the value of the underlying stock and sells a call option to generate premium income to cover the cost of the premium for the put option. As a result, the premium received on the call option pays for the premium paid on the put option (thus, the term *zero-cost* or *cashless*).

G. FUTURES

LO E.41.8 Describe the characteristics, uses, and taxation of futures.

A **futures contract** is an agreement between two parties to make or take delivery of a specified amount of a commodity or financial asset at a future time, place, and unit price. In addition to commodities (e.g., corn or wheat), futures contracts are written on financial assets, such as U.S. Treasury securities, indexes, and foreign currencies. Using commodity futures is the easiest and most common way to gain economic exposure to commodities. To complete the futures contract, delivery of the commodity or asset may be made, but more often, the buyer (or holder) simply purchases an offsetting contract and cancels the original position. Only about 1% of all futures contract positions involve the delivery of the underlying commodity. Futures contracts, which are standardized as to size, quality, and delivery, are traded on exchanges such as the New York Mercantile Exchange or Chicago Mercantile Exchange.

As with options, investors can take a long or short position in a futures contract. Purchasing a contract for future delivery is a long position (i.e., to take delivery of the commodity). Selling a contract for future delivery is a short position (i.e., to make delivery of the commodity). As with stocks, a long position will increase in value if the underlying commodity or asset increases in value, whereas a short position will increase in value if the underlying commodity or asset declines in value. Investors are usually required to have strong balance sheets and deposited funds with the broker, in addition to sufficient knowledge of the risks, before they are permitted to trade futures.

Hedging, a primary use of futures, involves purchasing a contract in the opposite position of that which is currently held and is used to reduce the risk from fluctuating commodity prices.

> **EXAMPLE** The most popular stock index futures is the S&P 500 Index Future. Settlement takes place in cash and is based on a multiplier of 250, therefore, the value of a contract is 250 times the level of the index stated in the contract. With an index level of 1,000, the value of each contract is $250,000. Each index point in the futures price represents a gain or loss of $250 per contract. A long stock index futures position on S&P 500 index futures at 1,051 would show a gain of $1,750 in the trader's account if the index were 1,058 at the settlement date ($250 × 7 = $1,750).

Futures contracts covering several other popular indices are traded, and the pricing and contract valuation are the same, although the multiplier can vary from contract to contract.

Taxation

The income taxation of futures contracts is even more complex than that of options. Nevertheless, for tax purposes, all futures contracts are marked to market, meaning that they are adjusted on a daily basis for contract price movements to ensure that both contract parties maintain sufficient collateral to guarantee their future adherence to the contract. At the end of the calendar year, net gains or losses on the contract are treated as 60% long-term and 40% short-term, regardless of the actual breakdown of the gain or loss. In addition, these gains and losses are considered capital gains or losses, regardless of the tax character of the underlying asset.

PRACTICE QUESTION

Choose the best answer for the question below.
The answer can be found at the end of this unit.

10. ADM needs large quantities of soybeans in the future for use in manufacturing products. Which of the following investment strategies should ADM employ to hedge its risk?

- A. ADM should buy soybean futures to hedge against higher soybean prices.
- B. ADM should sell soybean futures to hedge against lower soybean prices.
- C. ADM should sell soybean futures to hedge against higher soybean prices.
- D. ADM should buy soybean futures to hedge against lower soybean prices.

H. TANGIBLE ASSETS

LO E.41.9 Describe the characteristics of tangible assets.

Tangible assets take the form of either collectibles or, sometimes, precious metals (e.g., gold or silver). Collectibles (e.g., baseball cards) may provide the dual benefit to the investor of pleasure in maintaining a collection and possible capital appreciation. However, the collectibles market is usually characterized by an inefficient market and inherent lack of liquidity. Alternatively, precious metals derive their value from factors that are external to the financial markets (e.g., with the purchase of gold, an investor's fear of inflation). As a result, the price of precious metals often moves inversely (i.e., has a negative correlation) with the market prices of stocks. Therefore, investing in gold bullion or silver may be used as a hedge against a declining, or bearish, stock market.

PRACTICE QUESTION

Choose the best answer for the question below.
The answer can be found at the end of this unit.

11. Dane is concerned about a decline in the stock market. He has many holdings in growth stock mutual funds and would like to diversify his portfolio into an investment that offers a hedge against a bearish market. Which of the following investments would be the most appropriate for Dale?

- A. Fine art and paintings
- B. Gold coins
- C. Oil and gas futures
- D. Savings bonds

I. NATURAL RESOURCES

LO E.41.10 Explain the characteristics of natural resources.

An investment in **natural resources** includes an investment in oil and gas properties or timber lands. Investors may participate in this market in the following three ways:

- Investing in properties or lands via (typically) limited partnerships
- Investing in the stock of companies who develop the natural resources
- Investing in mutual funds that specialize in natural resources (a type of sector fund)

A major advantage of investing in natural resources is the pass-through of certain tax benefits, such as deductions for depletion or intangible drilling costs. Also, natural resources have historically exhibited some negative correlation with other financial assets (stocks and bonds). However, a major disadvantage of such an investment is the higher degree of risk, particularly if the activity involves exploratory drilling for oil wells.

PRACTICE QUESTION

Choose the best answer for the question below.
The answer can be found at the end of this unit.

12. Which of the following statements regarding an investment in tangible assets or natural resources is CORRECT?

A. The value of precious metals declines sharply during periods of high inflation.
B. The value of natural resources is generally negatively correlated with other financial assets.
C. Purchasing shares of a mutual fund that invests in gold mining corporations does not help diversify a bond portfolio.
D. All types of oil and gas investments involve the same amount of risk.

103 UNIT 4 ANSWERS TO PRACTICE QUESTIONS

1. C. The monthly NOI of Roger's potential commercial real property investment is $11,750, computed as follows.

Gross rental receipts:	$25,000
– Vacancy and collection	
Losses (5% of PGI):	– $1,250
Effective gross income:	$23,750
– Operating expenses:*	– $12,000
NOI:	$11,750

* Operating expenses do not include debt service or depreciation expense.

2. A. Potential gross income = $400/month × 100 units × 12 months + $20,000 (laundry and parking) = $500,000. Net income after vacancy and expenses: $500,000 × [1 – (0.07 + 0.30)] = $500,000 × 0.63 = $315,000. Sales price = $315,000 ÷ 0.09 = $3,500,000. Depreciation and financing expenses are not considered.

3. B. A REIT is a portfolio investment and generates investment income. In contrast, distributions from a RELP are subject to the passive income taxation rules. A RELP is managed by a general partner, whereas a REIT is managed by a board of directors. Some REITs are actively traded on the exchanges.

4. D. Tranche Z has the longest repayment period and receives no payments until the other tranches are repaid. Thus, Tranche Z carries the greatest amount of interest rate risk.

5. A. A guaranteed investment contract (GIC) is regarded as a conservative investment; however, they are not free of default risk.

6. C. The call money rate is a rate of interest charged by broker/dealers on borrowed money and is not a factor used in determining the price of a call option under Black-Scholes.

7. A. The most risky transaction is selling a naked call option. The loss when purchasing any type of option (call or put) is limited to the option premium paid. However, selling a naked call option exposes the investor to an unlimited loss because there is no limit to how much the underlying stock price can increase in the secondary market.

8. C. The option is currently out-of-the-money because the exercise price of the option ($65 per share) is currently greater than the current market price of the stock ($63 per share). Therefore, the option will not be exercised unless the market price increases to more than $65 per share within the 3-month period.

9. C. This option was allowed to expire because it was out-of-the-money. When the option expires, the investor's gain is the amount of premium received, or $250 ($2.50 × 100 shares). Recall each option contract represents 100 shares of underlying stock.

10. A. ADM needs, or is short, soybeans. Therefore, the company should buy soybean futures (take an opposite position) to hedge against higher soybean prices. This is referred to as a long hedge.

11. B. Precious metals derive their value from factors that are external to the financial markets. As a result, the price of precious metals often moves inversely (i.e., has a negative correlation) with the market prices of stocks. Therefore, investing in gold coins may be used as a hedge against a declining, or bearish, stock market.

12. B. The value of natural resources is generally negatively correlated with that of financial assets. Exploratory drilling for oil wells involves more risk than an investment in developed wells. Purchasing shares of a mutual fund that invests in any type of precious metals mining will provide portfolio diversification.

103 UNIT 4 POST-STUDY CHECKLIST

- ☐ Can I explain a guaranteed investment contract and identify its major purchasers?
- ☐ Can I explain the types, valuation, and taxation of real estate investments?
- ☐ Do I understand the differences between real estate limited partnerships and real estate investment trusts?
- ☐ Can I define and explain real estate mortgage investment conduits and collateralized mortgage obligations?
- ☐ Do I understand the types, valuation, and taxation of options?
- ☐ Do I understand the characteristics, uses, and taxation of futures?
- ☐ Can I explain the characteristics of tangible assets and natural resources?
- ☐ Can I illustrate the uses of hedging, protective puts, and zero-cost collars?

Am I able to define and understand the application of the following terms as they relate to investment planning?

- ☐ At-the-money
- ☐ Binomial option pricing model
- ☐ Black-Scholes option valuation model
- ☐ Call option
- ☐ Collateralized mortgage obligation (CMO)
- ☐ Derivatives
- ☐ Futures contract
- ☐ Guaranteed investment contract (GIC)
- ☐ Hedging
- ☐ In-the-money
- ☐ Intrinsic value
- ☐ Long-term equity anticipation securities (LEAPS)
- ☐ Natural resources
- ☐ Net operating income (NOI)
- ☐ Options
- ☐ Out-of-the-money
- ☐ Portfolio insurance
- ☐ Protective put
- ☐ Put-call parity
- ☐ Put option
- ☐ Real estate investment trust (REIT)
- ☐ Real estate limited partnership (RELP)
- ☐ Real estate mortgage investment conduit (REMIC)
- ☐ Tangible assets
- ☐ Time value
- ☐ Tranches
- ☐ Undeveloped land
- ☐ Zero-cost collar

UNIT 5

Types of Investment Risk and Quantitative Investment Concepts

REFER TO

CFP Board Principal Knowledge Topics – E. Investment Planning, E.34. Types of Investment Risk

CFP Board Principal Knowledge Topics – E. Investment Planning, E.35. Quantitative Investment Concepts

INTRODUCTION

Investment risk may broadly be categorized as either unsystematic or systematic risk; both types of risk together constitute total, or absolute, risk. Total risk is measured by standard deviation, which measures the variability of an asset's returns over time. Alternatively, systematic risk has its own risk measurement called beta, or the beta coefficient. In this unit, you will learn how to compute both standard deviation and beta and how to apply them in the construction of a portfolio.

Finally, you will learn (and apply) a number of investment formulas and computations used in the quantification and measurement of risk. Therefore, you will need to use your financial function calculator (e.g., HP10bII+) in making these computations.

LEARNING OBJECTIVES

After completion of this unit, you should be able to achieve the following learning objectives:

CFP® Board Principal Knowledge Topics – E. Investment Planning

E.34. Types of Investment Risk

LO E.34.1 Discuss investment risk and diversification.

LO E.34.2 Define and give examples of unsystematic and systematic risk.

E.35. Quantitative Investment Concepts

LO E.35.1 Explain how sensitivity analysis is used to evaluate an investment.

LO E.35.2 Discuss the relationship between covariance and the correlation coefficient and their importance to portfolio construction and management.

LO E.35.3 Explain the use of the coefficient of determination in portfolio evaluation.

LO E.35.5 Define and calculate the standard deviation of a single asset.

LO E.35.6 Explain beta and weighted beta and how they are applied to the construction of an investment portfolio.

LO E.35.7 Define the use of semivariance when addressing returns associated with an investment portfolio.

LO E.35.8 Calculate the standard deviation of a two-asset portfolio.

LO E.35.9 Evaluate and interpret probability distributions and statistical measures such as z-statistic, skewness, and kurtosis.

LO E.35.10 Explain the use of stochastic modeling in projecting future portfolio performance.

LO E.35.11 Explain and calculate expected return.

KEY TERMS

Beta
Business risk
Coefficient of determination
Correlation coefficient
Covariance
Default risk
Diversification
Exchange rate risk
Expected return
Financial risk
Interest rate risk
Investment manager risk
Median
Mode
Monte Carlo simulation
Negatively skewed distribution
Normal probability distribution
Platykurtic distribution
Political risk
Positively skewed distribution
Purchasing power risk
Reinvestment rate risk
Semivariance
Sensitivity analysis

Investment risk
Kurtosis
Leptokurtic distribution
Liquidity risk
Lognormal probability distribution
Market risk
Marketability risk
Mean
Skewness
Standard deviation
Stochastic modeling
Systematic risk
Tax risk
Unsystematic risk
Z-statistic

A. INVESTMENT RISK AND DIVERSIFICATION

LO E.34.1 Discuss investment risk and diversification.

Investment risk is the uncertainty that an investment's actual, or realized, return will be different from its expected return. The two most important investment strategies that assist investors in managing investment risk are diversification and asset allocation. **Diversification** is structuring an individual's investment portfolio to maximize risk/return. In other words, an investor should attempt to realize the greatest amount of return per unit of risk. This may be pursued by (1) structuring a portfolio that contains assets with low correlation to each other, (2) having a longer investment time horizon, or both. For example, an individual under age 40 who is saving for a retirement investment goal may purchase an aggressive investment (defined as an investment that exhibits a wide variation of actual returns) much more safely than an individual age 65 or over. Why? Because the younger individual has a much longer time to experience the probability of significant positive returns to offset the likelihood of several negative returns. Further, as we shall see, because each asset class may not move either in the same direction as another (known as correlation) or in the same amount, it is possible to combine asset classes to reduce an investor's overall risk. Studies have shown that an investor only needs about 15 to 20 assets to fully diversify a portfolio, as indicated below.

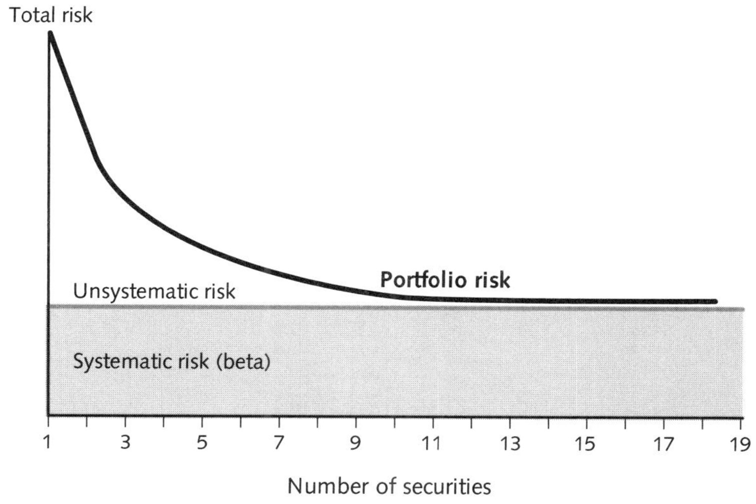

As a technique in portfolio management, **portfolio diversification** (i.e., committing to an array of separate investments) reduces unsystematic risk, such as business risk, and enhances returns. The securities in a diversified portfolio are selected, in part, because they do not tend to move up or down in relation to each other; when some go down, the loss is offset by those that rise. This kind of diversification is enhanced by the addition of foreign securities to a portfolio because they are usually not highly correlated with domestic equity.

There are many ways to classify investment and financial products. The investment pyramid (shown below), for example, categorizes products according to their risk and return potential. Another way is to group similar products into specific classes. These classes are generally defined as the following:

- *Cash and cash equivalents*—passbook savings and checking accounts; money-market accounts; money-market funds; certificates of deposit; T-bills
- *Fixed-income investments*—corporate bonds; municipal bonds; Treasury bonds; bond funds; mortgage-backed securities
- *Equities*—preferred and common stocks of all kinds: growth; income appreciation; stock mutual funds
- *Real assets*—real estate; collectibles; precious metals; stones

Each of these asset classes, as a whole, responds differently to different types of risk; therefore, diversifying or allocating investment resources among these classes is a proven way to reduce risk overall, dampen volatility, and improve the performance of one's portfolio. Fixed-income products, for example, are a hedge against deflation; equities are a hedge against inflation. To minimize market risk, one could diversify among all four asset categories (with additional diversification within the equities category). To minimize interest rate risk, one could diversify within the fixed-income category by staggering bond maturity dates. To minimize business risk, one could allocate among the four categories and purchase mutual funds. To reduce liquidity risk, one would keep a sufficient portion of assets in cash or cash equivalent assets.

Diversification is not a synonym for asset allocation. For example, an aggressive young professional may invest almost exclusively in common stock. That would be a single asset class. But, within that asset class of common stock, the portfolio might consist of shares of a dozen or more different companies in varied industries. Although asset allocation does not guarantee diversification (it is possible to be concentrated in one or two investments in each class), a proper asset allocation program will generally consist of enough securities in each class to offer broad diversification. Asset allocation will be covered in more detail in Unit 10.

Risk-Return Pyramid

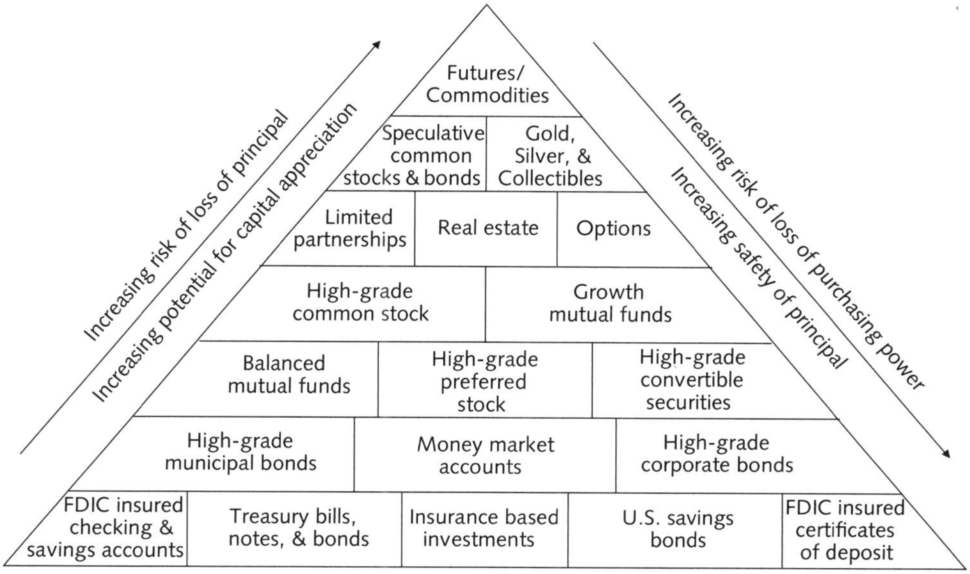

B. UNSYSTEMATIC AND SYSTEMATIC RISK

LO E.34.2 Define and give examples of unsystematic and systematic risk.

The total, or absolute, risk of any investment consists of two components:

- Unsystematic, or diversifiable, risk
- Systematic, or nondiversifiable, risk

This relationship may be summarized by the equation:

total risk = unsystematic risk + systematic risk

Total risk may be quantified, or measured, by standard deviation, whereas systematic risk may be measured by an investment or portfolio's beta coefficient, or beta. Because unsystematic risk may be effectively managed by the construction of a diversified portfolio, the risk with which the investor should be most concerned is systematic risk.

Unsystematic Risk

Unsystematic risk, also known as diversifiable risk, is risk that affects only a particular company, country, or sector and its securities. This risk is not correlated with stock market returns. Diversifying a portfolio's assets among various investments may greatly reduce unsystematic risk. The following are types of unsystematic risk.

- **Business risk**—the uncertainty of operating income.
- **Financial risk**—the risk that a firm's financial structure (debt versus equity) will negatively affect the value of an equity investment.

- **Liquidity risk**—liquidity is the ability to sell an asset quickly and without significant loss of principal. Because stock values may drop below the investor's purchase price, they are subject to some liquidity risk. Direct investments in real estate and closely held corporations are also subject to liquidity risk, primarily because the sales period for these assets may be extensive.
- **Marketability risk**—the inability of an investor to find a ready market to sell an investment to a willing buyer.
- **Default risk**—the potential inability of a debt issuer to make timely interest and principal repayments. Junk bonds are particularly subject to default risk. Bonds with more default risk, also known as credit risk, may also exhibit greater interest rate risk.
  An investment in common stock is not subject to default risk because the issuing corporation is not contractually bound to pay dividends.
- **Political risk**—the risk that the political and economic climate of a country will negatively affect an investment. Governments have the power to change laws affecting securities. These changes may adversely affect an investment's value. Investors need to be aware of any pending changes in the law that may affect the value of their investments.
- **Tax risk**—the uncertainty associated with a country's tax laws that may potentially affect the rate of return generated by an investment.
- **Investment manager risk**—the risk associated with the skills and philosophy of the individual manager of an investment fund or account. This includes changes in either the management team or investment style.

Systematic Risk

As previously mentioned, systematic risk is the more important of the two components of total risk. Also known as nondiversifiable risk, **systematic risk** reflects the uncertainty of returns associated with an investment in any type of asset. This part of risk is generally considered inescapable, because the risk of the overall investment market may not be completely avoided. Therefore, a portfolio manager hopes to minimize systematic risk.

Purchasing Power Risk

Purchasing power risk is the potential loss of the purchasing power of an investment due to inflation. The actual risk associated with inflation is generally not related to the current level of inflation (because an inflation premium is built into the purchase price of any investment) but to unanticipated changes in the levels of inflation.

Purchasing power risk mostly affects fixed income types of investment, such as bonds and CDs. Recall, cash and cash equivalents are the primary form of investment vehicle used to fund an individual's emergency fund. However, some investors, by virtue of an extremely risk-averse temperament, may tend to have a predominant part of their portfolio in cash and cash equivalents. Although these vehicles may assist in managing liquidity risk, they do suffer from purchasing power risk because they have limited opportunity for principal appreciation.

Reinvestment Rate Risk

Reinvestment rate risk is the risk that proceeds available for reinvestment must be reinvested at a lower rate of return than that of the investment vehicle that generated the proceeds. Reinvestment rate risk mostly affects fixed income types of investments, particularly those with long-term maturities in a changing interest rate environment. Another prominent investment that is subject to reinvestment rate risk is a mortgage-backed security, such as a GNMA (Ginnie Mae).

Note: A way to eliminate reinvestment rate risk is to invest in zero-coupon bonds.

Interest Rate Risk

Interest rate risk is the risk that the market price of an investment will decline as the result of changes in market interest rates. The most notable investment that is subject to interest rate risk is bonds, whose market prices move inversely with market interest rates.

Market Risk

Market risk is another word for systematic risk. Market risk is the risk of the overall securities marketplace and is sometimes simply referred to as volatility. The more volatile the movement of a security's return (as measured by beta), the greater its risk in comparison to a market index, such as the Standard & Poor's 500 Index. In addition, certain events, such as wars and economic collapse, could have a large impact on a client's portfolio. Forecasting and planning for these types of events may be difficult, but communicating their possibility over a long-term investment horizon is important for financial planners. If a sudden disruption in the market does take place, the financial planner should recommend the client stay focused on the long-term and not rush into making a financial decision based solely on emotion.

Exchange Rate Risk

Exchange rate risk is the risk that a change in the relationship between the value of the dollar and the value of the foreign currency during the period of investment will negatively affect the investor's return. This type of risk primarily affects those individuals who invest in foreign securities, such as foreign stocks, bonds, and ADRs. One method of minimizing exchange rate risk is to invest in Yankee Bonds. When a country intentionally changes the value of its currency relative to another country's currency (usually the American dollar), this process is known as devaluation or revaluation, depending on the directional change in the value of the currency. If a country's currency value declines with respect to another currency's value (i.e., it now takes more of the adjusted currency to exchange for the benchmark currency), it is referred to as devaluing the adjusted currency. If a country's currency value increases with respect to the referenced currency, it is referred to as revaluing the adjusted currency.

To memorize the components of systematic risk, remember the mnemonic *PRIME*, which uses the first letter of each risk source.

PRACTICE QUESTIONS

Choose the best answer for each of the questions below.
Answers can be found at the end of this unit.

1. All of the following are examples of nondiversifiable risks EXCEPT
- A. liquidity risk
- B. market risk
- C. interest rate risk
- D. purchasing power risk

2. Eos Company is a privately owned manufacturer of plastics used in the automotive industry. The company is currently financed with a mix of 90% equity and 10% debt. Which of the following risks is(are) experienced by the shareholders of Eos Company?
1. Liquidity risk
2. Market risk
3. Business risk
4. Default risk

- A. 1 only
- B. 3 only
- C. 2 and 4
- D. 1, 2, and 3

C. EXPECTED RETURN

LO E.35.11 Explain and calculate expected return.

Expected return is the return that the investor demands or expects to make and is computed by multiplying each of the investment's possible annual returns by the probability that they will occur and adding the results.

> **EXAMPLE** Assume an investment has a 20% probability of experiencing a negative 10% annual return and the same 20% probability of encountering a negative 5% annual return. Furthermore, assume the investment has a 20% chance of attaining a positive 5% annual return and a 40% chance of achieving a positive 10% return annually. Therefore, we would expect a return of a positive 2% for this investment, calculated as follows: $E(r) = (0.20 \times -0.10) + (0.20 \times -0.05) + (0.20 \times 0.05) + (0.40 \times 0.10) = 2\%$.

The terms *expected return* and *required return* may refer to the same concept. For example, an asset has an expected, or required, return based on its measure of risk. The terms may refer to different concepts as well. For example, an investor may expect a 10% return on her portfolio on the basis of historical results but may require only an 8% return to reach her financial goals. The context in which these terms are used is critically important in financial analysis.

D. STANDARD DEVIATION

LO E.35.5 Define and calculate the standard deviation of a single asset.

Standard deviation, also known as variance, is an absolute measure of the variability of the actual investment returns around the average or mean of those returns (otherwise known as the expected return of the investment). This measure is the single most accepted measure of total, or absolute, risk in investment theory and tells an investor how far from the mean the investment's actual return is likely to vary.

The formula for the *sample* standard deviation of an asset is:

$$S_r = \sqrt{\frac{\sum_{t=1}^{n}\left(r_t - \bar{r}\right)^2}{n-1}}$$

where

S_r = sample standard deviation
n = number of observations
r_t = actual return for period t
$\bar{r}$ = average return

Most financial calculators will calculate the sample standard deviation from a list of historical asset returns. Please see your calculator manual or *Understanding Your Financial Calculator*, published by Kaplan Schweser, for step-by-step directions.

EXAMPLE Assume that ABC stock has generated the following historical rates of return for the last four years:

Year 1: 15%
Year 2: 8%
Year 3: 2%
Year 4: 18%

The average or mean return of ABC stock is 10.75% (43 ÷ 4). The stock also has a sample standard deviation of 7.18%. An easy way to calculate standard deviation of historical returns is to use the sigma register (Σ+) on your financial calculator. Using this information, calculate the standard deviation as follows (HP 10bII+):

15 [Σ+]
8 [Σ+]
2 [Σ+]
18 [Σ+]
[shift] [Sx,Sy]
7.18215, or 7.18%

The *population* standard deviation of an asset also has a formula:

$$\sigma_r = \sqrt{\frac{\sum_{t=1}^{n}\left(r_t - \bar{r}\right)^2}{n}}$$

where

σ_r = population standard deviation
r_t = actual return for period t
$\bar{r}$ = average return
n = number of returns

In the previous example, the population standard deviation of the asset is 6.22% and may be found using your financial calculator. The denominators are slightly different for each calculation. For sample standard deviation *n-1* is used, while for population standard deviation *n* is used.

In the real world, finding the standard deviation of an entire population is generally unrealistic. Although σ (population standard deviation) tends to eliminate the statistical bias associated with *S* (sample standard deviation), it is likely that you will only be asked to compute *S* on the CFP® Exam.

PRACTICE QUESTION

Choose the best answer for the question below.
The answer can be found at the end of this unit.

3. Assets A and B have the following sample historical series of returns:

	A	B
Year 1	7%	4%
Year 2	12%	11%
Year 3	–1%	21%

Which asset, if any, is the most risky based on standard deviation?

A. Asset A
B. Asset B
C. Assets A and B, equally
D. Need more information

E. BETA COEFFICIENT (BETA)

LO E.35.6 Explain beta and weighted beta and how they are applied to the construction of an investment portfolio.

Beta is a relative measure of systematic risk. Beta may be used as a measure for the risk associated with a particular security; however, it is better used as a measure of risk within a diversified portfolio or a portfolio that has no unsystematic risk. In contrast, standard deviation is an appropriate measure of risk for all assets, including nondiversified portfolios.

The overall market has a beta of +1.0. Therefore, as a relative measure of risk, if a particular security or portfolio has a beta less than +1.0, the security or portfolio is not as volatile as the overall market. This type of asset would be considered a defensive asset. Alternatively, if a particular security or portfolio has a beta greater than +1.0, the security or portfolio is more volatile than the overall market. This type of asset would be considered an aggressive asset.

EXAMPLE A portfolio has a beta of 1.30. Therefore, the portfolio is 30% more volatile than the overall market. If the market was expected to return 10%, the portfolio would be expected to return 13%. If the portfolio had a beta of .80, it would be 20% less volatile than the overall market. If the market was expected to return 10%, the portfolio would be expected to return 8%.

The formula for the beta coefficient (beta) of a sample asset is:

$$\beta_i = \frac{COV_{im}}{\sigma_m^2} = \frac{\rho_{im}\sigma_i}{\sigma_m}$$

β_i = beta
σ_i = standard deviation of the investment
σ_m = standard deviation of the market
ρ_{im} = correlation coefficient between the investment and the market
COV_{im} = covariance between the investment and the market
Covariance = $\rho_{im}\sigma_i\,\sigma_m$

Some assets, such as gold, may actually exhibit a negative beta. An asset with a negative beta may protect the investor from a significant decline in the value of the portfolio in a bear market.

Weighted Beta

The beta of a portfolio of securities is referred to as a weighted beta, meaning that the portfolio beta is calculated by weighting the individual asset betas and adding the results. If the portfolio has a weighted beta of 1.0, then the portfolio is perfectly weighted with the market (as with an index mutual fund) and will move in exact lockstep with market returns. Normally, portfolios have weighted betas different than 1.0.

EXAMPLE Assume that you have constructed a portfolio consisting of $3,000 of Stock X, $4,000 of Stock Y, and $3,000 of Stock Z. Stock X has a beta of 0.64, Stock Y has a beta of 1.24, and Stock Z has a beta of 0.85. Therefore, the weighted beta for this portfolio is 0.943 calculated as follows:

	FMV	×	Beta	=	Product
Stock X	3,000	×	0.64	=	1,920
Stock Y	4,000	×	1.24	=	4,960
Stock Z	3,000	×	0.85	=	2,550
Total	10,000				9,430

Weighted Beta = 9,430 ÷ 10,000 = **0.9430**
Keystrokes for the HP 10bII+
[■][C ALL]
0.64 [INPUT]
3000 [Σ+]
1.24 [INPUT]
4000 [Σ+]
0.85 [INPUT]
3000 [Σ+]
[■][$\bar{x}_w$,b]

With a beta less than 1.0, the constructed portfolio is a bit less volatile than the overall market. You should also observe that adding a stock to the portfolio that is more volatile than the overall market (such as Stock Y) will not unduly affect the volatility of the portfolio so long as its value is not a large portion.

PRACTICE QUESTIONS

Choose the best answer for each of the questions below. Answers can be found at the end of this unit.

4. Jane's portfolio consists of 2 stocks, each comprising 50% of the portfolio. Stock 1 has an expected return of 4.5%, a standard deviation of 1.5%, and a beta of 0.65. Stock 2 has an expected return of 8%, a standard deviation of 3%, and a beta of 0.82. If the correlation coefficient between stocks 1 and 2 is 0.75, what is the beta for Jane's portfolio?

A. 0.01
B. 0.63
C. 0.74
D. 2.25

5. Adding investments with a negative beta to a well-diversified portfolio that currently has a beta of +1.0 will

A. cause the expected performance of the portfolio to improve in bear markets
B. cause the expected performance of the portfolio to decline in bear markets
C. cause the portfolio to experience more volatility in times of a bull market
D. cause the portfolio to experience more volatility in times of a bear market

F. STOCHASTIC MODELING

LO E.35.10 Explain the use of stochastic modeling in projecting future portfolio performance.

Stochastic modeling is a method of financial analysis that attempts to forecast how investment returns on different asset classes vary over time by using thousands of simulations to produce probability distributions for various outcomes. A popular form of stochastic modeling that uses computer-generated distributions is the **Monte Carlo simulation** (MCS). This simulation is an analytic and risk management tool widely used in finance. MCS incorporates computer programming to generate stochastic (probability) random value inputs in simulating thousands of iterations. In a Monte Carlo simulation, each of the variables is also given a probability distribution to allow for real-world uncertainty. Consider the uncertainty in retirement planning. Small changes in the projected rate of return will make a dramatic difference in the outcome. Life expectancy is also another important variable that may be incorrectly approximated. MCS uses a random number generator to provide an output with specific probabilities of outcomes. The simulation provides insight into the range of outcomes and provides the user (the investor or an analyst) with both a best-case and a worst-case scenario.

Advantages:

- Can clearly display tradeoffs of risk and return. The paths can be ranked from best to worst to assess the probability of any given outcome.
- Properly modeled tax analysis, which considers the actual tax rates of the investor as well as tax location of the assets (held in taxable or tax-deferred locations), can be assessed.
- Tax burden changes with market returns and withdrawals could be considered.
- A clearer understanding of short-term and long-term risk can be gained. For example, reducing the holdings of risky stock would reduce the short-term variability of the portfolio but increase the long-term risk of not having sufficient assets.
- Monte Carlo simulation can better model the real stochastic process where return over time depends not only on the starting value of the period but also on the additions or withdrawals to the portfolio at each future period.
- Points along the time line can be considered to answer questions such as "Do savings need to be increased?" "Can I retire earlier?" "Must I retire later?"

Disadvantages:

- Simplistic use of historical data, such as expected returns, for the inputs. Returns change and have a major effect on projected future values of the portfolio.
- Models that simulate the return of asset classes but not the actual assets held. Simulating the return of the Wilshire 5000 when a fund with fees will be held could significantly overstate the future value or time period over which distributions can be sustained.

G. SENSITIVITY ANALYSIS

LO E.35.1 Explain how sensitivity analysis is used to evaluate an investment.

Sensitivity analysis is used to evaluate the risk associated with a given investment and assesses the impact of different variables on an investment's returns. When evaluating a particular investment, investors may use forecasted cash flows to estimate its intrinsic value. However, many variables (e.g., business cycle) may either negatively or positively impact the forecasted cash flows and resulting valuation with varying degrees of sensitivity. Generally, investors, while performing sensitivity analysis, will calculate both the net present value (NPV) and the internal rate of return (IRR) of the forecasted cash flows. This calculation will be performed on the basis of three different assumptions: pessimistic, expected, and optimistic. By changing one of the input variables, subsequent changes in NPV or IRR can be reviewed and analyzed. Investors may choose an investment based on the reliability of the outcome for a given variable.

H. PROBABILITY DISTRIBUTIONS

LO E.35.9 Evaluate and interpret probability distributions and statistical measures such as z-statistic, skewness, and kurtosis.

A **normal probability distribution**, perfectly symmetrical, is characterized by a single peak in the center, which is the location of the arithmetic mean of the series of observations. The series of observations, normally referred to as a bell curve, implies that there is a 50% chance that an observation selected at random will fall to the right of the mean and a 50% chance that it will fall to the left of the mean. A bell curve is illustrated in the following figure.

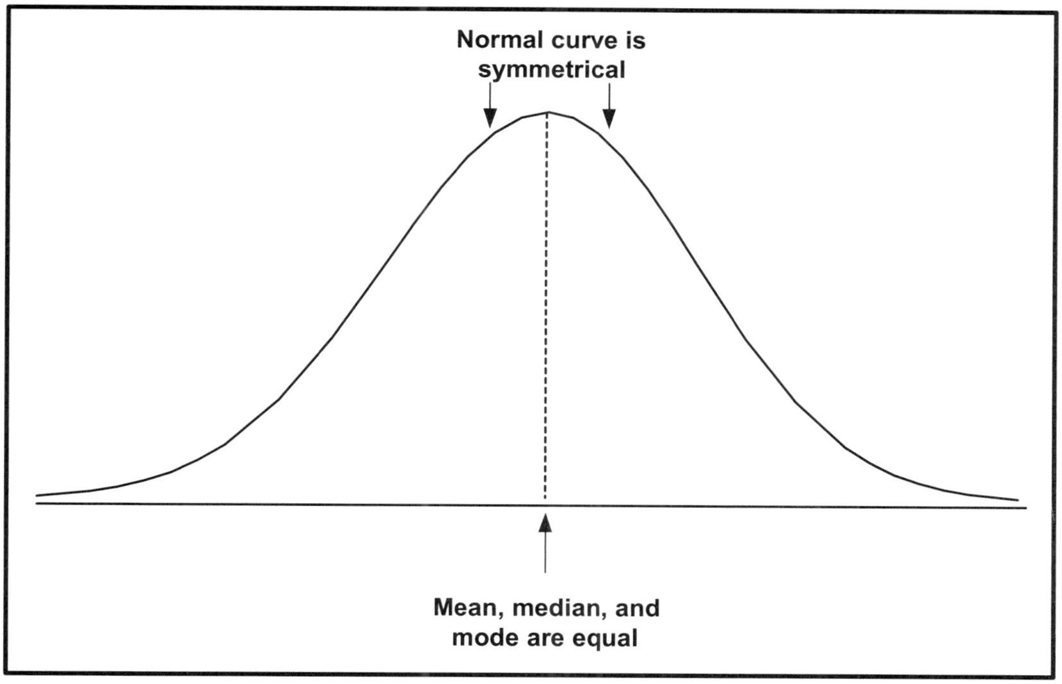

- The **mean** is an absolute value and is the best indicator of central tendency of a distribution. For example, if a stock returned 5%, then 8%, then 9%, and then 2%, the mean would be 6% (5 + 8 + 9 + 2 = 24 ÷ 4 = 6).
- The **median** is the central value of observations arranged in order of lowest to highest. For example, the median of 11, 7, 4, 13, and 8 is 8 (4, 7, 8, 11, 13).
- The **mode** is the observation value with the greatest frequency. For example, the mode of 2, 2, 2, 6, 7, 7, and 9 is 2.

You should also note that, when interpreting standard deviation, a return (observation) will occur 68% of the time within one standard deviation of the mean, 95% of the time within two standard deviations of the mean, and 99% of the time within three standard deviations of the mean.

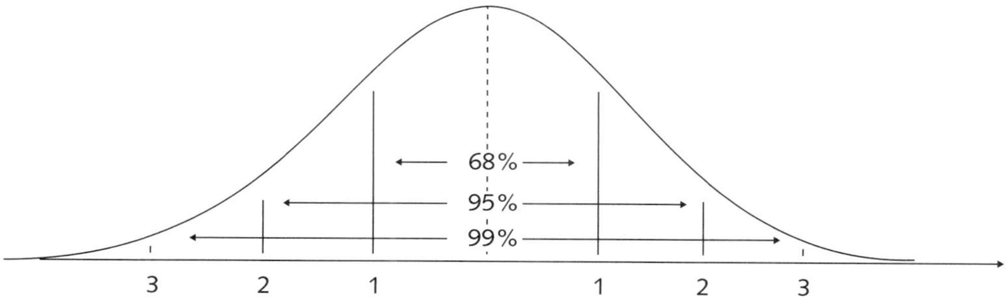

> **EXAMPLE** If the mean return for Nosilla, Inc., is 10% and the standard deviation is 5%, 68% of the outcomes will fall between 5% (10% - 5%) and 15% (10% + 5%).
>
> Approximately 95% of the outcomes will fall between 0% [10% – (2 × 5%)] and 20% [10% + (2 × 5%)].
>
> Approximately 99% of outcomes will fall between -5% [10% – (3 × 5%)] and 25% [10% + (3 × 5%)]. Returns falling outside of 3 standard deviations are considered outliers.

A normal probability distribution may be assumed by the investor whenever analyzing the possible range of annual returns for a portfolio. This is because the actual portfolio percentage return may be either negative (below zero) or positive at any given point in time.

PRACTICE QUESTION

Choose the best answer for the question below.
The answer can be found at the end of this unit.

6. Mysterious Company stock has a mean return of 9% and a standard deviation of 3%. Which statement is CORRECT?

A. Approximately 68% of Mysterious Company's returns will fall between 3% and 15%.
B. 5% of Mysterious Company's returns will be greater than 15%.
C. Half of Mysterious Company's returns will fall below 6%.
D. Mysterious Company is unlikely to experience a negative return.

Z-Statistic

The **z-statistic** (z-score) measures the number of standard deviations a data value is from the mean (either above or below). This score is obtained by subtracting the mean from a given data value and dividing this result by the standard deviation. If the data value is higher than the mean, then the z-score will be positive. If the data value is smaller than the mean, then the z-score will be negative. For example, a z-score of 1.46 means the data value is 1.46 standard deviations above the mean. A z-score of –2.56 means the data value is 2.56 standard deviations below the mean.

Lognormal Probability Distribution

A **lognormal probability distribution** is one in which the series of observations is skewed to the left of the arithmetic mean (i.e., the mean is to the right of the peak of the series). A lognormal probability distribution implies that there is a greater than 50% chance that an observation selected at random will fall to the left of the mean (indicating, in practical terms, a performance that is less than expected or predicted).

A lognormal probability distribution may be assumed by the investor whenever analyzing the ending (terminal) or future value of a portfolio. This is because the value of an unleveraged portfolio (i.e., one for which margin is not used) may not go below zero. Stated more simply, the ending value of the portfolio may go to zero, but not below it; because once the value has reached zero, the investor has lost the entire investment. However, in theory, the value of a portfolio (or individual stock) could rise toward infinity. In addition, the distribution of portfolio returns tends to be skewed to the right, and as a result, the mean is always greater than the median.

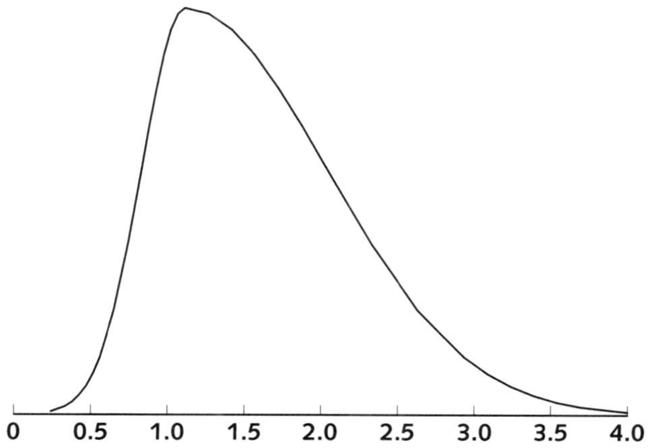

Skewness

Skewness measures how far the actual outcomes of a probability distribution deviate from the arithmetic mean or the asymmetry of the distribution. Recall, a normal distribution is not skewed, observations are equally distributed on both sides of the mean (peak). Effectively, what is being measured in decimal terms is how far the median return (i.e., the single outcome where there is an equal number of occurrences above and below that outcome) is from the mean return (i.e., the arithmetical average of all observed outcomes). When observations (rates of return) are skewed (asymmetrical), the distribution tends to have long tails on one side or the other. In **positively skewed distributions**, the median is below the mean (long tail is on positive side of the peak); in **negatively skewed distributions**, the median is above the mean (long tail is on negative side of peak). For a positively skewed distribution, there are more outliers to the right of the mean than to the left of the mean. For a negatively skewed distribution, there are more outliers to the left of the mean than to the right. Each of these distributions may be illustrated as shown in the following graphic.

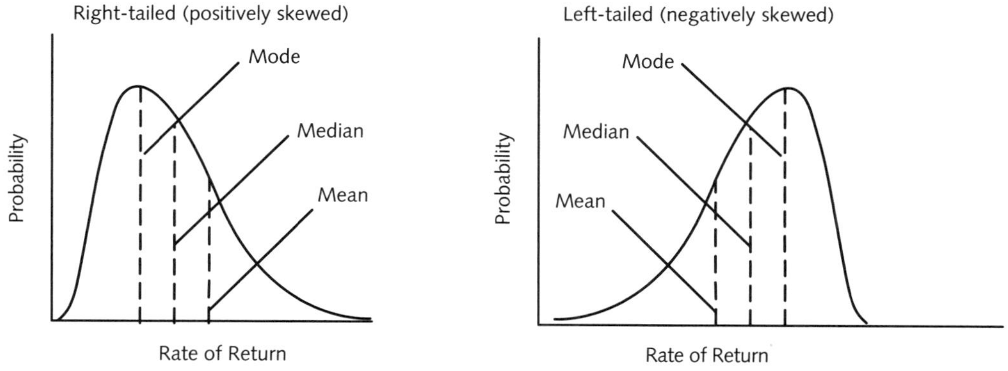

As one may easily observe from the graphic, the left tail of the negatively skewed distribution is considerably longer than that of the positively skewed distribution. Accordingly, an investment with positive skewness subjects the investor to a greater number of returns below the mean. An investment exhibiting a high positive skewness may have a larger than average number of positive price movements than an investment with low positive skewness.

Behavioral finance studies have found that many investors prefer assets with positive skewness. Investors may be willing to accept low expected returns given the chance for a few large returns. In contrast, an investment reflecting a negative skewness exposes the investor to the possibility of a greater number of returns above the mean return. However, an investment reflecting a negative skewness may subject an investor to large losses.

Kurtosis

Kurtosis measures the degree of peak in a distribution of returns. In other words, kurtosis measures the degree to which exceptional values (those much higher or lower than average) occur more frequently (high kurtosis) or less frequently (low kurtosis). A less peaked distribution indicates that more returns with large deviations from the mean have occurred, or are expected to occur, than with a normal distribution. This is also known as a **platykurtic distribution**. A more peaked distribution indicates that more returns are clustered around the mean than with a normal distribution. This is also known as a **leptokurtic distribution.**

Platykurtic and leptokurtic distributions are represented in the following graphic (in comparison to a normal probability distribution and normal tail). Investors who want to minimize volatility in their portfolios would prefer a leptokurtic distribution.

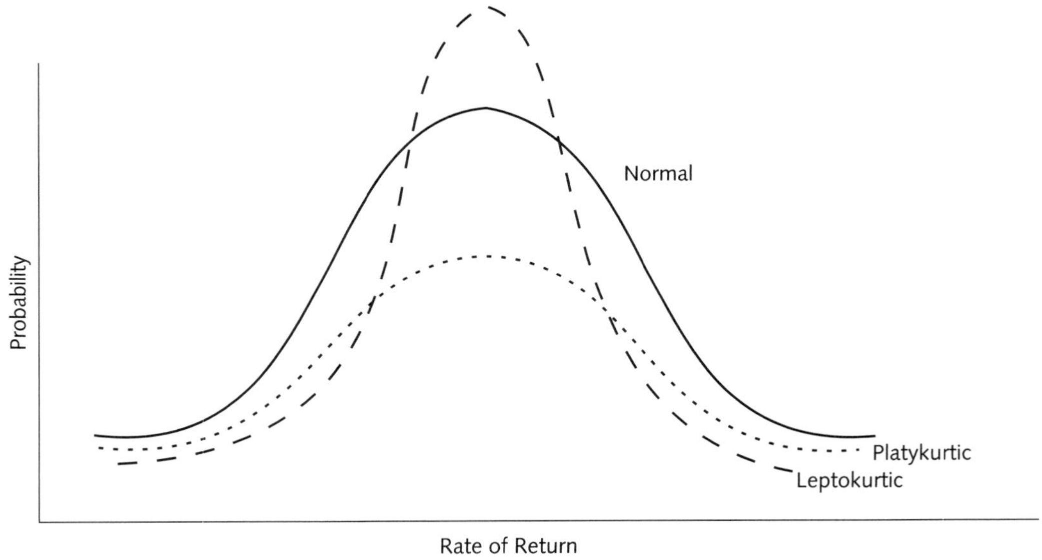

PRACTICE QUESTION

Choose the best answer for the question below.
The answer can be found at the end of this unit.

7. Which of the following statements about kurtosis is CORRECT?

I. Kurtosis describes the degree to which a distribution is not symmetric about its mean.

II. Kurtosis measures the peakedness of a distribution reflecting a greater or lesser concentration of returns around the mean.

A. I only
B. II only
C. Both I and II
D. Neither I nor II

I. SEMIVARIANCE

LO E.35.7 Define the use of semivariance when addressing returns associated with an investment portfolio.

The use of standard deviation as a measure of total risk has been criticized by some finance experts because it considers the series of possible returns in excess of the expected or mean return, in addition to those below the mean. However, in the real world, the primary consideration of the risk-averse investor is only with the series of possible returns below the mean (in other words, the downside risk, or downside deviation, of the investment). As a result, the statistical measure of **semivariance** has been developed to measure only those returns that are below the mean, with no consideration given to those above the mean. Semivariance is described as the average square deviation below the mean. When used in analysis, the lower the semivariance of a security, the less likely the security will incur a substantial loss in value.

J. COVARIANCE (COV) AND CORRELATION COEFFICIENT (R)

LO E.35.2 Discuss the relationship between covariance and the correlation coefficient and their importance to portfolio construction and management.

Covariance measures the extent to which two variables (the returns on investment assets) move together, either positively (together) or negatively (opposite). Covariance does not have boundaries. In essence, covariance measures the association between the variables. In addition, because we know there is a direct relationship between the covariance and the correlation coefficient, we also know that if the covariance between two assets is positive, so is the correlation coefficient.

The formula for covariance is:

$$COV_{ij} = \rho_{ij}\sigma_i\sigma_j$$

EXAMPLE Using ABC and XYZ stocks with a standard deviation of 7.18% and 12%, respectively, assume a correlation coefficient of 0.25 between the two stocks. Accordingly, we can derive a covariance between the two stocks of a positive 0.002154 (0.0718 × 0.12 × 0.25).

Even though you can determine whether units are increasing or decreasing, you cannot measure the *degree* to which the two variables move together; therefore, you should use the correlation coefficient. The **correlation coefficient** provides similar information on the movement of two assets' returns. This measures the strength of the straight-line or linear relationship between two variables. The overall range of values lie between –1.0 and +1.0.

Rewriting the previous formula provides us with a formula for correlation coefficient (*R*):

$$R \text{ (or } \rho_{ij}) = \frac{COV_{ij}}{\sigma_i \times \sigma_j}$$

EXAMPLE In our previous example, we have calculated a covariance between ABC and XYZ stocks of 0.002154 (and assumed a correlation coefficient of 0.25). However, we can also properly calculate the correlation coefficient by using the formula, or:

$$R \text{ (or } \rho) = \frac{0.002154}{0.0718 \times 0.12} = \frac{0.002154}{0.008616} = 0.25$$

To summarize:

- perfectly positively correlated assets have a correlation coefficient of +1.0 (in this event, the assets move exactly together and there is no reduction in the total risk of the portfolio);
- perfectly negatively correlated assets have a correlation coefficient of –1.0 (in this event, the assets move exactly opposite of one another and the total risk of the portfolio can be completely eliminated); and
- a correlation coefficient of 0.0 means there is no *linear* relationship between the returns of the assets.

Combining assets with less than perfect positive correlation can reduce the total risk of a portfolio. For example, assets M and N, with correlation of 0.89, may be combined to result in a portfolio with a standard deviation less than that of both M and N. The farther away the correlation between two assets is from +1.0, the greater the diversification benefits that may be attained.

PRACTICE QUESTION

Choose the best answer for the question below.
The answer can be found at the end of this unit.

8. Which of the following pairs of assets provides the greatest level of diversification?

A. Assets 1 and 2, with a correlation coefficient of +0.37
B. Assets 3 and 4, with a correlation coefficient of 0
C. Assets 5 and 6, with a correlation coefficient of –0.42
D. Assets 7 and 8, with a correlation coefficient of –0.78

K. STANDARD DEVIATION OF A TWO-ASSET PORTFOLIO

LO E.35.8 Calculate the standard deviation of a two-asset portfolio.

Both covariance and the correlation coefficient may be used to calculate the standard deviation of a two-asset portfolio. The standard deviation of a two-asset portfolio is computed using the following formula:

$$\sigma_p = \sqrt{W_i^2\sigma_i^2 + W_j^2\sigma_j^2 + 2W_i W_j \left[COV_{ij}\right]}$$

σ_p = standard deviation of the portfolio p

W_i = percentage of the portfolio invested in security i

W_j = percentage of the portfolio invested in security j

COV_{ij} = covariance between security i and j

Note: W_i and W_j must sum to 100%

Covariance = $\rho_{ij}\sigma_i \sigma_j$

ρ_{ij} = correlation coefficient between i and j

In this formula, W represents the weighting, or percentage, of each asset within the portfolio, and σ represents the standard deviation of those respective assets. In addition, to derive the answer, we need to know the covariance between the two assets within the portfolio.

EXAMPLE Continuing with our previous example of ABC stock, which has a mean return of 10.75% and a standard deviation of 7.18%, combine this stock in a portfolio with XYZ stock, which has a mean return of 20% and a standard deviation of 12%. Assume that these two stocks are combined in the portfolio and are weighted in the proportions of 80% for ABC stock and 20% for XYZ stock. Also assume that they exhibit a covariance of 0.002154. Therefore, the standard deviation of this two-asset portfolio is 6.76%, calculated as follows:

$$\sigma_p = [(0.8)^2(0.0718)^2 + (0.2)^2(0.12)^2 + 2(0.8)(0.2)(0.002154)]^{0.5}$$

$$= (0.003299 + 0.000576 + 0.0006893)^{0.5} = 0.00564^{0.5} = 0.06756, \text{ or } 6.76\%$$

(Note: raising a number to 0.5 is equivalent to taking the square root.)

In summary, the following table represents the combination of ABC stock and XYZ stock in the same portfolio.

	ABC stock	XYZ stock	Portfolio
Weighting	80%	20%	100%
Expected return [E(r)]	10.75%	20%	12.6%
Standard deviation (σ)	7.18%	12%	6.76%

You should observe closely what has occurred here. Specifically, by combining the two stocks in the same portfolio, we have created a portfolio with an expected return of 12.6%, greater than that of ABC stock. At the same time, our portfolio's standard deviation is less than that of either ABC stock and XYZ stock alone. The portfolio's standard deviation, or investment risk, is only 6.76%, whereas ABC's standard deviation is 7.18% and XYZ's standard deviation is 12%. How is this possible? The secret is the relatively low correlation between the returns of ABC and XYZ stocks.

The two-asset portfolio standard deviation formula can take a while to compute and is highly subject to making mistakes. For the CFP® exam, you may consider using a shortcut to approximate the answer. Compute the weighted average of the two assets' standard deviations given their respective weightings in the portfolio. Unless the two assets are perfectly positively correlated, the standard deviation of the portfolio must be less than the weighted average of the two assets' standard deviations. The recommendation is to select the answer just below the weighted average of the two assets' standard deviation. The shortcut takes a fraction of the time and is less prone to error.

L. COEFFICIENT OF DETERMINATION (R-SQUARED)

LO E.35.3 Explain the use of the coefficient of determination in portfolio evaluation.

The **coefficient of determination** (R-Squared or R^2), which is the square of the correlation coefficient, describes the percentage of variability in one variable (e.g., a stock) that is explained by the changes in a second variable (e.g., the overall market) or the strength of the relationship between the two variables. For example, if the coefficient of determination between ABC stock and the market is 70% (0.70), then 70% of ABC's movement in price may be explained by changes affecting the overall market. The remaining 30% (0.30) of price movement is explained by changes that do not affect the overall market, or unsystematic risk. Thus, the coefficient of determination is a very important percentage to understand, because it also tells us how to appropriately use beta as a measure of risk when selecting between multiple assets for inclusion in a portfolio. The higher the coefficient of determination (R^2) of the stock or portfolio, the more the overall market is an appropriate benchmark for the measurement of investment risk.

Use of R^2 in Portfolio Evaluation

The common measures of portfolio performance (Jensen, Treynor, and Sharpe) will be discussed in Unit 7, but they are important here with respect to what they use as a risk measure. The Jensen and Treynor methods use beta as the relevant risk measure; therefore, by definition, each method assumes a diversified portfolio with little unsystematic risk. Thus, the use of Jensen and Treynor is appropriate only where the R^2 of the stock or portfolio is approximately 0.75 or more.

In contrast to Jensen and Treynor, the Sharpe method uses standard deviation as the relevant risk measure and, therefore, may be used to evaluate any portfolio or stock. Thus, the use of the Sharpe method is required where the R^2 of the stock or portfolio is less than 0.75, but the Sharpe method may be used with any R^2.

PRACTICE QUESTIONS

Choose the best answer for each of the questions below.
Answers can be found at the end of this unit.

Answer both Questions 9 and 10 using the following facts: Portfolio A has a standard deviation of 55%, and the market has a standard deviation of 40%. Assume that the correlation coefficient between Portfolio A and the market is 0.50.

9. What percentage of the total risk of Portfolio A is unsystematic risk?

A. 25%
B. 50%
C. 75%
D. 100%

10. What portfolio measure is best used to evaluate the performance of Portfolio A?

A. Sharpe ratio
B. Jensen's alpha
C. Treynor ratio
D. Information ratio

103 UNIT 5 ANSWERS TO PRACTICE QUESTIONS

1. A. Liquidity risk is a type of unsystematic, or diversifiable, risk.

2. D. Eos Company shareholders own equity in Eos and, therefore, are not subject to default risk. Because Eos is privately held, liquidity risk is relevant. Market risk is a systematic risk, and the automotive industry is particularly subject to market fluctuations. Business risk is the risk associated with individual businesses.

3. B. The standard deviation for Asset A is 6.56%, and the standard deviation for Asset B is 8.54%. Therefore, on the basis of total risk, Asset B is riskier.

Using this information, calculate the standard deviation as follows (keystrokes are shown for the HP10bII+):

Asset A
7 [Σ+]
12 [Σ+]
1 [+/-][Σ+]
[shift] [Sx,Sy]
6.5574

Asset B
4 [Σ+]
11 [Σ+]
21 [Σ+]
[shift] [Sx,Sy]
8.5440

4. C. The portfolio beta is a weighted average: (0.50 × 0.65) + (0.50 × 0.82) = 0.74.

5. A. A negative beta means that the investment will move in an opposite direction from the overall market. Therefore, if the market is declining, then the asset should increase in value, thereby increasing the expected performance of the portfolio.

6. D. With a normal probability distribution, 68% of the returns fall within 1 standard deviation of the mean, 95% within 2 standard deviations, and 99% within 3 standard deviations. Therefore, Mysterious Company has less than a 1% chance of experiencing a negative return.

7. B. Only statement II is correct. The degree to which a distribution is not symmetric about its mean is measured by skewness. Excess kurtosis, which is measured relative to a normal distribution, indicates the peakedness of a distribution and also reflects the probability of extreme outcomes.

8. D. The greatest level of diversification will occur when the correlation coefficient is closest to –1.0. Therefore, Assets 7 and 8 offer the greatest level of diversification.

9. C. The coefficient of determination (R^2) of Portfolio A is 25% (0.25). This is derived by squaring the correlation coefficient (R) of 0.50 (0.50 × 0.50 = 0.25). Therefore, 25% is the percentage of returns of Portfolio A that may be explained by the market (or systematic risk). The remainder of the percentage of returns (movement) of Portfolio A is explained by factors independent of the market (or unsystematic risk). To determine this, subtract the systematic risk from 1.0 (1.0 – 0.25 = 0.75, or 75%).

10. A. As calculated in the answer to Question 9, the R^2 of Portfolio A is 0.25. This means that Portfolio A has a large amount of unsystematic risk; therefore, the Sharpe ratio is most appropriate as an evaluation tool because it uses standard deviation as its risk measure.

103 UNIT 5 POST-STUDY CHECKLIST

- ☐ Can I explain investment risk and diversification?
- ☐ Do I understand the various types of systematic and unsystematic risks?
- ☐ Can I explain and calculate expected return?
- ☐ Am I able to explain probability distributions?
- ☐ Can I calculate and interpret statistical measures such as z-statistic, skewness, and kurtosis?
- ☐ Can I explain the relationship between covariance and the correlation coefficient?
- ☐ Can I explain the use of the coefficient of determination in portfolio evaluation?
- ☐ Do I understand how to calculate the standard deviation for both a single asset and a two-asset portfolio?
- ☐ Do I understand how beta is used in the construction of an investment portfolio?
- ☐ Am I able to use semivariance in analyzing investment portfolio returns?
- ☐ Can I use stochastic modeling in projecting the future performance of a portfolio?
- ☐ Can I explain how sensitivity analysis is used to evaluate an investment?

Am I able to define and understand the application of the following terms as they relate to investment planning?

- ☐ Beta
- ☐ Business risk
- ☐ Coefficient of determination
- ☐ Correlation coefficient
- ☐ Covariance
- ☐ Default risk
- ☐ Diversification
- ☐ Exchange rate risk
- ☐ Expected return
- ☐ Financial risk
- ☐ Interest rate risk
- ☐ Investment manager risk
- ☐ Investment risk
- ☐ Kurtosis
- ☐ Leptokurtic distribution
- ☐ Liquidity risk
- ☐ Lognormal probability distribution
- ☐ Market risk
- ☐ Marketability risk
- ☐ Mean
- ☐ Median
- ☐ Mode
- ☐ Monte Carlo simulation
- ☐ Negatively skewed distribution
- ☐ Normal probability distribution
- ☐ Platykurtic distribution
- ☐ Political risk
- ☐ Positively skewed distribution
- ☐ Purchasing power risk
- ☐ Reinvestment rate risk
- ☐ Semivariance
- ☐ Sensitivity analysis
- ☐ Skewness
- ☐ Standard deviation
- ☐ Stochastic modeling
- ☐ Systematic risk
- ☐ Tax risk
- ☐ Unsystematic risk
- ☐ Z-statistic

Measures of Investment Returns

REFER TO

CFP Board Principal Knowledge Topics – E. Investment Planning, E.36. Measures of Investment Returns

INTRODUCTION

This unit considers the second part of the risk/return investment equation: measures of investment returns. Unlike investment risk, where less is best, the greater the return of an investment in the past, the greater chance the investment will outperform in the future. Among the numerous measures of investment return, some are more relevant for evaluating stock and mutual fund performance, while some are more relevant for evaluating bond performance.

Because of the nature of this unit, heavy use of your financial calculator is required. In addition, the time value of money principles you learned and used in *101 General Financial Planning Principles, Professional Conduct, and Regulation* are applicable in some of the computations.

LEARNING OBJECTIVES

After completion of this unit, you should be able to achieve the following learning objectives:

CFP® Board Principal Knowledge Topics – E. Investment Planning

E.36. Measures of Investment Returns

LO E.36.1 Contrast and calculate simple and compound rate of return.

LO E.36.2 Explain arithmetic and geometric mean.

LO E.36.3 Compare and contrast time-weighted and dollar-weighted returns.

LO E.36.4 Calculate and interpret both the nominal and real rate of return for an investment asset.

LO E.36.5 Define and calculate the various rates of returns dealing with stocks and mutual funds including total return, SEC yield, and holding period return.

LO E.36.6 Define and calculate the returns dealing with bonds including current yield, yield to maturity, yield to call, and taxable equivalent yield.

LO E.36.7 Calculate annual percentage rate and effective annual rate.

KEY TERMS

Annual percentage rate (APR)
Arithmetic mean
Compound rate of return
Current yield (CY)
Dollar-weighted return
Effective annual rate (EAR)
Geometric mean
Holding period rate of return (HPR)
Nominal rate of return
Real rate of return
SEC yield
Simple rate of return
Taxable equivalent yield (TEY)
Time-weighted return
Total return
Yield to call (YTC)
Yield to maturity (YTM)

A. SIMPLE VS. COMPOUND RATE OF RETURN

LO E.36.1 Contrast and calculate simple and compound rate of return.

A **simple rate of return** for an investment is computed by dividing its total return (income earned plus capital appreciation divided by the original investment) by the number of years that the investor has held the asset. The computation results in an annualized noncompounded rate of return. However, the simple rate of return ignores the time value of money.

EXAMPLE Jacob owned an investment that generated a total return of 60% over the past five years. Jacob's simple rate of return is 12% (60% ÷ 5).

In contrast, the **compound rate of return** computation for an investment assumes that all interim proceeds, such as interest and repayment of principal, are reinvested (thereby generating additional return) over the holding period. A compound rate of return is easily calculated with a financial calculator using the time-value-of-money keys or the uneven-cash-flow and net-present-value keys.

EXAMPLE Melissa deposits $1,000 in a one-year CD that pays an annual interest rate of 4% compounded quarterly. You have determined that, at the end of one year, Melissa will have a total of $1,040.60 (1,000 +/–PV; 1 × 4 N; 4 ÷ 4 I/YR; solve for FV). Therefore, Melissa's compound rate of return is 4.06% (1,000 +/–PV; 1,040.60 FV; 1 N; solve for I/YR).

B. ARITHMETIC VS. GEOMETRIC MEAN

LO E.36.2 Explain arithmetic and geometric mean.

The **arithmetic mean**, which is a noncompounded return, is calculated by dividing the sum of the periodic returns by the total number of periods being evaluated. The arithmetic mean does not assume reinvestment of returns.

EXAMPLE Assume that an investor has earned the following series of returns on an investment:

Year 1:	15.20%
Year 2:	9.10%
Year 3:	6.50%
Year 4:	18.30%
Year 5:	16.80%
	65.90%

Therefore, the investor's arithmetic mean return is 13.18% (65.90% ÷ 5).

The arithmetic mean is the same as the average, or mean, return we used in the last unit when we computed various measures of investment risk.

The **geometric mean**, on the other hand, assumes compounding of returns. The formula for geometric mean is as follows:

$$\text{geometric mean} = \sqrt[n]{(1+r_1)(1+r_2)(1+r_3)\ldots(1+r_n)} - 1$$

where r_i = the periodic return for year i, and n = the number of periods

An easy method to solve for the geometric mean is to use the time-value-of-money keys on your financial calculator, as demonstrated below.

> **EXAMPLE** Continuing with the returns in the previous example, the geometric mean of 13.09% may be computed as follows (assume an investment of $1):
> PV = –1
> FV = (1 + 0.152)(1 + 0.091)(1 + 0.065)(1 + 0.183)(1 + 0.168) = 1.8495
> n = 5
> Solve for i = 13.0865, or 13.09%

You should note that the geometric mean will always be lower than the arithmetic mean, except when the returns for all periods are equal, in which case the geometric and arithmetic means will be equal. The reason for this difference in percentage returns is that the arithmetic mean does not take into consideration the compounding effect of the returns. When analyzing a security's returns, the geometric mean would be the preferred measurement over the arithmetic mean.

PRACTICE QUESTION

Choose the best answer for the question below.
The answer can be found at the end of this unit.

1. August Corporation's common stock experienced the following returns over the past 3 years: 6%, –10%, 20%. Which row correctly identifies the August Corporation's arithmetic and geometric mean?

	Arithmetic Mean	Geometric Mean
A.	5.33%	4.61%
B.	4.61%	5.33%
C.	12.00%	7.00%
D.	7.00%	12.00%

C. TIME-WEIGHTED VS. DOLLAR-WEIGHTED RETURN

LO E.36.3 Compare and contrast time-weighted and dollar-weighted returns.

A **time-weighted return** is determined without regard to any subsequent cash flows of the investor. As such, it measures the performance of the investment over a period of time (and not of the investor as in a dollar-weighted approach). Most returns reported on mutual funds are time-weighted because the portfolio manager does not have any control over the future cash flows to the fund with respect to investor dollars.

In contrast, a **dollar-weighted return** considers subsequent contributions to and withdrawals from an investment, including sales of, for example, stock. As a result, the dollar-weighted approach focuses on the return of the investor (not the investment, as in the time-weighted approach) over a period of time, and usually results in a rate of return different than the time-weighted method.

EXAMPLE Connie purchased one share of XYZ stock for $50. One year later, the stock paid a dividend of $4, and Connie purchased an additional share for $65. At the end of the second year, Connie sold XYZ stock for $75 per share. The stock did not pay a dividend in the second year. What was the time-weighted return for XYZ stock over the two-year period?

CF_0 = –50 (value of the stock at the beginning of the investment period)
CF_1 = 4 (dividend paid on stock at end of year 1)
CF_2 = 75 (value of stock at the end of year 2)
Solve for IRR = 26.5398, or 26.54%

Alternatively, the dollar-weighted return to Connie was 22.63%, calculated as follows:

CF_0 = –50 (value of the stock at the beginning of the investment period)
CF_1 = 4 – 65 = –61 (dividend less purchase of additional stock)
CF_2 = 75 × 2 = 150 (value of stock holdings at the end of year 2)
Solve for IRR = 22.6328, or 22.63%

PRACTICE QUESTIONS

Choose the best answer for each of the questions below.
Answers can be found at the end of this unit.

2. Larry invested $5,000 in ABC mutual fund one year ago. The fund paid dividends of $100, $150, $50, and $100 at the end of each quarter, all of which were distributed to Larry. At the time of the last dividend payment, his fund had grown to $5,175. What was the dollar-weighted return for this investment?

A. 2.85% ×4
B. 3.50%
C. 11.38%
D. 14.00%

3. Arthur purchases 200 shares of HMS stock for $23 per share. He then makes subsequent purchases at the end of the following years:

Year 1: 50 shares at $26 per share

Year 2: 75 shares at $29 per share

Year 3: 25 shares at $36 per share

At the end of the fourth year, HMS is trading at $41 per share. What is the annualized time-weighted return on the stock over the 4-year period? (Assume that no dividends were paid over the 4-year period.)

A. 13.85%
B. 14.25%
C. 15.00%
D. 15.55%

D. NOMINAL VS. REAL (INFLATION-ADJUSTED) RETURN

LO E.36.4 Calculate and interpret both the nominal and real rate of return for an investment asset.

The **nominal rate of return** of an investment is simply its stated rate of return for a given period without accounting for inflation. This rate is the same as the coupon rate of a bond. If a taxable investment is at issue, the nominal rate also reflects the before-tax rate of return. Conversely, the **real rate of return** takes inflation into account; that is why the real rate of return is sometimes called the inflation-adjusted rate of return.

Some planners compute the real rate of return by simply taking the nominal rate of return and subtracting the annual inflation rate. However, more properly (and for purposes of the CFP® Exam), the real rate of return is calculated using the formula:

$$\left[\frac{(1+R_n)}{(1+I)}-1\right]\times 100$$

where

R_n = the absolute return
I = the rate of inflation for the period

EXAMPLE Renee owns a corporate bond with a coupon rate of 6%. If the annual inflation rate is 3.5%, her real rate of return on the bond is 2.42%, calculated as follows:

$$\left(\frac{1+0.06}{1+0.035}-1\right)\times 100=(1.0242-1)\times 100=2.4155\text{, or }2.42\%$$

Note that the planner can get close to this rate by simply subtracting 3.5% (inflation rate) from 6% (nominal rate) for a rate of 2.5%, but this result is not precisely correct. Over a considerable number of years, for example, in performing a retirement needs analysis computation, this approximation can lead to significant dollar error.

After-Tax Inflation-Adjusted Rate of Return

A two-step process may be used to integrate the effect of taxes and inflation on an investment's rate of return.

1. Compute the after-tax rate of return by using the formula:

$$r_{\text{after-tax}} = r_{\text{nominal}} \times (1 - \text{investor's marginal tax rate})$$

If the investor resides in a state that imposes state income taxes, the marginal tax rate should also reflect state taxes (in addition to federal taxes).

2. Multiply the nominal rate by (1– investor's marginal tax rate) and use this product as the numerator in the inflation-adjusted rate of return formula and derive the after-tax, inflation-adjusted amount.

EXAMPLE Continuing with the previous example, now assume that Renee is in a 15% federal marginal income tax bracket (she lives in a state that does not impose state income taxes). Therefore, her after-tax rate of return on the corporate bond is 0.051, or 5.1% (0.06 × [1 – 0.15]). In turn, her after-tax, inflation-adjusted rate of return is 1.55%, calculated as follows:

$$\left(\frac{1+0.051}{1+0.035}-1\right)\times 100=(1.0155-1)\times 100=1.55, \text{ or } 1.55\%$$

PRACTICE QUESTION

Choose the best answer for the question below.
The answer can be found at the end of this unit.

4. Susan is earning a before-tax (nominal) return of 10% on a recently purchased investment. Her combined federal and state marginal income tax rate is 37%. What is her after-tax rate of return on this investment?

A. 3.7%
B. 6.3%
C. 6.7%
D. 2.7%

E. ANNUAL PERCENTAGE RATE AND EFFECTIVE ANNUAL RATE

LO E.36.7 Calculate annual percentage rate and effective annual rate.

The nominal **annual percentage rate (APR)** is the yearly cost of funds expressed as a percentage. However, the nominal APR does not take compounding into consideration. If a lender advertises a 1.25% monthly rate, the APR is 15% (1.25% × 12).

The **effective annual rate (EAR)** is the annual percentage rate taking into consideration the impact of compounding. This calculation provides the annual rate of interest of an investment or debt when compounding occurs more than once per year.

$$\text{effective annual rate} = [1 + (i \div n)]^n - 1$$

where

i = annual interest rate
n = number of periods

If an investor has a certificate of deposit paying monthly interest based on annual rate of 2.05%, the effective annual rate will be more than 2.05% due to the effect of compounding. This is a result of a greater principal onto which the interest is calculated each month. The resulting effective annual rate is 2.069%.

EXAMPLE Gregory carries a balance on his credit card. The nominal APR is 12.99% compounded daily. The effective annual rate is actually 13.87%, calculated as follows:

effective annual rate = $[1 + (0.1299 \div 365)]^{365} - 1 = 0.1387$, or 13.87%

Keystrokes for the HP 10bII/HP 10bII+

0.1299 ÷ 365 =

+ 1 =

Shift × (this is the y^x function)

365 =

– 1 =

0.1387

F. RETURNS DEALING PRIMARILY WITH STOCKS AND MUTUAL FUNDS

LO E.36.5 Define and calculate the various rates of returns dealing with stocks and mutual funds including total return, SEC yield, and holding period return.

In addition to the compound annual rate of return measurement (discussed earlier), there are three other types of investment returns frequently quoted with respect to stocks and/or mutual funds. They are total return, SEC yield, and holding period return.

Total Return

Total return includes the income from dividends or interest plus any capital appreciation over a given time period, usually one year.

EXAMPLE A common stock purchased for $20 with an annual dividend of $1, which was paid in cash, is sold after one year for $24. The total return on the investment is $5: $1 in dividends + $4 in capital appreciation. As a result, the total return is 25% ($5 ÷ $20).

Whether an investor values the income or capital growth component of total return more highly (or both are valued equally) depends on his tax status and cash flow needs. For example, a recently retired individual is more likely to value income than capital growth, whereas a young wage-earner in a higher tax bracket is more likely to find capital appreciation more attractive than a high income payout.

SEC Yield

The **SEC yield** is a standardized calculation that the SEC requires mutual funds to report and allows investors to compare yields among various investments. This yield is based on the most recent 30-day period covered by the fund's SEC filings and represents the interest and dividends earned during that particular period, *after* expenses have been deducted. Mutual funds are required to disclose this rate in their prospectuses.

Holding Period Rate of Return (HPR)

The **holding period rate of return (HPR)** (sometimes referred to as the single period return) is simply the total return of an investment for the given period over which the investment is owned. However, the measurement has a major weakness because it fails to consider the timing of when the cash flows actually occurred. As a result, if the holding period of the investment is more than one year, the HPR overstates the true return of the investment on an annual basis. Conversely, if the investment's holding period is less than one year, the HPR understates the true return.

The formula for the holding period return of any investment is as follows:

$$\text{HPR} = \frac{\text{ending value} - \text{beginning value} \pm \text{cash flows}}{\text{beginning value}}$$

EXAMPLE Michael purchases a U.S. Treasury bond for $1,050 and sells the bond later for $980. During the holding period, Michael received interest payments totaling $160. Therefore, Michael's holding period rate of return (HPR) is 8.57%, computed as follows:

$$\text{HPR} = \frac{\$980 - \$1{,}050 + \$160}{\$1{,}050} = \frac{\$90}{\$1{,}050} = 0.0857\text{, or } 8.57\%$$

As you can readily see from the above example, in computing HPR, we do not have a time period that may be referenced. In other words, we do not know how long Michael owned the bond and, therefore, cannot compare the performance of the bond to other investments.

Alternate Formula

$$\text{HPR} = [(1 + r_1) \times (1 + r_2) \times \ldots (1 + r_n)] - 1$$

HPR = holding period return
r = rate of return for given period
n = number of periods

EXAMPLE Jim owns an investment with the following returns over the past 5-year period:

Year 1: 12%
Year 2: –9%
Year 3: 3%
Year 4: 5%
Year 5: –7%

What is Jim's HPR over the 5-year period?

HPR = [(1 + 0.12) × (1 – 0.09) × (1 + 0.03) × (1 + 0.05) × (1 – 0.07)] – 1
HPR = [1.12 × 0.91 × 1.03 × 1.05 × 0.93] – 1
HPR = 1.0251 – 1 = 0.0251, or 2.51%

PRACTICE QUESTIONS

Choose the best answer for each of the questions below.
Answers can be found at the end of this unit.

5. A bond that was purchased for par is now selling for $1,075. The bond made semiannual coupon payments of $60 during the year. What is the holding period rate of return for the owner of this bond at the end of the first year?

A. 7.5%
B. 13.5%
C. 19.5%
D. 60.0%

6. Michael purchased 800 shares of ABC stock at $75 per share. The stock paid a $1.20 dividend per share at the end of the year. During this same year, there was a 2-for-1 stock split. If the value of Michael's investment at the end of the year was $66,000, what was his holding period rate of return (HPR)?

A. 8.3%
B. 10.0%
C. 12.0%
D. 13.2%

G. RETURNS DEALING PRIMARILY WITH BONDS

LO E.36.6 Define and calculate the returns dealing with bonds including current yield, yield to maturity, yield to call, and taxable equivalent yield.

The four types of investment return computations frequently cited with respect to bonds are current yield (CY), yield to maturity (YTM), yield to call (YTC), and taxable equivalent yield (TEY).

Current Yield (CY)

The **current yield (CY)** of a bond is the return represented by the amount of annual interest income paid in relation to the current market value of the bond. Current yield is calculated by dividing the annual interest payment on the bond (as reflected by its coupon rate multiplied by the par value of the bond) by the bond's current market price.

$$CY = \frac{\text{annual interest}}{\text{current market price}}$$

EXAMPLE Jeff has a bond with a coupon rate of 3% that is currently trading at $965. Therefore, the current yield (CY) on Jeff's bond is 3.11%, calculated as follows:

$$CY = \frac{\$30}{\$965} = 0.0311, \text{ or } 3.11\%$$

You should also note that the current yield of 3.11% is higher than the coupon rate, or nominal yield, of 3% on Jeff's bond. This is because the bond is currently trading at a discount in the secondary market.

Yield to Maturity (YTM)

The **yield to maturity (YTM)**, internal rate of return, is the total return earned on a bond that is held to maturity. A major assumption when calculating YTM is that all interest payments on the bond are reinvested at the calculated YTM. For example, if the calculated YTM is 7%, any interest payments generated from the bond are also assumed to be reinvested at 7%.

The easiest method to calculate the YTM of any bond is by using your financial function calculator.

EXAMPLE Today, Tom purchased a five-year bond with a coupon rate of 6% paid semiannually. The bond is currently trading in the secondary market for $1,050. Therefore, the YTM on Tom's bond is 4.86%, calculated as follows:

PV = –1,050
FV = 1,000
PMT = 6% × 1,000 ÷ 2 = 30 (periodic payment – semiannual)
n = 5 × 2 = 10 (number of periods)
Solve for i = 2.43 × 2 = 4.86% (You must multiply periodic rate of 2.43 by number of periods per year to arrive at annual rate)

The YTM on Tom's bond is lower than its coupon rate, because the bond is currently trading at a premium in the secondary market.

Yield to Call (YTC)

The **yield to call (YTC)** on a bond takes into account the possibility that the bond may be called by the issuer before its maturity date. The actual formula for YTC is the same as that for YTM except that the par value of the bond is replaced by the call price and the maturity date is replaced by the first potential call date.

> **EXAMPLE** Continuing with our previous example involving Tom, now assume that the bond may be called after three years for $1,030 (103% of par). Therefore, the YTC is 5.12%, calculated as follows:
>
> PV = –1,050
> FV = 1,030
> PMT = 6% × 1,000 ÷ 2 = 30
> $n = 3 \times 2 = 6$
> Solve for $i = 2.56 \times 2 = 5.12\%$

You should note that, at times, YTC may be higher than YTM for premium bonds with a premium call price (as with Tom's bond). Note: For yield relationships, refer to the figure in Unit 8.

Taxable Equivalent Yield (TEY)

Some bonds, like municipals, return federally tax-free income. As a result, investors require a method of comparing the yield on municipal bonds with the yield of those that are fully taxable (e.g., corporate issues). As previously discussed in Unit 2, the **taxable equivalent yield (TEY)** formula permits this comparison.

$$\text{TEY} = \frac{\text{tax-exempt yield}}{1 - \text{marginal tax rate}}$$

> **EXAMPLE** Lucy owns a municipal bond, trading at par, with a 5% coupon rate and is in the 28% federal marginal income tax bracket. Therefore, the TEY for this bond is 6.94%, calculated as follows:
>
> $$\text{TEY} = \frac{0.05}{1 - 0.28} = 0.0694, \text{ or } 6.94\%$$

PRACTICE QUESTIONS

Choose the best answer for each of the questions below.
Answers can be found at the end of this unit.

7. Jerry Roberts purchased a 30-year junk bond for $977.36 with a stated coupon rate of 8.5%. What is the YTM for this bond if Jerry receives semiannual coupon payments and expects to hold the bond to maturity?

A. 4.36%
B. 5.68%
C. 8.71%
D. 8.93%

8. Bond ABC is selling at par, offers an 8% coupon, and matures in 20 years. Bond ABC has a call feature that allows the bond to be called after 10 years at a price of $1,050. Which of the following statements is CORRECT?

YTC = 8.34
YTM = 8%

A. The YTC for Bond ABC is 8.34%, which is less than Bond ABC's YTM.
B. The YTC for Bond ABC is 8.34%, which is more than Bond ABC's YTM.
C. The YTC for Bond ABC is 8.00%, which is equal to Bond ABC'S YTM.
D. The YTC for Bond ABC is 8.00%, which is more than Bond ABC's YTM.

9. Franklin is considering investing in bonds. He may purchase a corporate bond paying a 7% coupon or a municipal bond paying 5.3%. If Franklin's marginal federal income tax rate is 31% and his state does not collect income taxes, Franklin would prefer

A. the municipal, because its taxable equivalent yield is 16.06%
B. the municipal, because its taxable equivalent yield is 7.68%
C. the corporate, because its after-tax yield is 10.45%
D. the corporate, because its after-tax yield is 21.21%

$\frac{.053}{1-.31} = 7.68$

103 UNIT 6 ANSWERS TO PRACTICE QUESTIONS

1. A. Arithmetic mean: (6% – 10% + 20%) ÷ 3 = 5.33%.
Geometric mean: PV = –1, n = 3, PMT = 0, FV = (1.06)(0.90)(1.20) = 1.1448.
Solve for i = 0.0461, or 4.61%.

2. C. The dollar-weighted rate of return equals 11.38%, calculated as follows:
CF_0 = (5,000)
CF_1 = 100
CF_2 = 150
CF_3 = 50
CF_4 = 5,275 (5,175 + 100)
IRR = 2.8455 × 4 = 11.3820, or 11.38%

3. D. Because time-weighted returns do not consider the cash flows of the investor (Arthur), only appreciation and dividends on the investment are relevant.
CF_0 = –23 (beginning share value)
CF_1 = 0
CF_2 = 0
CF_3 = 0
CF_4 = 41 (ending share value)
IRR = 15.5484, or 15.55%

4. B. Susan's after-tax rate of return on the investment is 6.3%, calculated as follows:
0.10 × (1 – 0.37) = 0.10 × 0.63 = 0.063, or 6.3%

5. C. The holding period return (HPR) for the bond owner is 19.5%, computed as follows:

$$\text{HPR} = \frac{\$1{,}075 - \$1{,}000 + \$60 + \$60}{\$1{,}000} = \frac{\$195}{\$1{,}000} = 19.5\%$$

6. D. Michael's HPR was 13.2%, computed as follows:

$$\text{HPR} = \frac{\$66{,}000 - \$60{,}000 + (\$1.20 \times 800 \times 2)}{\$60{,}000} = \frac{\$7{,}920}{\$60{,}000} = 13.2\%$$

Note that the dividend (or positive cash flow) is based on 1,600 shares because of the subsequent 2-for-1 stock split after Michael purchased the initial shares of ABC stock.

7. C.
PV = –977.36
FV = 1,000
PMT = 8.5% × 1,000 ÷ 2 = 42.50
n = 30 × 2 = 60
Solve for i = 4.3569 × 2 = 8.71%

8. B. Because ABC is selling at par, its YTM = 8.0%. ABC's YTC: PV = –1,000, FV = 1,050, n = 10 × 2 = 20, PMT = 8% × 1,000 ÷ 2 = 40. Solve for i = 4.17% × 2 = 8.34%.

9. B. One can either compare the taxable equivalent yield of the municipal bond with the nominal yield for the corporate bond or compare the after-tax yield of the corporate bond with the nominal yield of the municipal bond. The taxable equivalent yield of the municipal bond = 5.3% ÷ (1 – 0.31) = 7.68%, which is more than the nominal yield of the corporate bond. The after-tax yield of the corporate bond is 7% × (1 – 0.31) = 4.83%.

103 UNIT 6 POST-STUDY CHECKLIST

- ☐ Can I calculate simple and compound rate of return?
- ☐ Am I able to differentiate arithmetic and geometric mean?
- ☐ Do I understand the difference between time-weighted and dollar-weighted returns?
- ☐ Can I calculate and interpret the nominal and real rate of return?
- ☐ Am I able to calculate the various rates of returns associated with stocks and mutual funds?
- ☐ Do I understand the various types of bond returns including current yield, yield to maturity, yield to call, and taxable equivalent yield?
- ☐ Can I explain the relationship between annual percentage rate and effective annual rate?

Am I able to define and understand the application of the following terms as they relate to investment planning?

- ☐ Annual percentage rate (APR)
- ☐ Arithmetic mean
- ☐ Compound rate of return
- ☐ Current yield (CY)
- ☐ Dollar-weighted return
- ☐ Effective annual rate (EAR)
- ☐ Geometric mean
- ☐ Holding period rate of return (HPR)
- ☐ Nominal rate of return
- ☐ Real rate of return
- ☐ SEC yield
- ☐ Simple rate of return
- ☐ Taxable equivalent yield (TEY)
- ☐ Time-weighted return
- ☐ Total return
- ☐ Yield to call (YTC)
- ☐ Yield to maturity (YTM)

Portfolio Management Theory

REFER TO

CFP Board Principal Knowledge Topics – E. Investment Planning, E.35. Quantitative Investment Concepts

CFP Board Principal Knowledge Topics – E. Investment Planning, E.36. Measures of Investment Returns

CFP Board Principal Knowledge Topics – E. Investment Planning, E.37. Asset Allocation and Portfolio Diversification

CFP Board Principal Knowledge Topics – E. Investment Planning, E.39. Portfolio Development and Analysis

INTRODUCTION

Portfolio management theory builds on a foundation of assumptions about investors' behavior and was first introduced by Harry Markowitz in 1952. At its core, modern portfolio theory proceeds from the premise that investors will behave rationally. Pricing models have been introduced to determine what should be the proper market price for investment assets. The most familiar and useful of these models is the capital asset pricing model, known as CAPM, which derives from the work of Markowitz and others, including William Sharpe, after whom the Sharpe ratio was named.

LEARNING OBJECTIVES

After completion of this unit, you should be able to achieve the following learning objectives:

CFP® Board Principal Knowledge Topics – E. Investment Planning

E.35. Quantitative Investment Concepts

LO E.35.4 Explain the coefficient of variation and how it is used as a measure of total risk.

LO E.35.12 Discuss capital market theory, the capital market line, the capital asset pricing model (CAPM), and the security market line.

LO E.35.13 Explain the application of the arbitrage pricing theory.

E.36. Measures of Investment Returns

LO E.36.8 Discuss, calculate, and evaluate the common types of performance measures including Jensen's alpha, the Sharpe ratio, the Treynor ratio, and the information ratio.

LO E.36.9 Define and calculate risk-adjusted return.

E.37. Asset Allocation and Portfolio Diversification

LO E.37.1 Explain the assumptions of modern portfolio theory including the development of indifference curves and the efficient frontier.

LO E.37.2 Define the efficient market hypothesis, discuss its three forms, and provide examples of anomalies.

E.39. Portfolio Development and Analysis

LO E.39.5 List the various security market indexes and averages and how they are used to compare actual investment performance to a benchmark.

LO E.39.6 Explain the role of each of the security markets.

KEY TERMS

Anomalies
Arbitrage pricing theory (APT)
Best efforts
Capital asset pricing model (CAPM)
Capital market line (CML)
Coefficient of variation (CV)
Dilution
Dow Jones Industrial Average (DJIA)
Efficient frontier
Efficient market hypothesis (EMH)
Firm commitment
J.P. Morgan Indices
Market risk premium
Modern portfolio theory
MSCI EAFE® Index
Primary market
Risk-adjusted return
Russell 2000 Index
Secondary market
Security market line (SML)
Sharpe ratio

Indifference curves
Information ratio
Initial public offering (IPO)
Jensen's alpha
S&P 500 Index
Stock risk premium
Treynor ratio
Wilshire 5000 Index

A. MODERN PORTFOLIO THEORY (MPT)

LO E.37.1 Explain the assumptions of modern portfolio theory including the development of indifference curves and the efficient frontier.

The research of Professor Harry Markowitz provided a framework for measuring the risk-reduction benefits of diversification. Using the standard deviation of returns as the measure of investment risk, he investigated how combining risky securities into a portfolio affected the portolio's risk and expected return. One important conclusion of his model is that unless the returns of the risky assets are perfectly positively correlated, risk is reduced by diversifying across assets. In 1952, Markowitz first developed the foundations of **modern portfolio theory (MPT)** by stipulating the following assumptions.

- Investors consider each investment opportunity as being represented by a probability distribution of expected returns over a specified holding period.
- Investors estimate the risk of the portfolio on the basis of the variability (i.e., standard deviation) of returns.
- Investors base decisions solely on expected return and risk; therefore, their indifference curves are a function of expected return and the expected variance of returns only. (Note: This assumption is often captured by the concept of mean-variance optimization.)
- Investors base their indifference to alternative investments on the maximization of wealth over a specified period, and this indifference diminishes as they get beyond this period.
- For a given level of risk, investors prefer higher returns to lower returns.

MPT is based on the use of statistical measures including mathematical concepts such as beta and correlation. The key point is that many investments are required to effectively diversify a portfolio, and that number depends primarily on the correlation between the investments.

Markowitz used risk (as measured by standard deviation) and expected return as the basis for determining appropriate combinations of assets, or portfolios. The universe of these portfolios is, in turn, plotted on a risk-return parabola known as the **efficient frontier**. Specifically, this curve represents that set of portfolios that has the maximum rate of return for every given level of risk. In pictorial terms, the efficient frontier is depicted as follows:

Efficient Frontier

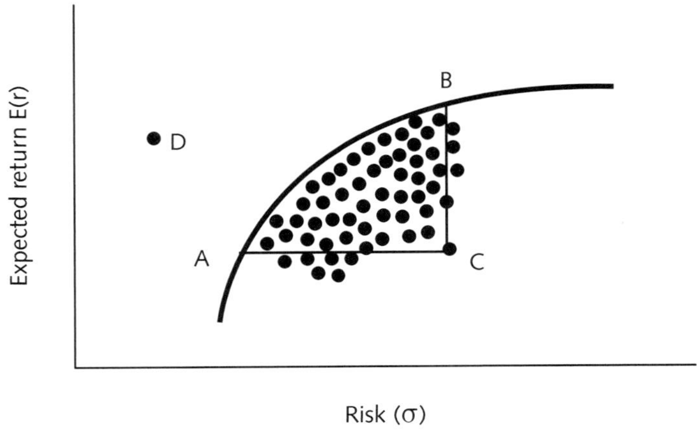

Every portfolio residing on the efficient frontier has either a higher rate of return for equal risk or lower risk for an equal rate of return than another portfolio below or underneath the frontier. For example, in the previous graphic, Portfolios A and B are both equally efficient and dominate Portfolio C because:

1. Portfolio A has an equal expected rate of return as Portfolio C but with a significantly lower level of assumed risk; and
2. Portfolio B has an equal level of assumed risk as Portfolio C but with a significantly higher expected rate of return.

Therefore, Portfolio C is inefficient; it is attainable but not optimal.

Portfolio D is unattainable because it resides above the efficient frontier. This portfolio is arguably efficient, but the expected rate of return is unattainable because it is located outside the universe of available portfolios.

Each risk-averse investor (a fundamental assumption of modern portfolio theory) will choose to establish a portfolio lying somewhere on this efficient frontier by implementing her own set of indifference curves. **Indifference curves**, which represent the risk-reward trade-off that the investor is willing to make, will cross the efficient frontier in two locations, lie tangent to the efficient frontier, or not intersect the efficient frontier at all. The portfolio that lies at the point of tangency is the optimal portfolio for the investor.

The efficient frontier, an investor's indifference curves, and an optimal portfolio are illustrated in the figure below.

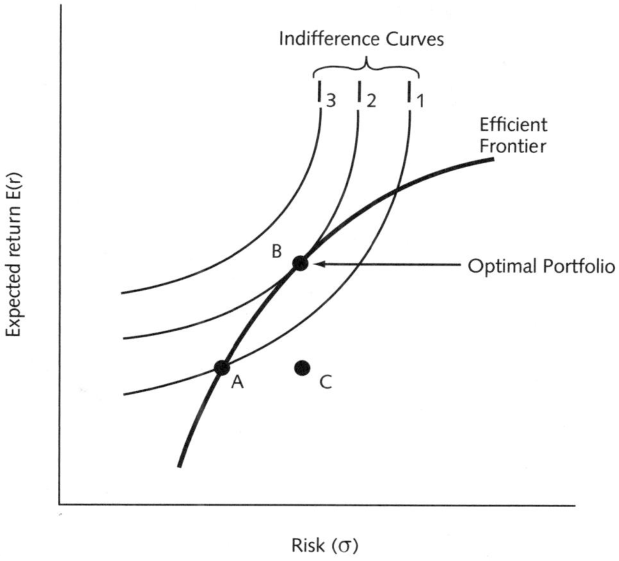

In the figure, Portfolios A and B are both efficient, but Portfolio C is not. Portfolio A is more efficient than Portfolio C because it has the same expected return but much less risk. Portfolio B is more efficient than Portfolio C because it has a much higher expected return for the same level of risk.

Portfolios may exist below the efficient frontier (such as Portfolio C in the previous figure). However, these portfolios are said to be inefficient. Portfolios may not exist above the efficient frontier, however, because the efficient frontier consists of all portfolios maximizing the highest investment return for a given level of investor risk. Therefore, any portfolio above the efficient frontier is said to be unattainable.

Different investors may have different indifference curves. For example, if the investor is very risk averse (i.e., conservative), the curve will tend to be very steep, indicating that a relatively large amount of additional return is necessary to entice the investor to assume the additional risk of a potential investment. Alternatively, if the investor is more risk tolerant (i.e., moderate or aggressive), the curve will tend to be less steep or flat, indicating that a smaller amount of additional return is necessary to entice the investor to assume additional risk.

PRACTICE QUESTIONS

Choose the best answer for each of the questions below. Answers can be found at the end of this unit.

1. Which statement based on the indifference curves graphic below is CORRECT?

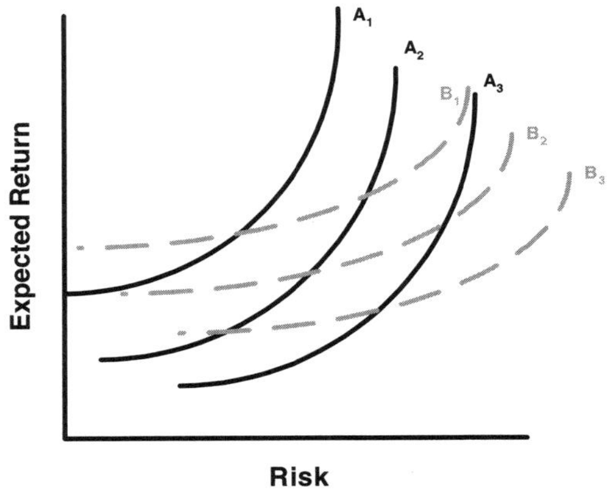

A. Investor B (dashed curves) is more risk tolerant than investor A (solid curves).
B. Investor B (dashed curves) is more risk averse than investor A (solid curves).
C. No information on the relative risk tolerance of investor B (dashed curves) and investor A (solid curves) can be derived.
D. The optimal portfolio lies at the intersection of curves A_2 and B_2.

2. Which of the following correctly describes the graphic below?

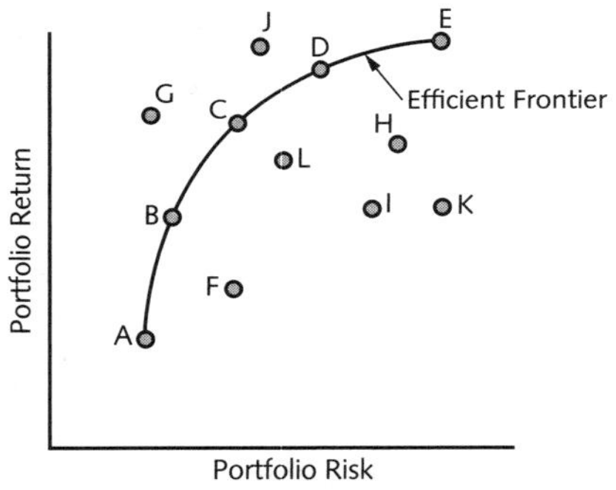

	Unattainable	Attainable	Efficient
A.	C	I	G
B.	F	A	D
C.	J	B	E
D.	G	L	H

B. CAPITAL MARKET THEORY

LO E.35.12 Discuss capital market theory, the capital market line, the capital asset pricing model (CAPM), and the security market line.

William Sharpe continued the work of Harry Markowitz and added to modern portfolio theory with a branch of research known as capital market theory. Sharpe said it was possible to identify a portfolio on the Markowitz efficient frontier that would be considered the market portfolio (M). In turn, this market portfolio consists of all risky assets (i.e., those with both unsystematic and systematic risk). A line could then be drawn from the risk-free rate of return (r_f) on the vertical axis, or Y-axis, through portfolio M. This line becomes the new efficient frontier and is known as the **capital market line (CML)**. The CML is calculated as follows:

$$r_p = r_f + \sigma_p \left[\frac{r_m - r_f}{\sigma_m} \right]$$

r_p = expected return of the portfolio
r_f = risk-free rate of return
r_m = market rate of return
σ_p = standard deviation of the portfolio
σ_m = standard deviation of the market

The CML is illustrated in the figure below.

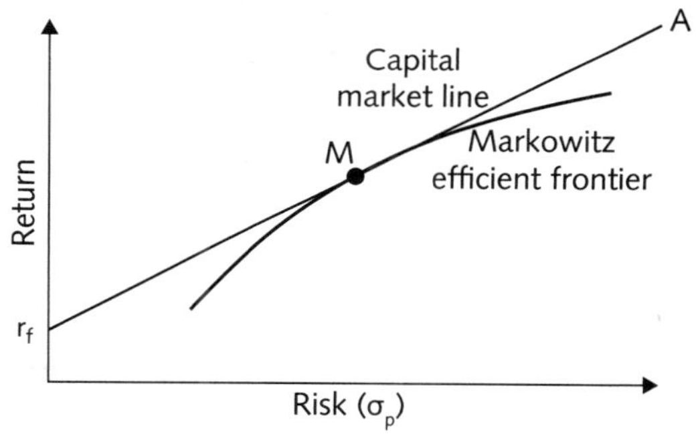

Note that the CML, like Markowitz's efficient frontier, uses standard deviation as the risk measure along the horizontal axis, or X-axis.

As the investor proceeds along the CML (toward point A), he is becoming more aggressive in making investments, including making use of margin and leveraging his investment assets (borrowing portfolio). As the investor proceeds back along the CML toward the risk-free rate of return (r_f), he is becoming conservative in making investments and is investing more in risk-free government securities (lending portfolio).

Capital Asset Pricing Model

The end result of capital market theory (and the practical application of Sharpe's work) was the derivation of the **capital asset pricing model (CAPM)**, which is written as follows:

$$r_i = r_f + (r_m - r_f)\beta_i$$

r_i = expected rate of return
r_m = market rate of return
r_f = risk-free rate of return
β_i = beta

The CAPM allows the investor to determine an asset's expected rate of return, a form of risk-adjusted return encapsulating how much risk the investor should assume to obtain a particular return from an investment. The model is made up of two separate components. One component is known as the **stock risk premium** and is the part of the model reflected by the following formula: $(r_m - r_f)\beta_i$, where r_m is the market return, r_f is the risk-free return, and β_i is the beta coefficient of the stock. The other component is the **market risk premium** and is the part of the model reflected by the following formula: $r_m - r_f$, where r_m is the market return and r_f is the risk-free return. The stock risk premium is the inducement necessary to entice the individual to invest in a particular stock, whereas the market risk premium is the incentive required for the individual to invest in the securities market in general.

EXAMPLE Assume that the return on the market is currently 10%, the 90-day Treasury bill rate of return is 4.5%, and the beta coefficient of Stock X is 1.2. Therefore, the expected return on Stock X using the CAPM is 11.1%, calculated as follows:

r_i = 0.045 + [(0.1 – 0.045) × 1.2] = 0.045 + (0.055 × 1.2) = 0.045 + 0.066 = 0.111, or 11.1%

Of this amount, the stock risk premium is 6.6%, and the market risk premium is 5.5%. This is the amount of additional return that the investor will need to invest (in excess of the risk-free rate of return) in the specific stock and overall market, respectively.

You should note that the CAPM accounts for the impact of systematic risk *(as measured by beta)* only and does not take into consideration unsystematic risk, which is assumed to have been diversified away.

The major contribution of the CAPM to investment theory was the creation of a quantitative investment risk measure and a statistical association with the investment's expected rate of return. The CAPM links together risk and return and helps investors make prudent investment decisions. Specifically, the CAPM allows us to calculate the expected rate of return for an investment and compare it to an investor's required rate of return for that investment. For example, if the CAPM expected rate of return is higher than the investor's required rate of return, all other investment considerations being equal, a positive investment decision is warranted. Conversely, if the CAPM expected rate of return is lower than the investor's required rate of return, the investment should be rejected.

Like Markowitz, Sharpe also stipulated that certain assumptions must be present for the CAPM to be used. The most important of these assumptions are outlined below.

- All investors have the same expectations—that is, they estimate identical probability distributions for a given investment.
- Investors can always borrow or lend money at the risk-free rate of return as represented by the yield on U.S. short-term securities, such as the 13-week (90-day) Treasury bill.
- No taxes or transaction costs are involved in buying or selling investment assets, meaning that these expenses are not relevant in investment decision making.
- At all times, capital markets are in equilibrium, meaning that all investments are properly priced, taking into account the commensurate level of investor risk. Thus, CAPM establishes a theoretical baseline by which to evaluate the suitability of any investment for any investor.

Security Market Line

The CML is a representation of the relationship of risk and return for all efficient portfolios. However, this reflects the *macro* level of the economy and does not focus on individual securities or portfolios that are more appropriate for the average investor. As a result, Sharpe needed to develop something at the *micro* level to quantify the risk/return relationship for individual securities. This is the purpose of the **security market line (SML)**, which depicts the relationship of risk and return for individual efficient portfolios and has the same formula as that for the CAPM. The graph of the CAPM is called the SML, with intercept equal to the risk-free rate and slope equal to the market risk premium. The SML may be illustrated as follows:

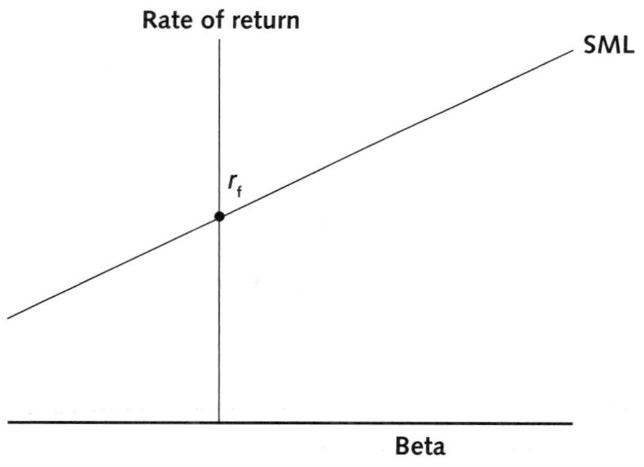

You should observe that, unlike the CML, the SML uses beta as its risk measurement on the horizontal axis. If security markets are in equilibrium (an assumption of Sharpe's capital market theory), all individual assets should plot along the SML. If this is not the case (i.e., the asset does not plot along the SML), the asset is considered to be either undervalued (i.e., the asset plots above the SML) or overvalued (i.e., the asset plots below the SML) and an investment opportunity or mistake results. Ultimately, market forces will drive the price of the asset either down or up to the SML.

PRACTICE QUESTIONS

Choose the best answer for each of the questions below.
Answers can be found at the end of this unit.

3. George is considering adding ABC stock to his portfolio. ABC has a standard deviation of 4.5% and a beta of 0.85. If the market rate of return is 12% and the 90-day T-bill has a yield of 3%, what are the market risk premium and the stock risk premium for ABC?

	Market Risk Premium	Stock Risk Premium
A.	12%	7.65%
B.	9%	7.65%
C.	12%	13.50%
D.	9%	13.50%

4. Troy requires a 15% return to meet his financial goals. He is interested in a mutual fund with a beta of 1.3. If the market return has averaged 11% over the past 10 years and the Treasury bill rate is currently 4%, should Troy invest in this fund?

A. No, the fund's expected rate of return is less than Troy's required rate of return.
B. No, Troy's required rate of return is less than the fund's expected rate of return.
C. Yes, the fund's expected rate of return is more than Troy's required rate or return.
D. Yes, Troy's required rate of return is more than the fund's expected rate of return.

C. ARBITRAGE PRICING THEORY (APT)

LO E.35.13 Explain the application of the arbitrage pricing theory.

The CAPM explains the returns on stock as a result of only one factor: the volatility of a stock relative to the market as a whole (as measured by beta). What if there are other unanticipated factors that explain the expected return of a stock? Those other unanticipated factors are what the **arbitrage pricing theory (APT)** attempts to quantify.

Proponents of APT assert that the expected returns on securities are based on a variety of unexpected or unanticipated factors. In turn, these factors affect the amount of risk premium that an investor will demand to entice him to make a potential investment. Many potential factors affect the expected return of a security; some of these factors affect all securities, whereas others affect only a specific industry or sector of the economy. However, among the most prevalent factors are an unanticipated change in the inflation rate, an unexpected change in the level of unemployment, and an unexpected change in the level of industrial production.

According to the APT, once all of these unanticipated factors are considered (as specified in the formula by F_n), the sensitivity of the security's expected return (b_1, b_2, and so forth) is entered in the formula as a coefficient. Then, all of this is added to the risk-free return (shown in the formula as a_0) to determine the total expected return. The formula for APT is as follows:

$$r_i = a_0 + b_1F_1 + b_2F_2 + \ldots + b_nF_n + e$$

EXAMPLE Terry has determined that the following unanticipated factors (and resulting risk premium) most affect the amount of expected return on his stock. In addition, he has estimated the following sensitivity coefficients for each of these factors:

Factor	Sensitivity Coefficient	Risk Premium
Inflation	110% (1.1)	5%
Unemployment	80% (0.8)	7%
Industrial production	50% (0.5)	6%

The current risk-free rate is 2%. Therefore, using APT, the expected return on Terry's stock is 16.10%, computed as follows:

$r_i = 0.02 + (1.1 \times 0.05) + (0.8 \times 0.07) + (0.5 \times 0.06)$
$= 0.02 + 0.055 + 0.056 + 0.03$
$= 0.1610$, or 16.10%

D. RISK-ADJUSTED RETURN

LO E.36.9 Define and calculate risk-adjusted return.

Several methods exist to determine a stock or mutual fund's **risk-adjusted return**, with the final answer dependent on whether standard deviation or beta is used in the denominator. A simple risk-adjusted rate of return calculation for a stock or mutual fund using beta is to divide the stock or mutual fund's nominal rate of return by its beta coefficient.

EXAMPLE ABC Mutual Fund has a total return of 8% annually over the course of the last year and features a beta of 0.80 and an R^2 with the market of 0.90. Therefore, its risk-adjusted return is 10% (0.08 ÷ 0.80). If the S&P 500 Index's risk-adjusted return is only 9% over this same period of time, then ABC Mutual Fund has outperformed the index on a risk-adjusted basis.

Selecting an appropriate index for benchmarking entails regressing the portfolio's returns against an index's returns and evaluating the resulting coefficient of determination (R^2). In addition to having similar investment philosophies and goals, the benchmark and the portfolio should have a coefficient of determination that is meaningful (≥ 0.75).

E. PERFORMANCE MEASURES

LO E.36.8 Discuss, calculate, and evaluate the common types of performance measures including Jensen's alpha, the Sharpe ratio, the Treynor ratio, and the information ratio.

Jensen's Alpha

Jensen's alpha, also known as Jensen's performance index, is a measure of the risk-adjusted value added by a portfolio manager. Specifically, alpha is measured as the portfolio's actual or realized return in excess of (or deficient to) the expected return calculated by the capital asset pricing model (CAPM). A positive alpha means that the portfolio manager has added value on an absolute basis, compared with the required return based on the level of investment risk undertaken; a negative alpha means that the manager has underperformed. If alpha is positive, the portfolio plots above the SML; conversely, if alpha is negative, the portfolio plots below the SML. Because beta is used in calculating Jensen's alpha, it is only appropriate for evaluating diversified portfolios and stocks that constitute diversified portfolios.

The formula for Jensen's alpha is: CAPM

$$\alpha_p = \bar{r}_p - \left[\bar{r}_f + \left(\bar{r}_m - \bar{r}_f\right)\beta_p\right]$$

α_p = alpha, which represents the return that is able to be earned above or below an unmanaged portfolio with identical market risk

β_p = beta for portfolio p

$\bar{r}_p$ = average rate of return for portfolio p

$\bar{r}_m$ = market's rate of return

$\bar{r}_f$ = risk-free rate of return

Note: The last section of the equation, $[\bar{r}_f + (\bar{r}_m - \bar{r}_f)\beta_p]$, is equivalent to the capital asset pricing model. Thus, alpha is equal to the difference between the actual (realized) return and the expected return given the level of risk undertaken by the portfolio.

EXAMPLE Calculate Jensen's alpha to determine the extent to which portfolio P outperformed or underperformed its CAPM benchmark:

Realized portfolio P mean return	10%
Portfolio P beta	0.50
Market portfolio mean return	12%
Risk-free rate	4%

Jensen's alpha for portfolio P equals 2%.

Alpha = 0.10 – [0.04 + (0.12 – 0.04)0.5] = 0.10 – 0.08 = 0.02, or 2%.

Treynor Ratio

The **Treynor ratio** is computed as follows:

$$T_p = \frac{\overline{r}_p - \overline{r}_f}{\beta_p}$$

T_p = Treynor ratio for portfolio p

$\overline{r}_p$ = average rate of return

$\overline{r}_f$ = risk-free rate of return

β_p = beta for portfolio p

The Treynor ratio uses beta in its denominator and, therefore, may be used only to compare the performance of diversified portfolios or stocks that constitute diversified portfolios. Unlike the absolute measure achieved with Jensen's alpha, the Treynor ratio is a relative performance measure. Only when used to evaluate an asset's performance relative to another potential investment or a benchmark does it convey useful information. As with Jensen, the higher the Treynor ratio, the better the risk-adjusted performance of the asset.

> **EXAMPLE** Assume the current risk-free rate of return is 3% and Portfolio B has realized an actual return of 12%. The portfolio also exhibits a beta coefficient of 0.60. Accordingly, this means that Portfolio B's Treynor ratio is 0.15, calculated as follows: (0.12 – 0.03) ÷ 0.60. If the portfolio's Treynor ratio is higher than the Treynor ratio of the market, then the manager of Portfolio B has outperformed the market.

Sharpe Ratio

The **Sharpe ratio** is computed as follows:

$$S_p = \frac{\overline{r}_p - \overline{r}_f}{\sigma_p}$$

S_p = Sharpe ratio for portfolio p

$\overline{r}_p$ = average rate of return

$\overline{r}_f$ = risk-free rate of return

σ_p = standard deviation for portfolio p

The Sharpe ratio uses standard deviation in its denominator and, therefore, may be used to compare the performance of all portfolios. Similar to the Treynor ratio, the Sharpe ratio is a relative performance measure, and the higher the ratio, the better the risk-adjusted performance. Unlike Treynor and Jensen, which use beta as the risk measure, Sharpe uses standard deviation. Because beta is meaningful with respect to diversified portfolios only, an undiversified portfolio or an individual stock's risk-adjusted return may appear superior when measured with either Treynor or Jensen and inferior when measured with Sharpe. Jensen and Treynor should only be relied on when beta correctly reflects most of the investment's risk—that is, when the R^2 (coefficient of determination) of the investment with respect to the market is at least 0.75.

EXAMPLE Assume the same facts and actual return of Portfolio B as in the previous example. However, Portfolio B now has a standard deviation of 6.5%. Accordingly, Portfolio B's Sharpe ratio is 1.38, calculated as follows: (0.12 – 0.03) ÷ 0.065. If the Sharpe ratio of Portfolio B is higher than the Sharpe ratio of the market, then the manager of Portfolio B has outperformed the market.

Information Ratio

The **information ratio** measures the portfolio's average rate of return in excess of a comparison (benchmark) portfolio divided by the standard deviation of the excess return. The formula is as follows (as indicated on CFP Board-provided formula sheet):

$$IR = \frac{R_P - R_B}{\sigma_A}$$

IR = information ratio
R_p = average rate of return for portfolio p for a given period
R_B = average rate of return for the benchmark portfolio; CAPM's required rate of return may be used
σ_A = standard deviation of the excess return during a given period

If CAPM is used as the benchmark return, you should note that the numerator of the information ratio is alpha (the excess return over the risk-free return) and the denominator is the standard deviation of this excess return. Therefore, the information ratio is alpha divided by standard deviation. An investment with a high positive alpha and a low standard deviation will result in a high information ratio. The ratio reduces to the Sharpe ratio when the benchmark portfolio is a constant-return, risk-free asset and is extremely difficult to interpret when alpha for the subject portfolio is negative. Therefore, the information ratio should be used only when alpha is positive (i.e., the portfolio manager has added value) and beta is meaningful.

PRACTICE QUESTION

Choose the best answer for the question below.
The answer can be found at the end of this unit.

5. Portfolio A has a standard deviation of 5.5%, a beta of 1.15, an actual return of 8%, and an expected return of 10%. Portfolio B has a standard deviation of 7.5%, a beta of 1.50, an actual return of 9%, and an expected return of 12%. Assume a risk-free rate of return of 2.75% and an R^2 of 0.40 with respect to the market. Given this information, which of the following statements is CORRECT?

A. Portfolio A has a higher Sharpe ratio than Portfolio B indicating that Portfolio A outperformed Portfolio B.

B. Portfolio B has a higher Sharpe ratio than Portfolio A indicating that Portfolio B outperformed Portfolio A.

C. Portfolio A has a higher Jensen's alpha than Portfolio B indicating that Portfolio A outperformed Portfolio B.

D. Portfolio B has a higher Treynor ratio than Portfolio A indicating that Portfolio B outperformed Portfolio A.

F. COEFFICIENT OF VARIATION (CV)

LO E.35.4 Explain the coefficient of variation and how it is used as a measure of total risk.

The **coefficient of variation (CV)** is a computation of the relative measure of total risk (as measured by standard deviation) per unit of expected return and is used to compare investments with varying rates of return and standard deviations. When using this ratio to compare two alternatives, the one with the lower CV is usually the preferable choice.

$$CV = \frac{\text{standard deviation of asset}}{\text{expected return of asset}}$$

EXAMPLE Using ABC and XYZ stocks, ABC stock has a mean return of 10.75% and a standard deviation of 7.18% and XYZ has a mean return of 20% and a standard deviation of 12%. Therefore, if we are basing an investment decision solely on total risk, we would likely choose ABC stock, because it has a lower standard deviation. However, in determining the CV for each stock, we find that ABC stock has a CV of 0.6679, whereas XYZ stock has a CV of only 0.6. This means that ABC stock has more total risk per unit of expected return; thus, we may instead choose to invest in XYZ stock.

You should be careful not to confuse the coefficient of variation (CV) with covariance (COV). CV is a measure of relative risk per unit of expected return, whereas COV is a measure of how returns on assets move together. The former is used as a cross-check on an investment decision, whereas the latter is the basis for optimal portfolio diversification.

PRACTICE QUESTION

Choose the best answer for the question below.
The answer can be found at the end of this unit.

6. Stock P offers an expected return of 20%, a standard deviation of 6%, and a beta coefficient of 1.3. Stock Q offers an expected return of 16%, a standard deviation of 4%, and a beta coefficient of 0.95. Which stock would you recommend for purchase and why?

A. Stock P, because it has a lower coefficient of variation
B. Stock Q, because it has a lower coefficient of variation
C. Stock P, because it has a higher coefficient of variation
D. Stock Q, because it has a higher coefficient of variation

G. EFFICIENT MARKET HYPOTHESIS (EMH)

LO E.37.2 Define the efficient market hypothesis, discuss its three forms, and provide examples of anomalies.

In its purest form, the **efficient market hypothesis (EMH)** suggests that investors are unable to outperform the market on a consistent basis. The fundamental assumption of the theory, which was developed by Eugene Fama of the University of Chicago, is that current stock prices reflect all available information for a company and that prices rapidly (or immediately) adjust to reflect any new information. In addition, any new information must be unexpected; therefore, any changes in the stock price resulting from this new information will be random (i.e., the random walk theory). If prices move in random fashion, any investment strategies or market techniques used to take advantage of market inefficiencies are theoretically useless. This hypothesis is the basis for the buy-and-hold strategy. The three forms of the EMH are presented below.

- The *weak form* holds that current stock prices have already incorporated all historical market data and that historical price trends are, therefore, of no value in predicting future price changes. Although fundamental analysis and insider information may produce above-market returns under the weak form, technical analysis is of no value. Indeed, none of the forms of EMH attributes any value to technical analysis.
- The *semistrong form* holds that current stock prices not only reflect all historical price data but also reflect data from analyzing financial statements, industry, or current economic outlook. Thus, even fundamental analysis is of no value in this form, and only insider information may produce above-market returns. Technical analysis is also of no value.
- The *strong form* holds that current stock prices reflect all public and private information. Therefore, even insider traders are unlikely to consistently outperform the market. In addition, neither technical analysis nor fundamental analysis is of any value. (You should note that this form has effectively been negated in recent years given the considerable illegal profits made by investors who possess insider trading information.)

The three forms of EMH and which types of market information each considers relevant in attaining above-market rates of return are summarized in the table below.

Form of EMH	Relevant Information
Weak	Insider information and fundamental analysis
Semistrong	Insider information
Strong	Nothing

Anomalies

Anomalies are unexpected market results or trends that tend to contradict the EMH. In other words, if the EMH is absolutely true in all its forms, it cannot explain these results or trends, reflecting that the market may not be as efficient as the hypothesis stipulates. The more prevalent anomalies are outlined below.

- The *price-to-earnings (P/E) ratio effect* suggests that higher returns may be attainable with portfolios comprising securities with low P/E ratios. This effect is also a fundamental premise of value investing.

- The *small or neglected firm effect* relates to the number of security analysts who follow smaller companies. When fewer analysts follow a stock, the security may not be as efficiently priced and may result in undervalued stocks. There is some evidence that this anomaly holds, given the investment opportunities presented by international investing (because international stocks are less closely followed than domestic stocks) in recent years.
- The *January effect* suggests that stocks have a tendency to decline during the month of December and move up significantly in early January. This anomaly is likely the result of tax selling and buying, which are most prevalent during the months when the anomaly is observed.
- The *Value Line® enigma* relates to stocks that are rated 1 on Value Line's scale of 1–5 ratings (with 1 being the highest rating and a recommended buy). Historically, these stocks have had a tendency to outperform lower rated stocks by Value Line, a noted source of investment research.

PRACTICE QUESTIONS

Choose the best answer for each of the questions below.
Answers can be found at the end of this unit.

Sally: none
Michael: Strong/Sem.
Anita: Weak

7. Sally, Michael, and Anita use different methods for choosing assets for their investment portfolios. Sally uses technical analysis to determine when to buy and sell the stocks in her portfolio. Michael is committed to a passive investment strategy and a well-diversified portfolio of randomly selected stocks. Anita ignores historical volume and price information but reviews the financial statements of the firms in which she is interested. Which of the following statements best describe(s) Sally, Michael, and Anita?

1. Anita accepts the strong form of the efficient market hypothesis (EMH).
2. Michael accepts the semistrong form of the EMH.
3. Sally accepts the weak form of the EMH.
4. Both Anita and Sally accept the semistrong form of the EMH.

A. 2 only
B. 1 and 4
C. 2 and 3
D. 2, 3, and 4

8. An individual who is a proponent of the efficient market hypothesis (EMH) will likely invest in which of the following?

A. Growth mutual funds
B. Sector mutual funds
C. Balanced mutual funds
D. Index funds

9. Which of the following forms of the efficient market hypothesis, if any, supports technical analysis?

A. Weak
B. Semistrong
C. Strong
D. None of these

H. SECURITY MARKET INDEXES AND AVERAGES

LO E.39.5 List the various security market indexes and averages and how they are used to compare actual investment performance to a benchmark.

Averages and indexes are constructed to inform investors about changes in the market and serve as benchmarks for the performance of investors' portfolios and the performance of money managers, such as mutual fund money managers. The most well-known of these price-weighted indexes is the **Dow Jones Industrial Average (DJIA)**. Higher priced stocks within this index have more influence on the overall movement of this index than lower priced stocks.

- Price weighted index—that is, a $50 stock has five times the impact of a $10 stock (DJIA is a price-weighted index)
- Market capitalization weighted index—that is, a stock with a market capitalization value of $25 million will have 10 times the impact of a stock with a market capitalization value of a $2.5 million company (S&P 500 Index is a market capitalization weighted index)

Averages are calculated by determining the average stock price for a group of stocks. For instance, the DJIA consists of 30 stocks. To determine the DJIA, the 30 stock prices are added and then divided by an adjusted divisor. The divisor was originally 30, equaling the number of stocks for the average. However, the denominator for the DJIA, which is now less than 1.00, has changed dramatically since its inception as a result of stock splits, stock dividends, and substitutions of stocks.

The DJIA has several inherent shortcomings. The measure fails to reflect payment of cash dividends, ignores stock dividends of less than 10%, fails to account for the number of shares outstanding, and consists of a biased sample of stocks (mostly blue-chip companies). As mentioned earlier, another shortcoming of this index is that higher priced stocks within the DJIA have more influence than lower priced stocks within the index. Although the DJIA does have fundamental shortcomings, it is highly correlated with other broader market indexes, such as the S&P 500. The correlation coefficient between the DJIA and the S&P 500 is greater than 95%. A high correlation indicates that the DJIA is an adequate representation of the market in spite of its fundamental weaknesses.

The **S&P 500 Index** is a market capitalization weighted index. This index comprises 500 different stocks from the NYSE and the Nasdaq and includes only large companies. The S&P 500 is determined by summing the market capitalization value (which is the share price multiplied by the number of shares outstanding) of the 500 companies, dividing by the base year value, and then multiplying this amount by 10 (the initial index value). If the value of the S&P 500 increased from 100 to 200, this change would indicate that the market capitalization value of the securities had doubled. This method automatically adjusts for stock splits and dividends by focusing on market capitalization values instead of the individual stock share prices of each of the 500 companies within the index. The S&P 500 Index is used by most professionals as a benchmark for U.S. large-cap equity investments and is composed of industrial stocks, transportation stocks, utilities, and financial institutions.

The **Russell 2000 Index** is a well-known index that is used to benchmark small capitalization companies. This index is a market capitalization weighted index and is a subset of the Russell 3000 Index, which represents the majority of U.S. equities.

The **MSCI EAFE® Index** (Morgan Stanley Capital International Europe, Australasia, and Far East) was created as a measure of the international securities markets. This index provides an indication of how a portfolio consisting of companies outside the United States might perform over time and is probably the most well-known measure of international markets.

The **Wilshire 5000 Index** is another well-known index that is used as a measure of the U.S. broad market. This index consists of over 5,000 U.S.-based companies and is often used as a measure of the overall market within the United States.

The **J.P. Morgan Indices** track emerging markets, government debt, and corporate asset classes.

PRACTICE QUESTION

Choose the best answer for the question below.
The answer can be found at the end of this unit.

10. Mildred is the portfolio manager of a small-cap fund which invests strictly within the U.S. Which index would provide the best benchmark for Mildred's fund?

A. Russell 2000
B. MSCI EAFE®
C. S&P 500
D. Wilshire 5000

I. SECURITY MARKETS

LO E.39.6 Explain the role of each of the security markets.

The purpose of the **primary market** is to facilitate the initial sale of securities issued to the public. If a business finds that its product or service is in great demand, the owners may decide to go public and do an **initial public offering (IPO)** of its stock. To do this, first, the owners engage an investment banking firm to underwrite the stock offering; that is, to purchase all the public shares at a pre-established price and then resell them to the public (presumably at a significant profit). The proposed stock sale is publicized in the financial press with ads commonly known as tombstones because they are in heavy print with a notable black border. The day before the actual sale of the company's shares to the actual public, the underwriter typically prices the issue, or establishes the price that it will pay for each share. This may be done either on a **firm commitment** basis (the underwriter will purchase any shares that remain unsold) or using the underwriter's **best efforts** (the underwriter will make every effort to sell all the shares, but the company does not receive any money for unsold shares). Technically, when the investment banker agrees to sell the company's stock using best efforts, the banker does not underwrite the securities at all because it does not buy any securities. Rather, the banker acts only as a broker to sell whatever stock it can at the stipulated price.

If a company has already issued shares but wants to raise additional capital through the sale of more stock, it does so by what is called a secondary or seasoned offering. Companies are often loath to issue more stock because the larger the supply of stock outstanding, the less valuable each share is that has already been issued (not to mention the commensurate reduction in earnings per share). This is called **dilution**. For this reason, a company typically issues new shares only if its capital structure of debt and equity needs rebalancing to comply with debt covenants.

The purpose of the **secondary market** is to provide investors with a method of buying and selling previously issued securities. The secondary market consists of four distinct markets. The first market is the exchange (auction) market where listed securities trade and includes the New York Stock Exchange (NYSE) and the Over-The-Counter (OTC) market. The second market provides a method of trading unlisted securities (OTC and NASDAQ). The third market consists of stocks traded both on the organized exchanges and on the OTC market. Finally, the fourth market is generally used by institutions (e.g., pension funds) that trade in very large volumes among themselves without the help of brokers (INSTINET).

PRACTICE QUESTION

Choose the best answer for the question below.
The answer can be found at the end of this unit.

11. Myron, age 68, enjoys participating in an investment club. The club actively trades securities for its members with the goal of modest capital appreciation. In which market do the club's trades take place?

A. Primary
B. Secondary
C. Futures
D. Currency

103 UNIT 7 ANSWERS TO PRACTICE QUESTIONS

1. A. The indifference curves illustrate the increase in the amount of return demanded by the investor for changes in the portfolio's risk. The steeper the curve is, the more risk averse (less risk tolerant) the investor.

2. C. Portfolios on the efficient frontier are both attainable and efficient. Those below the efficient frontier are attainable but not efficient. Those above the efficient frontier are unattainable.

3. B. Market risk premium = $r_m - r_f$ = 12% – 3% = 9% Stock risk premium = $(r_m - r_f)\beta_i$ = 9% × .85 = 7.65%

4. A. Expected rate of return for the mutual fund using CAPM: $r_f + (r_m - r_f)\beta_i$ = 0.04 + (0.11 – 0.04)1.3 = 0.131, or 13.1%. Because the expected rate of return is less than Troy's required rate of return, he should not purchase shares in the fund.

5. A. Because R^2 is less than 0.75, the Sharpe ratio must be used to compare the performance of the portfolios.
The formula for Sharpe's ratio: $S_p = (r_p - r_f) \div \sigma_p$
Sharpe for Portfolio A = (0.08 – 0.0275) ÷ 0.055 = 0.9545
Sharpe for Portfolio B = (0.09 – 0.0275) ÷ 0.075 = 0.8333
As a result, the Sharpe ratio for Portfolio A is higher than Portfolio B indicating that Portfolio A outperformed Portfolio B.

6. B. Stock P has a CV of 0.30 (0.06 ÷ 0.20), whereas Stock Q has a CV of only 0.25 (0.04 ÷ 0.16). Therefore, Stock Q has a lower CV and is the better purchase on the basis of that measure only. Beta does not enter into the CV computation.

7. A. Under the weak form of the EMH, access to fundamental analysis and insider information can achieve superior results. Under the semistrong form of the EMH, only access to insider information can achieve superior results. Under the strong form of the EMH, not even access to insider information can achieve superior results. Anita uses fundamental analysis, which is supported only by the weak form of EMH. Michael does not use fundamental or technical analysis. His strategy is supported by the semistrong and strong forms of the EMH. Sally uses technical analysis, which is rejected by all forms of the EMH.

8. D. An individual who believes in the EMH will likely invest in index funds. Inherent in this strategy is a belief that an investor cannot outperform the market with active portfolio management techniques. The remaining choices all incorporate an active portfolio management philosophy.

9. D. The efficient market hypothesis is in direct contradiction to technical analysis because the hypothesis is founded on the belief that all historical price and volume data (which are used by technical analysts) is already accounted for in the current stock price.

10. A. The Russell 2000 is an index of small capitalization U.S. stocks. The MSCI EAFE® is an index of European, Australasian, and Far East stocks. The S&P 500 is an index of large capitalization U.S. stocks. The Wilshire 5000 is a broad market index.

11. B. The purpose of the secondary market is to provide investors with a method of buying and selling previously issued securities. The purpose of the primary market is to facilitate the initial sale of securities issued to the public.

103 UNIT 7 POST-STUDY CHECKLIST

- ☐ Do I understand the role of each of the security markets?
- ☐ Can I calculate and interpret the coefficient of variation?
- ☐ Am I able to explain the assumptions of modern portfolio theory including the development of indifference curves and the efficient frontier?
- ☐ Can I explain capital market theory, the capital market line, the capital asset pricing model, and the security market line?
- ☐ Do I understand the efficient market hypothesis, its three forms, and its anomalies?
- ☐ Do I understand the application of the arbitrage pricing theory?
- ☐ Can I calculate and evaluate Jensen's alpha, the Sharpe ratio, the Treynor ratio, and the information ratio?
- ☐ Do I understand the various security market indices and averages and how they are used in portfolio analysis?
- ☐ Can I calculate and analyze risk-adjusted return?

Am I able to define and understand the application of the following terms as they relate to investment planning?

- ☐ Anomalies
- ☐ Arbitrage pricing theory (APT)
- ☐ Best efforts
- ☐ Capital asset pricing model (CAPM)
- ☐ Capital market line (CML)
- ☐ Coefficient of variation (CV)
- ☐ Dilution
- ☐ Dow Jones Industrial Average (DJIA)
- ☐ Efficient frontier
- ☐ Efficient market hypothesis (EMH)
- ☐ Firm commitment
- ☐ Indifference curves
- ☐ Information ratio
- ☐ Initial public offering (IPO)
- ☐ Jensen's alpha
- ☐ J.P. Morgan Indices
- ☐ Market risk premium
- ☐ Modern portfolio theory
- ☐ MSCI EAFE® Index
- ☐ Primary market
- ☐ Risk-adjusted return
- ☐ Russell 2000 Index
- ☐ Secondary market
- ☐ Security market line (SML)
- ☐ Sharpe ratio
- ☐ S&P 500 Index
- ☐ Stock risk premium
- ☐ Treynor ratio
- ☐ Wilshire 5000 Index

UNIT 8

Bond Valuation Concepts

REFER TO

CFP Board Principal Knowledge Topics – E. Investment Planning, E.38. Bond and Stock Valuation Concepts

CFP Board Principal Knowledge Topics – E. Investment Planning, E.39. Portfolio Development and Analysis

CFP Board Principal Knowledge Topics – E. Investment Planning, E.40. Investment Strategies

INTRODUCTION

In this unit, we will discuss how to derive a market value for a bond. Unlike stocks (the valuation of which will be discussed in Unit 9), the valuation of bonds is relatively easy because the future cash flows are contractually set in the bond indenture. Indeed, in the basic bond valuation formula, the only unknown is the investor's required rate of return necessary to make such a purchase. However, in valuing any security, we need to be sure that we are using the correct information. In the case of bond valuation, we need to compare what the bond should be yielding with similar quality debt obligations. Accordingly, we use bond rating agencies, such as Standard & Poor's, to assist in this process.

As you are also aware by now, a bond is a fixed-income security that is subject to interest rate risk (among other risks). How do we measure or quantify the sensitivity of this risk? In the bond market, interest rate sensitivity is captured by a concept known as duration, which is essentially the weighted-average number of years that it takes for a bond owner to receive a return of the initial investment on a present value basis. The concepts of duration and convexity are also central to this unit.

LEARNING OBJECTIVES

After completion of this unit, you should be able to achieve the following learning objectives:

CFP® Board Principal Knowledge Topics – E. Investment Planning

E.38. Bond and Stock Valuation Concepts

LO E.38.1 Determine the intrinsic value of a bond.

LO E.38.2 Explain the prevalent theories used to explain various yield curves.

LO E.38.3 Describe the relationship between interest rates and bond prices.

E.39. Portfolio Development and Analysis

LO E.39.1 Define duration and explain its relationship to coupon rate, yield to maturity, and term of the bond.

LO E.39.2 Explain convexity and its relationship to coupon rate, yield to maturity, and term of the bond.

LO E.39.3 Calculate the estimated change in the price of a bond given its present value, duration, and change in yield to maturity.

E.40. Investment Strategies

LO E.40.2 Discuss bond portfolio immunization.

KEY TERMS

Convexity
Duration
Flat yield curve
Inverted yield curve
Liquidity preference theory
Market segmentation theory
Modified duration
Normal (positive) yield curve
Portfolio immunization
Unbiased expectations theory
Yield curve

A. DETERMINING THE INTRINSIC VALUE OF A BOND

LO E.38.1 Determine the intrinsic value of a bond.

The basic formula used to determine the discounted present, or intrinsic, value (PV) of a bond is as follows:

$$PV = \frac{CF_1}{(1 + y)^1} + \frac{CF_2}{(1 + y)^2} + \cdots + \frac{CF_t}{(1 + y)^t}$$

where *CF* is the future cash flows (semiannual interest payments and par value) from the bond, *y* is the discount rate per period (YTM), and *t* is the number of cash flows to be evaluated.

You may wish to compute the intrinsic value of the bond using your financial function calculator and solving for the present value.

EXAMPLE A 10-year bond features a coupon rate of 5% (paid semiannually). If the comparable yield for this quality bond is currently 6%, what should be the intrinsic value (present value) of the 10-year bond?
$n = 10 \times 2 = 20$ (number of periodic payments)
$i = 6 \div 2 = 3$ (semiannual yield for comparable bonds)
PMT = 0.05 × 1,000 ÷ 2 = 25 (semiannual coupon payment)
FV = 1,000 (par value)
Solve for PV = 925.62, or $925.62

You should note that, in the above example, we could have anticipated that the bond would be trading at a discount to par because the investor's required rate of return of 6% exceeds the bond's coupon rate of 5%.

PRACTICE QUESTION

Choose the best answer for the question below.
The answer can be found at the end of this unit.

1. Wade purchased a noninvestment grade bond for $1,038.90 exactly 2 years ago today. The bond had a maturity of 5 years and a coupon rate of 10% (paid semiannually). Assuming the rates below are the prevailing rates for this type of bond at different maturity dates, how much could Wade sell his bond for today?

Maturity	1 year	2 years	3 years	5 years
Interest rates	6%	6.5%	7%	8.5%

A. $1,038.90
B. $1,060.08
C. $1,078.73
D. $1,079.93

B. BOND PRICES AND INTEREST RATES

LO E.38.3 Describe the relationship between interest rates and bond prices.

Bond prices and yields move in opposite directions: as a bond's price rises, its yield declines, and vice versa. When a bond trades at a discount, its current yield increases; when a bond trades at a premium, its current yield decreases. Similar effects occur to a bond's yield to maturity (YTM) and yield to call (YTC) if a bond trades at either a discount or premium. These concepts are illustrated in the following figure.

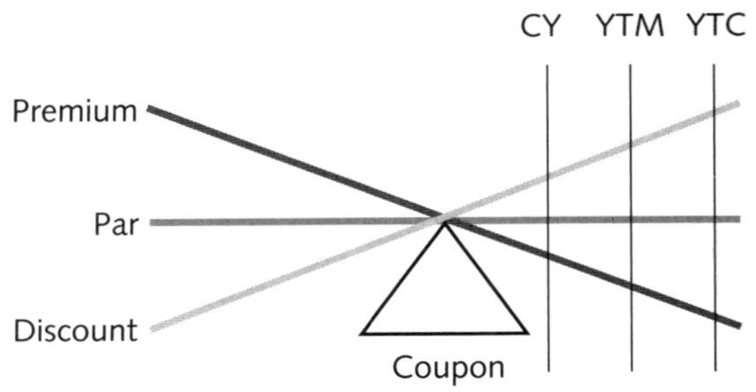

The effects shown in the graphic are also sometimes known as bond seesaws because they reflect all three bond investment returns [current yield (CY), yield to maturity (YTM), and yield to call (YTC)]. When bonds are at par, coupon and current yield are equal. When bonds are at a premium, the CY is less than the coupon. When bonds are at a discount, the CY is greater than the coupon.

EXAMPLE Assume that an investor purchases a 10-year, $1,000 par value bond with a coupon rate of 5%. If the prevailing market interest rates increase to 6%, a new purchaser of the bond will pay less than par ($1,000) so that its yield will equal 6% as well. Therefore, the new purchaser will be willing to pay only $925.62 for the current bond. Also, the current yield on this bond is 5.4%, or the annual interest in dollars ($50) divided by the bond's current market price ($925.62).

In this example, the bond's price decreased when interest rates increased. The 10-year, 5% coupon bond's value decreased from $1,000 to $925.62 as interest rates increased from 5% to 6%. Similarly, as interest rates fall, bond prices rise. This relationship between market interest rates and bond prices occurs because of the fixed nature of bond coupon payments. When bonds are issued, their coupon payments are set to match the prevailing market rate for bonds of similar credit quality and maturity. If market rates increase, the bond's coupon payments will not change. To attract a purchaser for a previously issued bond, the market price must drop to provide a YTM equal to the new market interest rate.

PRACTICE QUESTION

Choose the best answer for the question below.
The answer can be found at the end of this unit.

2. Which of the following correctly presents the relationships that exist between different yield measures?

1. For a premium bond: coupon rate > current yield > yield to maturity
2. For a par bond: coupon rate = current yield = yield to maturity
3. For a discount bond: coupon rate < current yield < yield to maturity
4. For a premium bond: current yield < yield to maturity < coupon rate

A. 4 only
B. 1 and 2
C. 2 and 4
D. 1, 2, and 3

C. YIELD CURVES

LO E.38.2 Explain the prevalent theories used to explain various yield curves.

A **yield curve** is a graph of interest rate yields for bonds of the same quality, ranging in maturity from 31 days to 30 years. A yield curve represents the plot of yield against maturity for a particular type of bond. This curve has a tendency to slope upward and outward, denoting that as the maturity date of bonds lengthen, the corresponding bond yields increase. The increased yields reflect the potential for changes in credit quality and the effect of purchasing power risk over time. If the curve assumes this shape, it is referred to as a normal, or positive, yield curve, indicating that long-term market interest rates are higher than short-term rates. In a normal curve, the difference between short-term and long-term interest rates is usually about three percentage points (300 basis points) but may be much larger or smaller at any given time.

A normal, or positively, sloped yield curve is shown in the figure below.

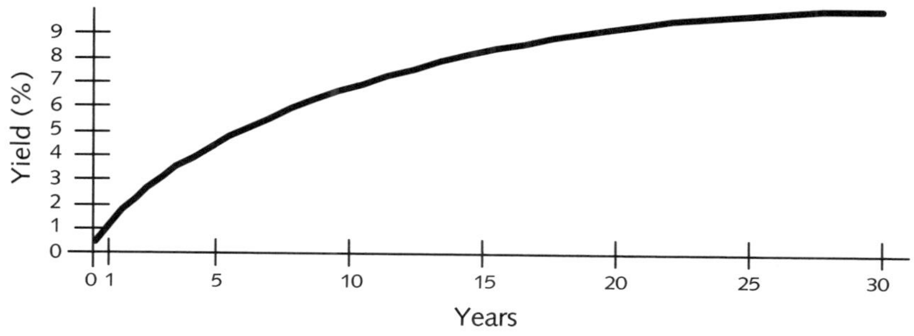

Sometimes, yield curves may be flat (denoting no difference in the yield of bonds relative to their maturity) or inverted (denoting that current short-term borrowing costs are higher than long-term borrowing costs).

The most important point about yield curves is that their shape varies according to changes in the economic cycle; therefore, they may be used to make predictions about the future state of the economy.

- A **normal (positive) yield curve** occurs during periods of economic expansion and generally predicts that market interest rates will rise in the future.
- A **flat yield curve** occurs when the economy is peaking and, therefore, no change in future interest rates (particularly down) is expected.
- An **inverted yield curve** occurs when the Federal Reserve has tightened credit in an inflationary economy; it predicts interest rates will fall and, sometimes, can signal an upcoming economic recession.

Normal Yield Curve (A)

Inverted Yield Curve (B)

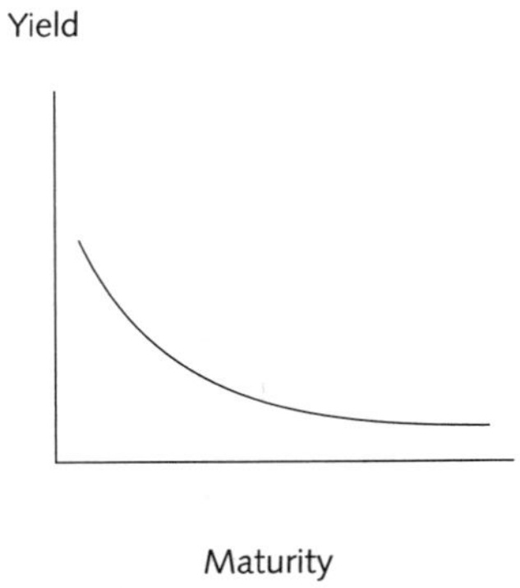

Horizontal Yield Curve (C)

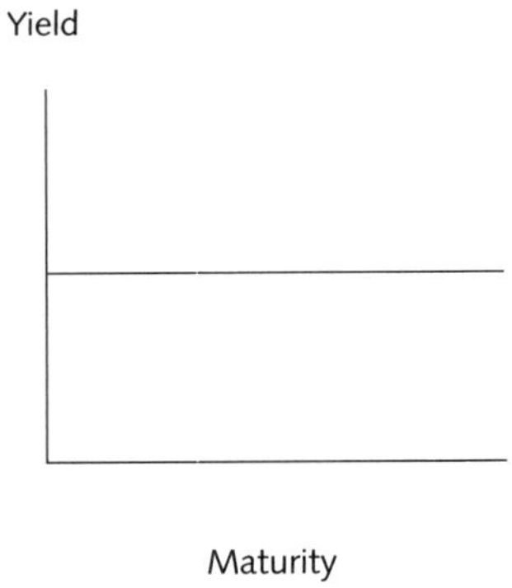

Humped Yield Curve (D)

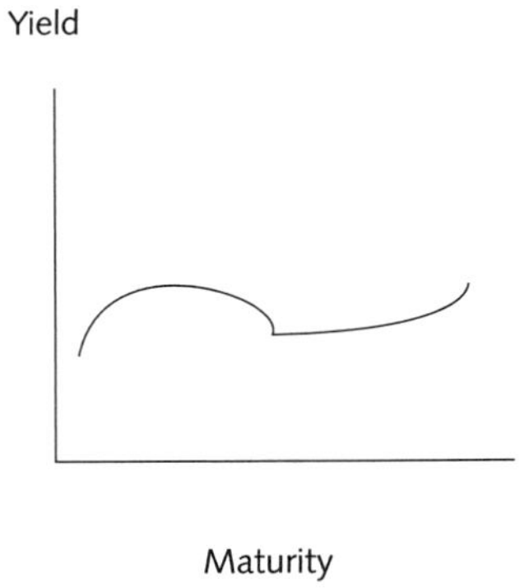

Yield curves and the consequences of their shape are also sometimes referred to as the term structure of interest rates. The *term structure of interest rates* (yield curve) is a theory that relates the term to maturity of a sample of same quality (or rated) bonds to their yield to maturity at a given point in time. Therefore, this theory represents a cross section of yields for a category of bonds that are comparable in all respects but their maturity date. Different yield curves may be constructed for a variety of bonds including Treasury bonds, government agency bonds, municipal bonds, AAA rated corporate bonds. However, the accuracy of the yield curve will depend on the overall comparability of the bonds in the sample.

Yield Curve Theories

Similar to the efficient market hypothesis (EMH) and its various forms, the term structure of interest rates theory also has several iterations. Specifically, there are three different academic arguments about why yield curves mutate into one of the four basic shapes pictured previously. The three predominant theories used to explain various yield curves are expectations theory, liquidity preference theory, and market segmentation theory. Although expectations theory and market segmentation theory may be used to explain any shaped yield curve, the liquidity preference theory only explains a normal, upward-sloping yield curve.

Unbiased expectations theory states that long-term rates consist of many short-term rates and that long-term rates will be the average (or geometric mean) of short-term rates. Accordingly, the expectations theory can explain the shape of any yield curve. As an example, investor expectations for increasing short-term future interest rates result in a positive or rising yield curve; conversely, investor expectations for declining short-term future interest rates will cause long-term rates to fall below current short-term rates, and the yield curve will turn negative (invert). Similar explanations may be offered for the flat and humped yield curves.

$$_1R_N=[1+{}_1R_1)(1+E(_2r_1))\ldots(1+E(_Nr_1))]^{1/N}-1$$

$_1R_N$ = rate of return for period N

N = number of periods

$_1R_1$ = interest rate for period 1

$E(_2r_1)$ = expected interest rate for period 2

$E(_Nr_1)$ = expected interest rate for given period

EXAMPLE Based on economic forecasts, U.S. Treasuries note interest rates for the next four years are expected to be as follows:

$_1R_1$	2.25%
$E(_2r_1)$	2.35%
$E(_3r_1)$	2.48%
$E(_4r_1)$	2.66%

What should be the current rate ($_1R_4$) for a four-year U.S. Treasury note?

$_1R_4 = [(1 + 0.0225)(1 + 0.0235)(1 + 0.0248)(1 + 0.0266)]^{1/4} - 1$

$_1R_4 = [1.1010]^{1/4} - 1$

$_1R_4 = 1.0243 - 1 = 0.0243$, or 2.43%

The **liquidity preference theory** is based on the expectations theory but incorporates a liquidity premium into the model. This theory holds that long-term bonds should provide higher returns than shorter-term obligations because investors are willing to sacrifice some yield to invest in short-term bonds in order to avoid the higher price volatility of longer-term issues. In other words, bondholders prefer short-term loans to the corporate issuer and, in order to induce investors to lend money for a longer term, it is necessary to offer higher yields. Furthermore, short-term bonds can more easily be converted into predictable amounts of cash should unforeseen market or economic events occur. As a result, the theory argues that the yield curve should always slope upward and that any other shape is only a temporary aberration.

Market segmentation theory relies on the laws of supply and demand for various maturities of borrowing and lending. These different maturities of borrowing and lending make up different markets and can be divided into three major categories:

- Short term, which is usually one year or less (e.g., commercial banks tend to lend short term, and consumer finance firms borrow short term)
- Intermediate term, which is usually one to five years (e.g., savings and loan institutions typically lend for the intermediate term, and manufacturers borrow for working capital needs)
- Long term, which is greater than five years (e.g., life insurance companies tend to lend for longer terms to match their liabilities; and expansion of plants, property, and equipment is usually financed with long-term debt)

Lenders in each market need to match their assets, or lending, with their liabilities, or debts. For example, commercial banks have many demand deposit accounts that are shorter-term maturities. Therefore, they need to match their lending term with their demand term. Borrowers attempt to match the term of indebtedness with the period for which they need to borrow the funds. Supply and demand in the various markets is considered to be independent, which allows for the yield curve to take on any shape and to change over time.

Specifically, this theory asserts that different institutional investors have different maturity needs that lead them to restrict their bond selections to only pre-determined maturity segments. That is, the shape of the yield curve is ultimately only a function of the investment policies of major institutional investors. In its strongest form, this theory maintains that the maturity preferences of these investors are so fixed that they never purchase securities outside their preferred maturity range to take advantage of yield differentials. As a result, the short- and long-term maturity portions of the bond market are effectively segmented.

PRACTICE QUESTIONS

Choose the best answer for each of the questions below.
Answers can be found at the end of this unit.

3. With respect to the term structure of interest rates, the market segmentation theory holds that
- A. an increase in demand for long-term borrowings could lead to an inverted yield curve
- B. expectations about the future of short-term interest rates are the major determinants of the shape of the yield curve
- C. the yield curve reflects the maturity demands of financial institutions and investors
- D. the shape of the yield curve is independent of the relationship between long- and short-term interest rates

4. According to the liquidity preference theory, which of the following statements is least accurate?
- A. All else equal, investors prefer short-term securities over long-term securities.
- B. Long-term rates should be higher than short-term rates because of the added risks.
- C. Investors perceive little risk differential between short-term and long-term securities.
- D. Borrowers will pay a premium for long-term funds to avoid having to roll over short-term debt.

D. DURATION

LO E.39.1 Define duration and explain its relationship to coupon rate, yield to maturity, and term of the bond.

The **duration** of a bond is the average time for a bondholder to receive the interest and principal payments from a bond in present value dollars. Duration measures a bond's sensitivity to changes in interest rates. The greater the bond's duration, the greater the bond's price volatility. Securities with the same duration have the same interest rate risk exposure. Duration is an important number for all bond investors because duration should be aligned with the time horizon of financial goals.

There are actually two types of duration—Macaulay duration and modified duration—although it is unlikely that CFP Board will make a distinction on the CFP® Exam. Rather, CFP Board is more interested in your understanding of the concepts and relationships of duration, which are outlined here.

- The coupon rate of a bond and its duration have an inverse relationship.
- The YTM of a bond and its duration have an inverse relationship.

- The term to maturity of a bond and its duration have a direct relationship.
- A zero-coupon bond will always have a duration equal to its term to maturity.

The algebraic formulas for duration are as follows:

$$D = \frac{\sum_{t=1}^{n} \frac{C_t(t)}{(1+i)^t}}{\sum_{t=1}^{n} \frac{C_t}{(1+i)^t}}$$

$$D = \frac{1+y}{y} - \frac{(1+y)+t(c-y)}{c\left[(1+y)^t - 1\right]+y}$$

These formulas may be used to calculate duration for long-term bonds when the use of the upcoming shortcut is impractical.

EXAMPLE Assume that a three-year $1,000 par value ABC corporate bond is currently trading on the secondary market for $974.22. The bond has a coupon rate of 7% (paying interest annually) and a YTM of 8%. Accordingly, the bond's duration is 2.8 years, computed as follows:

Year	Cash Flow (CF)	PV of CF @ YTM	PV × Year
1	$70.00	$64.81	$64.81
2	$70.00	$60.01	$120.03
3	$1,070.00	$849.40	$2,548.20
		$974.22	$2,733.04

Then, divide the sum in the last column ($2,733.04) by the present value (PV)/ market price of the bond ($974.22) to derive the specified duration of 2.8054 (rounded to 2.8) years. Note: You may use this shortcut to determine duration using simple time value of money calculations rather than using the previously presented algebraic formulas.

In the example above, you should also observe that the duration of the bond, 2.8 years, is less than its maturity date of 3.0 years. This result will always be true for coupon-paying bonds and is important to understand when immunizing a bond portfolio against interest rate risk. Although the duration of coupon-paying bonds is always less than their time to maturity, zero-coupon bonds have a duration that is always equal to their time to maturity. Finally, you can compute Macaulay duration on your calculator, but it is a lengthy and involved process, so refer to your owner's manual for further information.

PRACTICE QUESTION

Choose the best answer for the question below.
The answer can be found at the end of this unit.

5. Which of the following bonds would you recommend if the investor's time horizon is 10 years?
A. ABC bond: AAA rated, 5% coupon, 12-year maturity, duration 8.15 years
B. DEF bond: AAA rated, 4% coupon, 10-year maturity, duration 9.50 years
C. JKL bond: AAA rated, 4.5% coupon, 15-year maturity, duration 9.25 years
D. XYZ bond: AAA rated, 5% coupon, 15-year maturity, duration 9.35 years

E. CONVEXITY

LO E.39.2 Explain convexity and its relationship to coupon rate, yield to maturity, and term of the bond.

Convexity is a measure of the curvature of the relationship between a bond's YTM and its market price (value). Specifically, convexity helps explain the change in bond prices that is not accounted for simply by the bond's duration; in other words, convexity gives us a more precise measure of the change in the price of a bond, given a respective change in market interest rates. Convexity relationships are the same as those for duration and are summarized in the table below.

Factor	Duration	Convexity
Coupon rate	Inverse	Inverse
Yield to maturity	Inverse	Inverse
Time to maturity	Direct	Direct

Like duration, convexity is likely to be the greatest with the following types of bonds:

- Low coupon bonds
- Low YTM bonds
- Long maturity bonds

Bond portfolio managers have different convexity objectives as well as different duration objectives. Therefore, they will structure a bond portfolio to equal a specified level of both convexity and duration.

PRACTICE QUESTION

Choose the best answer for the question below.
The answer can be found at the end of this unit.

6. Convexity is likely to be the greatest with which types of bonds?
A. Low coupon bonds
B. Low YTM bonds
C. Long maturity bonds
D. All of these

F. ESTIMATED CHANGE IN THE PRICE OF A BOND

LO E.39.3 Calculate the estimated change in the price of a bond given its present value, duration, and change in yield to maturity.

The first step in determining the estimated change in the price of a bond paying semiannual interest is to convert its Macaulay duration into modified duration by use of the modified duration formula.

Modified duration is a relative measure for comparing different durations of bonds. The formula for modified duration is:

$$D_{mod} = \frac{\text{Macaulay duration}}{1 + y}$$

where *y* is the current YTM of the bond divided by the number of coupon payments in a year.

For example, if the bond in the previous example had made semiannual interest payments, its modified duration would have been 2.6923 (rounded to 2.7), computed as follows:

$$D_{mod} = \frac{2.8}{1 + (0.08 \div 2)} = \frac{2.8}{1 + 0.04} = 2.6923 \text{ (rounded to 2.7)}$$

Modified duration is the type of duration actually used in the estimated change in the price of a bond formula, although you may only be given (Macaulay) duration to plug into the formula on the exam.

Therefore, if given either form of duration, use the following formula:

$$\frac{\Delta P}{P} = -D\left[\frac{\Delta y}{1 + y}\right]$$

$\Delta P/P$ = percentage change in the price of a bond

D = duration of the bond

y = yield to maturity for the bond

Δy = change in YTM as a decimal

EXAMPLE If our bond from the previous example (current value of $974.22) has a Macaulay duration of 2.8 (i.e., the bond pays interest annually) and its YTM changes from 8% to 7.5% (i.e., market interest rates go down), what is the estimated change in the price of the bond? The answer is $986.88, calculated as follows:

$$\frac{\Delta P}{P} = -2.8 \times \frac{0.075 - 0.08}{1 + 0.08}$$

$$= -2.8 \times \frac{-0.005}{1.08}$$

$$= -2.8 \times -0.0046$$

$$= 0.01296, \text{ or } 1.3\%$$

Of course, we know that, given the inverse relationship of bond prices and the movement of market interest rates, this means that the price of our bond has to increase by 1.3%; specifically, the bond should sell for $986.88 ($974.22 × 1.013) in the secondary market.

We can also cross-check this result by simply solving for the intrinsic value (PV) of the bond using a 7.5% YTM:

$n = 3$
$i = 7.5$
PMT = 70
FV = 1,000
Solve for PV = 986.99, or $986.99

We are off by only $0.11, which is why duration will provide you with only an estimated change in the price of a bond given a respective change in interest rates. If we wanted to determine the exact change in price, we would need to compute the convexity of the bond.

Note: For the national exam, you may wish to use this time value of money calculation either as your primary method to solve for the new intrinsic value or as a cross-check to the formula method shown above.

PRACTICE QUESTION

Choose the best answer for the question below.
The answer can be found at the end of this unit.

7. What is the estimated change in the price of a zero-coupon $1,000 bond with a maturity date of 10 years when interest rates increase by 50 basis points? Assume the bond's YTM is 6%.

A. –4.70%
B. +4.70%
C. –5.00%
D. +5.50%

G. PORTFOLIO IMMUNIZATION

LO E.40.2 Discuss bond portfolio immunization.

Portfolio immunization is an interest-rate management technique, which offsets interest rate risk against reinvestment rate risk. Immunization is often used in pension fund management as pension liabilities come due. Rising interest rates result in a decrease in the value of the bond portfolio. However, rising interest rates also result in greater interest income from reinvesting the bond portfolio's coupons. Conversely, decreasing interest rates increase the value of the bond portfolio but decrease the interest income from reinvesting the coupons. You can see how there is an offset between interest rate risk and reinvestment rate risk. Full offset (or complete immunization from changes in interest rates) occurs when the duration of the portfolio equals the duration of the liability, thus, when the duration of the portfolio is equal to the investor's time horizon.

However, immunization is not a fully passive strategy. Rather, the duration of the portfolio declines at an overall faster rate than that of the duration of the liability. Accordingly, periodic rebalancing of the portfolio is often necessary to bring the portfolio duration in line with the liability duration.

The following relationships lead us to some basic principles used to maximize a bond portfolio's rate of return when interest rates are expected to change.

- The smaller the bond's coupon rate, the greater its relative price fluctuation.
- The longer the bond's term to maturity, the greater its relative price fluctuation.
- The smaller the bond's yield to maturity, the greater its relative price fluctuation.

If the investor expects a decline in market interest rates, the investor should attempt to construct a portfolio of long maturity bonds with low coupon rates. This will provide the investor with a portfolio that has the maximum interest rate sensitivity to take advantage of the capital gains experienced by bonds from the decrease in market interest rates. Conversely, if the investor expects an increase in market interest rates, the investor should attempt to construct a portfolio of short maturity bonds with high coupon rates. This will provide the investor with a portfolio that has the minimum interest rate sensitivity to minimize the capital losses experienced by bonds from the increase in market interest rates.

PRACTICE QUESTION

Choose the best answer for the question below.
The answer can be found at the end of this unit.

8. Yvette is saving for her son's college education. Her son is expected to start college in 8 years. Which bond portfolio would likely be immunized with respect to this goal?

A. Weighted average time to maturity of bonds is 8 years with coupon of 6%.
B. Weighted average time to maturity of bonds is 10 years with coupon of 0%.
C. Weighted average time to maturity of bonds is 7 years with coupon of 3%.
D. Weighted average time to maturity of bonds is 10 years with coupon of 5%.

103 UNIT 8 ANSWERS TO PRACTICE QUESTIONS

1. D. The intrinsic value of Wade's bond (what it should sell for today) is $1,079.93.
$n = 3 \times 2 = 6$ (number of periodic payments remaining)
$i = 7 \div 2 = 3.5$ (periodic interest rate based on comparable 3-year term bonds)
PMT = 0.10 × 1,000 ÷ 2 = 50 (semiannual coupon payment)
FV = 1,000
Solve for PV = 1,079.93, or $1,079.93
With only 3 years remaining until the maturity date of Wade's bond, you must use the interest rate associated with a maturity date of 3 years provided in the table.

2. D. Only statement 4 is incorrectly stated. Certain relationships exist between different yield measures depending on whether the bond is trading at par, at a discount, or at a premium.

3. C. The market segmentation theory holds that certain types of financial institutions and investors prefer to confine (most of) their investment activity to certain maturity ranges of the fixed-income market and that supply and demand forces within each segment ultimately determine the shape of the yield curve.

4. C. Rational investors feel that long-term bonds have more risk exposure than short-term securities (i.e., long-term securities are less liquid and subject to more price volatility). The other statements are correct.

5. B. DEF Bond, with a duration of 9.50 years, is the closest to the investor's time horizon of 10 years.

6. D. All of these bonds exhibit the greatest convexity. Bond portfolio managers have different convexity objectives, as well as different duration objectives.

7. A. The price of the bond should decrease by approximately 4.7%, calculated as follows:

$$\frac{\Delta P}{P} = -10 \times \frac{0.065 - 0.06}{1 + 0.06}$$

$$= -10 \times \frac{0.005}{1.06}$$

$$= -10 \times 0.0047$$

$$= -0.047, \text{ or } -4.7\%$$

8. D. To immunize the portfolio, the duration of the portfolio should closely match the investor's time horizon. In this case, the 10-year bonds with a coupon rate of 5% will have a duration that is closest to the investor's time horizon of 8 years. Coupon-paying bonds have durations that are less than their time to maturity. Zero-coupon bonds have durations equal to their time to maturity.

103 UNIT 8 POST-STUDY CHECKLIST

- ☐ Can I determine the intrinsic value of a bond?
- ☐ Can I explain the theories used to explain various yield curves?
- ☐ Can I explain the relationship between interest rates and bond prices?
- ☐ Am I able to define duration and its relationship to coupon rate, yield to maturity, and term of the bond?
- ☐ Do I understand convexity and its relationship to coupon rate, yield to maturity, and term of the bond?
- ☐ Can I calculate the estimated change in the price of a bond?
- ☐ Am I able to explain how to immunize a bond portfolio?

Am I able to define and understand the application of the following terms as they relate to investment planning?

- ☐ Convexity
- ☐ Duration
- ☐ Flat yield curve
- ☐ Inverted yield curve
- ☐ Liquidity preference theory
- ☐ Market segmentation theory
- ☐ Modified duration
- ☐ Normal (positive) yield curve
- ☐ Portfolio immunization
- ☐ Unbiased expectations theory
- ☐ Yield curve

UNIT 9

Stock Valuation Concepts

REFER TO

CFP Board Principal Knowledge Topics – E. Investment Planning, E.38. Bond and Stock Valuation Concepts

INTRODUCTION

Two general methods are used in valuing the proper price or trading value of an equity security (stock): (1) analytic formulas that attempt to determine the intrinsic value of the stock and (2) market-based methods that attempt to estimate the relative value of the stock with respect to its peers. Likely, the most popular of the relative valuation methods is the price-to-earnings ratio, which is applied not only to individual stocks but also to the broader market and market indexes to determine whether the market currently is undervalued (less expensive given historical trends) or overvalued (more expensive).

Asset-based methods may also be used to value stock. The most popular of these methods is to analyze the book value of the issuing corporation and, subsequently, compare this value with the market value of the stock. However, the stock of a corporation frequently trades in excess of the corporation's book value, so book value should only be used as a benchmark or reference point in determining the proper price at which the company's stock should trade.

LEARNING OBJECTIVES

After completion of this unit, you should be able to achieve the following learning objectives:

CFP® Board Principal Knowledge Topics – E. Investment Planning

E.38. Bond and Stock Valuation Concepts

LO E.38.4 Define and interpret the discounted earnings method of stock valuation.

LO E.38.5 Determine the intrinsic value of a stock using the constant growth dividend discount model, the multistage growth dividend discount model, the no-growth dividend discount model, and the discounted free cash flow model.

LO E.38.6 Define, calculate, and analyze the price-to-earnings ratio, price-to-earnings divided by growth ratio, price-to-free-cash-flow ratio, and price-to-sales ratio to determine if a security warrants a purchase.

LO E.38.7 Determine and analyze a company's book value.

LO E.38.8 Explain the difference between a stock's par value, market value, and intrinsic value.

LO E.38.9 Describe corporate/business accounting practices.

LO E.38.10 Differentiate between fundamental and technical analysis.

KEY TERMS

Balance sheet
Book value
Business statement of cash flows
Constant growth dividend discount model
Discounted earnings method
Discounted free cash flow model
Free cash flow to equity (FCFE)
Fundamental analysis
Income statement
Intrinsic value
Market value
Multistage growth dividend discount model
No-growth (perpetuity) dividend discount model
Par value
Price-to-earnings (P/E) ratio
Price-to-earnings divided by growth (PEG) ratio
Price-to-free-cash-flow (P/FCF) ratio
Price-to-sales (P/S) ratio
Pro forma income statement
Technical analysis

A. BUSINESS FINANCIAL STATEMENTS

LO E.38.9 Describe corporate/business accounting practices.

Balance Sheet

The **balance sheet** is a snapshot of the company's financial standing at a point in time and includes assets, liabilities, and stockholder's equity (net worth). The balance sheet and the business income statement are used by a security analyst who employs fundamental analysis as a method of valuing the company's securities.

Examples of business assets include:

- accounts receivable;
- inventory;
- land;
- buildings;
- machinery and equipment;
- leasehold improvements; and
- certain intangible assets, such as copyrights, patents, and business goodwill.

Examples of business liabilities include:

- accounts payable;
- notes payable;
- subordinated officer loans (sometimes referred to simply as *sub-off*); and
- certain contingent liabilities, such as lawsuits, warranties, and company guarantees of loan repayment.

Balance Sheet
ABC Company
as of December 31, 2017

Assets		Liabilities	
Current assets		**Current liabilities**	
Cash	$2,000	Notes payable	$5,000
Checking account	40,000	Accounts payable	25,000
Accounts receivable	50,000	Wages payable	100,000
Inventory	35,000	Taxes payable	6,200
Total current assets	$127,000	Total current liabilities	$136,200
Investments	38,000	**Long-term liabilities**	
		Notes payable	20,000
Property, plant, & equipment		Bonds payable	60,000
Land	50,000	Total long-term liabilities	$80,000
Buildings	150,000		
Equipment	135,000	**Total liabilities**	$216,200
Less: accumulated depreciation	(40,000)		
Total property, plant, & equipment	$295,000	**Stockholders' equity**	$343,800
Intangible assets			
Goodwill	100,000		
Total use assets	$100,000		
Total assets	$560,000	**Total liabilities and stockholders' equity**	$560,000

Income Statement

The **income statement** also known as the profit and loss statement (or simply, P&L statement) shows all income and expenses of the business over a period of time. In other words, the statement shows how profitable (or unprofitable) the business operations actually were for the stated period. Whether these profits are reported at the business entity level or by the individual businessowner(s) depend on whether the business is organized as a regular (C) form of corporation or as a sole proprietorship, partnership, or some other form of pass-through entity.

Income Statement GHI Company for Year Ending December 31, 2017		
Revenue		$500,000
Cost of goods sold		
Beginning inventory	$45,000	
Net purchases	120,000	
Less: ending inventory	(60,000)	
Less: Cost of goods sold		($105,000)
Operating expenses		
Selling expenses	$75,000	
General and administrative expenses	105,000	
Total operating expenses		($180,000)
Income from operations		$215,000
Other expenses		
Interest	$5,000	
Income tax expense	62,000	
Total other expenses		($67,000)
Net income		$148,000

Business Statement of Cash Flows

The **business statement of cash flows** assists in the reconciliation of the business income statement to changes between two balance sheets. For a given period, the business statement of cash flows reflects the inflows and outflows of the business and the net changes in cash between two balance sheets. This statement also identifies the changes in some of the accounts from one balance sheet to the next. Typically, the business statement of cash flows has three components: (1) cash flow from business operations, (2) cash flow from business investment activities, and (3) cash flow from financing activities, such as the issuance of additional debt (bonds) or equity (stocks).

Statement of Cash Flows RST Company for Year Ending December 31, 2017	
Cash flows from business operations	
Net earnings	$1,000,000
Adjustments	
Change in depreciation	5,000
Decrease in accounts receivable	7,500
Increase in accounts payable	7,500
Increase in taxes payable	1,000
Increase in inventory	(15,000)
Net cash flows from operating activities	$1,006,000
Cash flows from business investment activities	
Equipment	(250,000)
Cash flows from business financing activities	
Notes payable	5,000
Cash flows for year ending December 31, 2017	$761,000

Pro Forma Income Statement

A **pro forma income statement** is similar to the business income statement except that it projects for the future rather than reports the past. Pro forma income statements are an important tool for planning future business operations. If the projections accurately predict a decline in business profitability, the business entity or businessowner(s) can make operational changes, such as increasing prices or decreasing costs, before these events actually occur. The pro forma statement is created by first estimating gross profit and total expenses for the coming year or years and then accounting for the amount of taxes due on the net profit.

XYZ Company
Five-Year Pro Forma Income Statement

	2018	2019	2020	2021	2022
Sales	$1,000,000	$1,150,000	$1,322,500	$1,520,875	$1,749,006
Cost of goods sold	380,000	437,000	502,550	577,933	664,622
Operating income	620,000	713,000	819,950	942,942	1,084,384
Expenses					
Administrative	204,600	235,290	270,584	311,171	357,847
Marketing	248,000	285,200	327,980	377,177	433,754
Total expenses	452,600	520,490	598,564	688,348	791,601
Earnings before interest and taxes (EBIT)	167,400	192,510	221,386	254,594	292,783
Taxes	62,806	72,227	83,061	95,520	109,848
Net income	$104,594	$120,283	$138,325	$159,074	$182,935

PRACTICE QUESTIONS

Choose the best answer for each of the questions below.
Answers can be found at the end of this unit.

1. Which of the following statements regarding a business' financial statements is(are) CORRECT?

1. As a rule, an income statement has three components: (1) cash flows from operations; (2) cash flows from investing; and (3) cash flows from financing.
2. The income statement is also known as a P&L (profit and loss) statement.
3. The net worth on a personal statement of financial position is analogous to stockholders' equity or retained capital on a business' balance sheet.
4. A pro forma income statement is similar to a business' balance sheet, except that it projects into the future rather than reporting on the past.

A. 1 only
B. 2 and 3
C. 1, 2, and 4
D. 2, 3, and 4

2. All of the following are examples of assets unique to a business EXCEPT

A. accounts receivable
B. inventory
C. machinery and equipment
D. notes payable

B. SECURITY ANALYSIS

LO E.38.10 Differentiate between fundamental and technical analysis.

Security analysts use two primary forms of analysis to determine whether a particular security should be purchased, or, if already owned, should be sold—fundamental analysis and technical analysis.

Fundamental Analysis

Fundamental analysis is the process of determining the fair market value, or intrinsic value, of a security and looking for mispricings. For example, a fundamental analyst would likely use one of the dividend discount models (presented shortly) to determine the proper price at which a stock should be trading.

Factors considered by the fundamental analyst in determining the fair market value of a security include:

- statistics gathered from the overall economy or economic environment;
- interest rates and business cycles information;
- monetary policy conducted by the Federal Reserve Board, including the current amount of the money supply;
- fiscal policy conducted by Congress;
- industry analysis; and
- stock market tendencies.

Fundamental analysts also use ratios, such as the price-to-earnings ratio, in their analysis process. The ratios needed for securities analysis include the firm's return on equity, return on assets, gross profit margin, and numerous others. A summary of the financial ratios used by the fundamental analyst follows.

Liquidity Ratios	
Current ratio	$\frac{\text{Current assets}}{\text{Current liabilities}}$
Acid test or quick ratio	$\frac{\text{Current assets} - \text{inventory}}{\text{Current liabilities}}$
Activity Ratios	
Inventory turnover ratio	$\frac{\text{Cost of goods sold}}{\text{Average inventory}}$
Accounts receivable turnover	$\frac{\text{Sales}}{\text{Average accounts receivable}}$
Fixed asset turnover	$\frac{\text{Annual sales}}{\text{Fixed assets}}$
Profitability Ratios	
Operating profit margin	$\frac{\text{Earnings before interest and taxes (EBIT)}}{\text{Sales}}$
Net profit margin	$\frac{\text{Net income}}{\text{Sales}}$
Return on assets (ROA)	$\frac{\text{Net income}}{\text{Total assets}}$
Return on equity (ROE)	$\frac{\text{Net income}}{\text{Equity}}$
Debt Ratios	
Debt ratio	$\frac{\text{Total debt}}{\text{Total assets}}$
Debt-equity ratio	$\frac{\text{Total debt}}{\text{Total equity}}$
Ratios for Bond Analysis*	
Times interest earned	$\frac{\text{Earnings before interest and taxes (EBIT)}}{\text{Annual interest charges}}$
*Also see inventory turnover ratio and accounts receivable turnover	
Ratios for Stock Analysis**	
Payout ratio	$\frac{\text{Dividends}}{\text{Earnings}}$
Price-to-earnings ratio	$\frac{\text{Market price per share}}{\text{Earnings per share}}$
**Also see ROE, ROA, and net profit margin	

Fundamental analysts may be further differentiated according to where they begin (and finish) their analysis. A *top-down fundamental analyst* begins with researching the overall economy and current state of the secondary market. Specifically, such an analyst then selects an industry (or industry sector) that he believes will perform best over an upcoming time frame. Finally, the analyst then screens a database of securities within that industry to find acceptable companies (and acceptable stocks) in which to recommend investment.

The other type of fundamental analyst, the *bottom-up fundamental analyst*, essentially conducts his analysis in a manner opposite that of the top-down proponent. The bottom-up analyst first begins with an examination of the company fundamentals (e.g., by using ratio analysis) and then considers the financial prospects for the industry in which the company operates. Indeed, because of emphasis first and foremost on the security itself, the bottom-up analyst is sometimes known as a stock-picker. Finally, this type of analyst then considers the prospects for the overall economy.

Technical Analysis

Technical analysis is an attempt by analysts to determine the demand side of the supply-demand equation for a particular stock and, therefore, to predict the direction of its future market price. Such analysis is based on a belief that studying the history of security trades and security markets will provide buying opportunities. Technical analysts believe that the history of the stock price will tell the entire story of the security and that there is no need to be concerned with such things as ratio analysis.

In its simplest form, technical analysis involves the preparation of charting past price and volume data for a particular security or industry sector. Because of their reliance on these charts, technical analysts are sometimes called chartists. These charts produce certain trends and concepts that may be used to determine the future activity in (and price of) a particular security. According to technicians, these trends will generally continue until some major event causes a reversal of the trend. Such terms as *moving average*, *trendline*, and *support and resistance level* are then used by technical analysts to determine when the time is right for the purchase (or possible sale) of the security.

Technical analysts use certain theories or sentiment indicators to describe overall market trends including the following.

- *Dow theory*—Developed by Charles Dow, this theory is based on the premise that measures of stock prices, such as averages and indexes, should move coincidentally. As such, if prices in several indexes are increasing at the same time, a bull market is underway. Likewise, if those indexes are declining simultaneously, a bear market has begun.
- *Odd-lot theory*—Typically, small individual investors engage in odd-lot trading (i.e., less than 100 shares at once). Adherents of this theory, however, believe that these investors invariably buy and sell in this manner at the wrong time. Therefore, when odd-lot traders buy, odd-lot analysts believe that selling is appropriate. Odd-lot theory is an example of contrarian investing, which is also a hallmark of technical analysis.
- *Short-interest theory*—Short interest refers to the number of market shares that have been sold short, in a specific period of time. Therefore, because short positions must eventually be covered, some technical analysts believe that short interest reflects future market demand. A high amount of short interest is considered bullish, and a low amount of short interest is considered bearish.
- *Mutual fund cash position theory*—Technical analysts may monitor the cash positions of mutual funds and trade against them (contrarian) accordingly. If funds have large cash balances, technicians view this as a bullish signal and will buy securities. If funds have small cash balances, technicians will view this as a bearish signal and sell securities.

Technical charting implies three basic assumptions:

1. Markets discount the fundamentals
2. Markets trend
3. Trends repeat

Technical analysis assumes that since the financial markets are forward-looking, the fundamentals have already been discounted in the price. Technical analysts view price trends as leading indicators of the fundamentals. In fact, the study of these price trends is the foundation of technical analysis. The technical analyst's objective is to identify trends early and trade in their direction (known as "the direction of least resistance"). Trends may be intraday or up to several months and even years.

Much of technical analysis is the study of market psychology. Investors are expected to respond to similar market situations in a consistent manner. This is why historical trends are followed closely and form the basis for why trends repeat.

Charts are not merely trendlines and support and resistance levels. In analyzing price charts, the analyst looks for distinctive patterns (which may not be so distinctive to other analysts) that signal potential future price movements. As mentioned previously, the technical analyst strives to identify new trends or trend reversals.

PRACTICE QUESTIONS

Choose the best answer for each of the questions below.
Answers can be found at the end of this unit.

3. Which of the following describes the flow of the top-down valuation process?

A. Economic analysis, industry analysis, company analysis
B. Company analysis, industry analysis, economic analysis
C. Economic analysis, company analysis, industry analysis
D. Pick the best stocks regardless of the industry or economic conditions

4. Which of the following approaches would be emphasized by an investor who believes in the importance of fundamental security analysis?

A. Support and resistance levels
B. Financial statement review
C. The strong form of the efficient market hypothesis (EMH)
D. Indexing

C. DETERMINING THE INSTRINSIC VALUE OF A STOCK

LO E.38.5 Determine the intrinsic value of a stock using the constant growth dividend discount model, the multistage growth dividend discount model, the no-growth dividend discount model, and the discounted free cash flow model.

The intrinsic value of stock may be determined by using one or more models. They are:

- the constant growth dividend discount model;
- the multistage (variable) growth dividend discount model;
- the no-growth (perpetuity) dividend discount model; and
- the discount free cash flow model.

Constant Growth Dividend Discount Model

This model, also known as the Gordon model, is used to determine the intrinsic value of a stock when dividends are growing at a constant rate. In practice, companies rarely sustain constantly growing dividends. However, the model is often used as a starting point in determining the value of a company and is most appropriate for valuing mature companies.

The formula for the constant growth dividend discount model is:

$$V = \frac{D_1}{r - g}$$

where V is the intrinsic value of the stock, D_1 is the dividend paid at the end of period 1 (or the next year), r is equal to the investor's required rate of return, and g is equal to constant dividend growth rate.

The **constant growth dividend discount model** is based on a number of assumptions. The growth rate (g) cannot be equal to or greater than the investor's required rate of return (r). As the growth rate (g) of the dividend approaches the investor's required rate of return (r), the value or market price of the stock will approach infinity, therefore negating the practical use of the model.

The model assumes that the investor's required rate of return (r) is known and remains constant. If the investor's required rate of return increases, the value of the common stock will be reduced. If the investor's required rate of return decreases, the value of the common stock will increase.

If information is provided regarding the current year dividend (or end of period 0), the formula $[D_0 \times (1 + g)]$ may be used in substitution of D_1 in model.

EXAMPLE Assume that XYZ stock is currently paying (year 0) a dividend of $2 per share and that the dividend will grow at a constant rate of 6% annually. What should the stock be selling for if the investor's required rate of return is 10%?

$$V = \frac{\$2 \times (1 + 0.06)}{0.10 - 0.06} = \frac{\$2.12}{0.04} = \$53$$

Therefore, the investor should not pay more than $53 for the stock, or the investment will be imprudent.

We can also determine what the expected return of the stock (r in the subsequent formula) should be if we know the constant rate of the stock's dividend. Specifically, this formula may be written as:

$$r = \frac{D_1}{P} + g$$

where all entries are the same as in the constant growth model except that P, or the current price or trading value of the stock, is also assumed.

EXAMPLE Continuing with the previous example, assume that XYZ stock is currently trading at $55 per share. We determine the expected return on the stock to be 9.85% as follows:

$$r = \frac{\$2.12}{\$55} + 0.06 = 0.0385 + 0.06 = 0.0985, \text{or } 9.85\%$$

Of course, we knew that the expected return on the stock had to be less than the investor's required rate of return of 10% or the stock would not be selling for more than the previously computed amount of $53 per share. In other words, XYZ is currently overvalued on the basis of the investor's required rate of return, and the investor would likely not buy the stock at its current price.

PRACTICE QUESTIONS

Choose the best answer for each of the questions below.
Answers can be found at the end of this unit.

5. Jeff is interested in BEC stock. BEC's earnings and dividends are expected to grow at a constant rate of 6% per year for the foreseeable future. If Jeff's required rate of return is 11%, what is the intrinsic value of BEC stock if it is currently paying a dividend of $1.20?

A. $25.44
B. $24.00
C. $20.00
D. $10.91

6. XYZ stock has a current dividend of $1.75 that has been growing at a constant rate of 8% per year. If the stock is currently selling for $100 and your required rate of return is 10%, would you buy the stock at today's price (why or why not)?

A. Yes, because the stock is undervalued on the basis of the constant growth dividend discount model
B. Yes, because the stock is a good buy on the basis of its risk-return relationship
C. No, because the stock is overvalued on the basis of the constant growth dividend discount model
D. No, because the stock is not a good investment on the basis of its risk-return relationship

Multistage Growth Dividend Discount Model

The **multistage growth dividend discount model** assumes that the growth rate of the stock's dividend is not constant but rather changes (either up or down). For most companies, the dividend growth rate is not constant over time, rather, they increase or decrease the dividends they distribute based on the profits generated or investment opportunities. This model is most appropriate for valuing companies in the growth phase. To determine the intrinsic value of a stock using this model, you must follow a three-step process.

1. Compute the value of each future dividend until the growth rate stabilizes.
2. Use the constant growth dividend discount model to compute the remaining intrinsic value of the stock at the beginning of the year when the dividend growth rate stabilizes.
3. Use the uneven cash flow method to solve for the net present (intrinsic) value of the stock.

EXAMPLE Continuing with the XYZ stock example, now assume that its dividend is expected to grow for only three years at 6% annually and then at 7% annually thereafter. Furthermore, assume that the investor's required rate of return has now changed to 9% (therefore, we would expect the intrinsic value of the stock to increase). Note: all numbers are rounded up to the nearest cent.

1. Compute the value of each future dividend until the growth rate stabilizes (Years 1–3). Recall, the current dividend is $2.00.
   D_1 = $2.00 × 1.06 = $2.12
   D_2 = $2.12 × 1.06 = $2.25
   D_3 = $2.25 × 1.06 = $2.39
2. Use the constant growth dividend discount model to compute the remaining intrinsic value of the stock at the beginning of the year when the dividend growth rate stabilizes (Year 4).
   D_4 = $2.39 × 1.07 = $2.56
   V = $2.56 ÷ (0.09 – 0.07) = $128.00
3. Use the uneven cash flow method to solve for the net present (intrinsic) value of the stock.
   CF_0 = $0
   CF_1 = $2.12
   CF_2 = $2.25
   CF_3 = $2.39 + $128.00 = $130.39
   I/YR = 9%
   Solve for NPV = $104.52
   In this example, the intrinsic value of the stock is $104.52.

No-Growth (Perpetuity) Dividend Discount Model

When the dividend is expected to remain constant (i.e., no anticipated growth), the **no-growth (perpetuity) dividend discount model** may be used to calculate the stock's intrinsic value.

To determine the intrinsic value of the stock using this model, simply substitute zero for *g* in the constant growth dividend discount model as follows:

$$V = \frac{D_1}{r - 0} = \frac{D_1}{r}$$

The new formula is the dividend for the first period (D_1) divided by the investor's required rate of return. However, because the dividend is constant, it could be the dividend for any subsequent period; therefore, D may be substituted for D_1 in the formula.

EXAMPLE Now assume that our XYZ stock always pays a $2 dividend per share. Because the investor's required rate of return is 10%, this means that the intrinsic value of the stock using the perpetuity model is $20 per share ($2 ÷ 0.10).

You should note that the no-growth model is also used when computing the intrinsic value of preferred stock because, as discussed earlier, preferred stock is in perpetuity and has no maturity date.

Discounted Free Cash Flow Model

What happens if a company's stock does not currently pay (nor is ever anticipated to pay) a dividend? In this case (for example, with a closely held corporation), none of the previous three dividend discount models will apply. As an alternative, a company's free cash flow to equity may be discounted to find the stock's intrinsic value. **Free cash flow to equity (FCFE)** is the company's operating cash flow less its current year's capital investments and debt repayments (including any outstanding or cumulative preferred dividends payable). Accordingly, this cash flow is potentially available for distribution by the company in the form of a dividend.

The **discounted free cash flow model** is mathematically equivalent to the constant growth dividend discount model except that the current year's dividend (D_0) or next year's dividend (D_1) is replaced by FCFE on a per share basis. Therefore, the formula may be written as follows:

$$V = \frac{\text{FCFE}_1}{r - g} = \frac{\text{FCFE}_0 \times (1 + g)}{r - g}$$

EXAMPLE PLV Corporation has an estimated FCFE for next year of \$3 per share. In addition, its FCFE is expected to grow at a constant rate of 3% per year for the foreseeable future. Your client has a required rate of return of 14%. Therefore, the intrinsic value of PLV Corporation's stock to your client is \$27.27 per share, calculated as follows:

$$V = \frac{\$3}{0.14 - 0.03} = \frac{\$3}{0.11} = \$27.2727 = \$27.27$$

PRACTICE QUESTIONS

Choose the best answer for each of the questions below. Answers can be found at the end of this unit.

7. KRF Corporation offers \$100 preferred stock that will always pay a \$1.50 potential dividend to any investor. If an investor has a required rate of return of 12%, how much should the investor pay for KRF preferred stock?

A. \$1.68
B. \$12.50
C. \$15.00
D. \$100.00

8. CAR stock is currently paying a dividend of $1 per share. Assume the stock's dividend is expected to grow for 3 years at 5% per year. After 3 years, the dividend is expected to grow at a constant 2% rate. The investor's required rate of return is 8%. What is the intrinsic value of CAR stock?

A. $18.45
B. $20.83
C. $22.98
D. $19.67

D. DISCOUNTED EARNINGS MODEL

LO E.38.4 Define and interpret the discounted earnings method of stock valuation.

The **discounted earnings model**, or *capitalized earnings method*, discounts earnings instead of cash flows as in the dividend growth models. This model is a simplistic method for valuing a corporation and, by extension, its outstanding stock. The same formula as the perpetuity model is used, but inserts E (for earnings of the company) in the numerator for D_1 and R_D (for discount rate) in the denominator for r so that the resulting formula reads as follows:

> **EXAMPLE** JEM Corporation generated before-tax earnings of $10 million last year. Your client, a sophisticated investor, has determined a capitalization rate of 8% to use in valuing this company. Accordingly, he believes the company to be worth $125 million ($10 million ÷ 0.08). If the company has 2.5 million outstanding shares of common stock, this stock should be worth $50 per share ($125 million ÷ 2.5 million).

Several problems exist with respect to the capitalized earnings method for valuing companies as follows.

- Earnings, as determined by generally accepted accounting principles (GAAP), do not necessarily represent the cash flows of the corporation. In other words, earnings reported by the corporation may be manipulated for several reasons, including an objective of income tax savings.
- This method also fails to account for the residual value of any corporate assets at the end of the reporting period. These assets also add to the value of the corporation in the event of dissolution or liquidation.

One final point: the capitalization or discount rate used by an investor to value companies is the reciprocal of a multiple of earnings that is willing to be paid by the investor. For example, if the investor used a capitalization rate of 8%, that means he is willing to pay 12.5 times earnings (100 ÷ 8) for the corporation. Similarly, if the investor used a capitalization rate of 10%, that means he is willing to only pay 10 times earnings for that same corporation, reflecting a higher risk premium to make the investment.

E. MARKET-BASED MODELS OF RELATIVE VALUATION

LO E.38.6 Define, calculate, and analyze the price-to-earnings ratio, price-to-earnings divided by growth ratio, price-to-free-cash-flow ratio, and price-to-sales ratio to determine if a security warrants a purchase.

Market-based models of relative valuation sometimes simply go by the name *ratio analysis*. All of these valuation measures are heavily used by fundamental security analysts when making buy or sell recommendations. For the CFP® exam, you will be expected to know four of these ratios, or relative valuation models:

- Price-to-earnings (P/E) ratio
- Price-to-earnings divided by growth (PEG) ratio
- Price-to-free-cash-flow (P/FCF) ratio
- Price-to-sales (P/S) ratio

You can see that the first word in all these ratios is price, which is what you are attempting to determine for the stock or potential investment.

Price-to-Earnings (P/E) Ratio

The **price-to-earnings (P/E) ratio** may be used to compare a company's current market price to its earnings per share (EPS).

$$P/E \text{ ratio} = \text{current market price} \div EPS$$

EXAMPLE If ABC stock is currently trading for $50 per share and has an EPS of $2.50, the P/E ratio would be 20 ($50 ÷ $2.50).

The P/E ratio provides an investor with an idea of what the market is willing to pay for the company's earnings. A higher ratio could indicate an overpriced stock, while a lower ratio could indicate a buying opportunity.

In addition, an investor could use a variation of the formula to determine the estimated market price of a stock:

$$V = EPS \times P/E \text{ ratio}$$

where V is the estimated market price of the stock, EPS is the earnings per share of the stock, and P/E ratio is the price-to-earnings ratio established by the market or industry sector to which the stock belongs.

Price-to-Earnings Divided by Growth (PEG) Ratio

The **price-to-earnings divided by growth (PEG) ratio** is calculated by dividing a company's P/E ratio by the firm's expected growth rate of earnings. This ratio is a measure of relative valuation that can be used to compare companies with different growth rates. In formula terms:

$$PEG = P/E \div g$$

> **EXAMPLE** Acme stock has a P/E ratio of 6.67 and an expected earnings growth rate of 10% for next year, therefore, its PEG ratio is 0.667 (6.67 ÷ 10). Note: the whole number 10 is used rather than .10 in this equation.

We would then compare the PEG ratio of Acme stock to its peers to determine whether the stock is a good buy. Proponents of the PEG ratio generally believe that companies with a low PEG ratio (for example, lower than 1.00) will have higher future rates of return and are good value stocks.

Price-to-Free-Cash-Flow (P/FCF) Ratio

Another relative measure of stock valuation is that of how effectively the issuing company uses its free cash flow to generate earnings growth. This is known as the **price-to-free-cash-flow (P/FCF) ratio** and is written as:

$$\frac{P}{FCF} = \frac{1+g}{r-g}$$

where P is the price of the company's stock, FCF is the free cash flow (per share) of the company, g is the expected growth rate of the company's earnings, and r is the investor's required rate of return.

> **EXAMPLE** Acme stock has an expected earnings growth rate of 10% for next year. The investor's required rate of return is 14%. We determine its P/FCF ratio to be 27.50, calculated as follows:
>
> $$\frac{P}{FCF} = \frac{1+0.10}{0.14-0.10} = \frac{1.10}{0.04} = 27.50$$

Then, as with the other ratios, we would compare this P/FCF ratio to Acme stock's peers to determine if a purchase is warranted. For example, if the ratio is lower than that of the stock's peers, we may wish to purchase the stock.

Finally, in the valuation process, free cash flow is generally preferred over accounting earnings as a relevant measure of growth because accounting earnings may be manipulated by the issuing company or may vary from industry to industry.

Price-to-Sales (P/S) Ratio

The **price-to-sales (P/S) ratio** is an indication of how much an investor is willing to pay for a specific revenue stream, in this case the company's annual sales. One shortcoming of this ratio is that it does not take into account the subject company's net income. For example, a company may have significant sales but may still have negative earnings because of taxes, outstanding charges, and other business-related expenses. For this reason, the price-to-sales ratio is not generally considered to be a good complement to the P/E ratio (as are the other measures discussed).

The formula for the P/S ratio is:

$$P/S = \frac{\text{market price per share}}{\text{sales per share}}$$

EXAMPLE Acme stock has a current market price per share of $17.83 and a sales per share of $2.70. This means that Acme stock has a P/S ratio of 6.60, calculated as follows:

$$P/S = \frac{\$17.83}{\$2.70} = 6.60$$

As with all the other ratios discussed, the P/S ratio of Acme stock is then compared to its industry peers to determine whether the stock appears to be undervalued or overvalued. Similar to the price-to-free-cash-flow ratio, a ratio lower than that of its peers indicates a value buy.

PRACTICE QUESTION

Choose the best answer for the question below.
The answer can be found at the end of this unit.

9. Alphabet stock is selling for $67 per share. Alphabet's earnings per share last year were $8.90. Comparable firms in the same industry have P/E ratios of 8.0. Which of the following statements is CORRECT?

A. Alphabet stock is undervalued because its P/E ratio is greater than 8.0.
B. Alphabet stock is undervalued because its intrinsic value is $71.20.
C. Alphabet stock is overvalued because its P/E ratio is less than 8.0.
D. Alphabet stock is overvalued because its intrinsic value is $71.20.

F. SUMMARY OF VALUATION METHODS

In summary, you should be able to identify the difference between intrinsic value (stand-alone) methods and relative value (comparison) methods.

Intrinsic Value Methods	Relative Value Methods
1. Constant Growth Dividend Discount Model	1. Price-to-Earnings (P/E) Ratio
2. Multistage (Variable) Growth Dividend Discount Model	2. Price-to-Earnings Divided by Growth (PEG) Ratio
3. No-Growth/Perpetuity Dividend Discount Model	3. Price-to-Free-Cash-Flow (P/FCF) Ratio
4. Discounted Free Cash Flow Model	4. Price-to-Sales (P/S) Ratio

G. BOOK VALUE

LO E.38.7 Determine and analyze a company's book value.

The **book value** of a company refers to the amount of equity available to its shareholders—that is, the amount that the shareholders have invested in the company. The value is determined by subtracting company liabilities from company assets and is the equivalent of net worth as determined on an individual's statement of personal financial position. Generally, book value does not represent an accurate measure of the fair market value of the company because book value is determined using historical costs. In addition, different inventory accounting methods, such as FIFO or LIFO, may yield a different value for company assets, therefore affecting the book value of the corporation.

A company's balance sheet reflects the assets owned by the company and its liabilities (or claims against those assets). After these assets and liabilities are reported, the stockholder's equity portion may be computed. Then, once the stockholder's equity portion is divided by the total number of common shares outstanding, the book value per share may be derived.

H. SUMMARY OF VALUES

LO E.38.8 Explain the difference between a stock's par value, market value, and intrinsic value.

In summary, you should note the difference between a stock's par value, market value, and intrinsic value.

- A stock's **par value** is the specified value of the stock on the stock certificate or corporate charter. This value is often a dollar per share and has no economic meaning in terms of actual value.
- A stock's **market value** is the price of its stock as determined by investors in the secondary market.
- A stock's **intrinsic value** is its discounted present value based on future cash flows as determined (usually) by some form of the dividend discount model.

103 UNIT 9 ANSWERS TO PRACTICE QUESTIONS

1. B. A business statement of cash flows, not the income statement, has these three components. A pro forma income statement, which projects into the future, is similar to a business' income statement.

2. D. Notes payable are an example of a business liability.

3. A. Top-down analysis works from the macro to the micro level—economic analysis, industry analysis, company analysis.

4. B. Fundamental analysts attempt to determine the intrinsic value of a security and, therefore, review the financial statements of companies to help them determine this value. If an investor believes in the strong form of EMH, fundamental analysis is of no use. Support and resistance levels are used by technical analysts.

5. A. Using the constant growth dividend discount model: Intrinsic value = $D_0(1 + g) \div (r - g)$ = \$1.20 (1.06) ÷ (0.11 – 0.06) = \$25.44

6. C. On the basis of the constant growth dividend discount model, the intrinsic value of XYZ stock is \$94.50, calculated as follows:

$$V = \frac{\$1.75 \times (1 + 0.08)}{0.10 - 0.08} = \frac{\$1.89}{0.02} = \$94.50$$

Because XYZ stock is currently selling for \$100 per share, it is overvalued in the market and the investor should not buy the stock.

7. B. Using the perpetuity model, an investor should pay no more than \$12.50 for the preferred stock of KRF Corporation. The \$12.50 is derived by dividing the \$1.50 first year dividend (or any year) by the investor's required rate of return of 12%.

8. A. Using the multistage growth dividend discount model, the intrinsic value of CAR stock is \$18.45

1. Compute the value of each future dividend until the growth rate stabilizes (Years 1-3).
   D_1 = \$1.00 × 1.05 = \$1.05
   D_2 = \$1.05 × 1.05 = \$1.10
   D_3 = \$1.10 × 1.05 = \$1.16
2. Use the constant growth dividend discount model to compute the remaining intrinsic value of the stock at the beginning of the year when the dividend growth rate stabilizes (Year 4).
   D_4 = \$1.16 × 1.02 = \$1.18
   V = \$1.18 ÷ (0.08 – 0.02) = \$19.67
3. Use the uneven cash flow method to solve for the net present (intrinsic) value of the stock.
   CF_0 = \$0
   CF_1 = \$1.05
   CF_2 = \$1.10
   CF_3 = \$1.16 + \$19.67 = \$20.83
   I/YR = 8%
   Solve for NPV = \$18.45

9. B. Alphabet's P/E ratio is \$67 ÷ \$8.90 = 7.53. Because its P/E is lower than comparable firms, Alphabet is considered undervalued. Alphabet's intrinsic value is \$8.90 × 8.0 = \$71.20.

103 UNIT 9 POST-STUDY CHECKLIST

- ☐ Can I analyze, review, and interpret business financial statements?
- ☐ Can I differentiate between fundamental and technical analysis?
- ☐ Do I understand the problems associated with the discounted earnings method of stock valuation?
- ☐ Can I calculate the intrinsic value of a stock using the constant growth dividend discount model, the multistage growth dividend discount model, the no-growth dividend discount model, and the discounted free cash flow model?
- ☐ Am I able to calculate and analyze the price-to-earnings ratio, price-to-earnings divided by growth ratio, price-to-free-cash-flow ratio, and price-to-sales ratio to determine if a security warrants a purchase?
- ☐ Can I determine and analyze a company's book value?
- ☐ Can I explain the difference between a stock's par value, market value, and intrinsic value?

Am I able to define and understand the application of the following terms as they relate to investment planning?

- ☐ Balance sheet
- ☐ Book value
- ☐ Business statements of cash flows
- ☐ Constant growth dividend discount model
- ☐ Discounted earnings method
- ☐ Discounted free cash flow model
- ☐ Free cash flow to equity (FCFE)
- ☐ Fundamental analysis
- ☐ Income statement
- ☐ Intrinsic value
- ☐ Market value
- ☐ Multistage growth dividend discount model
- ☐ No-growth (perpetuity) dividend discount model
- ☐ Par value
- ☐ Price-to-earnings (P/E) ratio
- ☐ Price-to-earnings divided by growth (PEG) ratio
- ☐ Price-to-free-cash-flow (P/FCF) ratio
- ☐ Price-to-sales (P/S) ratio
- ☐ Pro forma income statement
- ☐ Technical analysis

UNIT 10

Asset Allocation, Portfolio Development, and Investment Strategies

REFER TO

CFP Board Principal Knowledge Topics – E. Investment Planning, E.37. Asset Allocation and Portfolio Diversification

CFP Board Principal Knowledge Topics – E. Investment Planning, E.39. Portfolio Development and Analysis

CFP Board Principal Knowledge Topics – E. Investment Planning, E.40. Investment Strategies

INTRODUCTION

Investment strategies are the practical applications of this course material. These strategies encompass formula investing, including dollar cost averaging for small investors, as well as the timing of investment purchases and sales to generate maximum return. The use of short selling and margin by investors will also be covered.

Finally, proper asset allocation and portfolio diversification have been shown to be the long-term key to generating superior investment performance. The two primary types of asset allocation discussed in this unit are strategic and tactical. Nevertheless, a major part of any asset allocation strategy is to minimize taxes on the portfolio (if the assets are held outside of a tax-deferred account, such as an IRA).

LEARNING OBJECTIVES

After completion of this unit, you should be able to achieve the following learning objectives:

CFP Board Principal Knowledge Topics – E. Investment Planning

E.37. Asset Allocation and Portfolio Diversification

LO E.37.3 Explain how investors use strategic asset allocation to meet their investment objectives.

LO E.37.4 Discuss the objectives of tactical asset allocation as an investment strategy.

LO E.37.5 Discuss asset allocation and model portfolios.

E.39. Portfolio Development and Analysis

LO E.39.4 Discuss the importance of an investment policy statement as an integral part of the overall financial planning process.

E.40. Investment Strategies

LO E.40.1 Differentiate between the types of orders investors use when either buying or selling securities.

LO E.40.3 Explain and apply investment strategies such as market timing, indexing, buy-and-hold, and sector rotation.

LO E.40.4 Evaluate the use of bond swaps.

LO E.40.5 Discuss the types of formula investing including dollar cost averaging; share averaging/averaging down; dividend reinvestment plans; and bond ladders, barbells, and bullets.

LO E.40.6 Explain the use of margin and when an investor would be subject to a margin call.

LO E.40.7 Explain and apply short selling techniques.

LO E.40.9 Discuss the strategies investors use to manage a concentrated portfolio.

LO E.40.10 Compare and contrast value and growth investing.

LO E.40.11 Describe the core and satellite investment strategy.

KEY TERMS

- Asset allocation
- Averaging down
- Bond barbells
- Bond bullets
- Bond ladders
- Bond swapping
- Buy-and-hold
- Core and satellite
- Dividend reinvestment plans (DRIPs)
- Dollar cost averaging (DCA)
- Formula investing
- Good-till-canceled order
- Growth investing
- Indexing
- Intermarket spread swap
- Investment policy statement
- Leverage
- Limit order
- Margin
- Market order
- Market timing
- Mean-variance optimization
- Pure yield pickup swap
- Rate anticipation swap
- Rebalancing
- Replication
- Sector rotation
- Share averaging
- Short selling
- Stop limit order
- Stop order
- Strategic asset allocation
- Substitution swap
- Tactical asset allocation
- Tax swap
- Value investing

A. THE INVESTMENT PLANNING PROCESS

LO E.39.4 Discuss the importance of an investment policy statement as an integral part of the overall financial planning process.

The investment planning process encompasses a variety of steps. These steps may include determining whether the client has the means to invest, determining the time horizon for investment based on the client's financial objective(s), and determining the appropriate level of risk and return for the portfolio based on the investor's risk tolerance and required return.

In addition, possible investment strategies that should be pursued by an investment advisor on behalf of the client begin with the formulation of a complete and thorough investment policy statement. An **investment policy statement**, a key component of a client's investment strategy, is a written document that sets forth a client's objectives, places boundaries on the portfolio's asset allocation and investment guidelines, as well as limitations on the investment manager. This statement gives guidance to the investment manager and provides a means for evaluating investment performance. An allocation among asset classes (and their respective weights) that is congruent with the client's primary investment objective is a part of any credible investment policy. In addition, review guidelines and rebalancing frequency are commonly included. Such a policy is not really optional because an investor has either implicitly (by default) or explicitly (in writing and as part of an investment policy statement) adopted some form of investment policy and asset allocation strategy.

Investment planning requires that the client's financial situation is analyzed so that the client's goals can be met while meeting his investment needs and requirements. In order to do an effective job of investment counseling, the advisor should examine and review the client's financial goals, risk tolerance and risk exposure, tax situation, liquidity and marketability needs, and financial statements.

In addition, all investment alternatives should be analyzed on an after-tax basis so that the returns from tax-exempt investments are comparable to taxable investments.

Alternatives to tax-exempt securities (i.e., municipal bonds) include tax-deferred investments, such as qualified plans, IRAs, insurance-based investments, and growth stocks (non-dividend-paying common stock). The purpose of investment planning is to match appropriate investment vehicles to the needs and goals of the client.

One of the first considerations in creating a financial plan is the need for an emergency fund. This fund should consist of liquid assets so as to be easily accessible in the event of an emergency (e.g., loss of job). If a client does not have an emergency fund or access to cash in case of an emergency, investments that have the potential for large price fluctuations, such as common stock, should make up a smaller portion of the overall portfolio. Likewise, investments that do not have efficient markets, such as real estate, should be limited.

The financial planner uses the client's financial information as a basis for creating a written plan to achieve the goals of the client. The client's financial statements should include a statement of financial position and statement of cash flows. These statements provide the planner with the resources available for accomplishing the client's goals.

The possibility exists that the planner, after reviewing the financial information, will determine that the client's goals are unrealistic based on the client's current financial position and earning capacity. In such a case, the goals should be revised to reflect more realistic objectives.

Expected resources may also be included in this analysis if they are relatively certain. These resources might include bonuses, promotions, or inheritances. In some cases, such as a large inheritance, the expected resource may allow the client to accomplish all objectives.

B. FORMULA INVESTING

LO E.40.5 Discuss the types of formula investing including dollar cost averaging; share averaging/averaging down; dividend reinvestment plans; and bond ladders, barbells, and bullets.

The term **formula investing** means that the investor does not actively trade or manage the portfolio but instead follows certain automatic rules regardless of market conditions.

Dollar Cost Averaging (DCA)

Dollar cost averaging (DCA) is the systematic process of purchasing securities over time by investing a predetermined amount of money at regular intervals. Often, this is accomplished through the use of an automatic withdrawal plan at the investor's bank or payroll deduction. The goal of the strategy is to reduce the effects of market price fluctuations. For example, when the market is increasing, shares purchased benefit from the price increases, and when the market is declining, the additional shares purchased are bought at lower prices and will yield more shares per dollar invested. However, this strategy does not guarantee a profit.

The effect of DCA is to increase the number of shares gradually over a long period. Because more shares are acquired when the price of the stock or mutual fund declines, the average cost per share is reduced. Subsequently, if the price of the stock or mutual fund share increases; the investor will earn greater profits on the lower-priced shares, thereby increasing the dollar-weighted rate of return.

Dollar cost averaging works best when markets are declining or fluctuating. DCA does not work well when the market is steadily increasing because in that event, the investor would be better off buying as many shares as possible up front when the price per share is lower. In addition, even in a declining market, the investor should not automatically assume that the market price of the stock or mutual fund will eventually increase. Rather, a stock or mutual fund that is declining in price may result from an underlying corporate earnings problem or a weakness in that particular market sector (e.g., technology). If this is the case, the investor needs to consider the ongoing expenditure of funds as a fixed cost that should not influence the purchase of any additional shares.

Averaging Down/Share Averaging

Some investors do not like to make periodic purchases of stock or mutual fund shares. Instead, they prefer to purchase additional shares only when the price of the shares *declines*. Accordingly, these investors are following a strategy of **averaging down**. This is a method by which the investor reduces the cost basis of an investment in one security by buying more shares as the price of that security decreases. As with dollar cost averaging, the investor will be rewarded if the price of the security subsequently increases. Of course, by only buying "on the dips" in the market, the investor may also miss out on a bull market, wherein share prices tend to move upward for a significant period of time. Finally, a variation of the averaging down strategy occurs when the investor purchases the same number of shares every time. If the investor does so, he is said to be following a policy of **share averaging**.

With dollar cost averaging, there is a *greater* total reduction in the average cost of shares than there is with share averaging. When the investor dollar cost averages, the amount spent is held constant, but the number of shares purchased varies. Conversely, when the investor share averages, the number of shares purchased is held constant, but the dollar amount varies. Because the investor purchases a fixed number of shares with share averaging, regardless of how low the price falls, the average cost of the overall shares is *not* reduced to the extent that it is with dollar cost averaging. Share averaging is also, by definition, not as easy to automate (e.g., by way of automatic monthly investing) as is dollar cost averaging because the amounts invested using share averaging are seldom the same.

Dividend Reinvestment Plans (DRIPs)

The term *dividend reinvestment* refers to dividends from a stock or mutual fund that are reinvested in the investment from which they were earned. **Dividend reinvestment plans (DRIPs)** are offered by many companies as a service to their shareholders. These plans provide several major benefits for a long-term investor.

- Dividends are automatically reinvested into the company's stock, thereby adding to the investor's share balance.
- Additional purchases of stock shares can be made without incurring brokerage commission.

Reinvested dividends are treated the same for income tax purposes as those dividends received in the form of cash. However, unlike cash dividends, the amount of reinvested dividends adds to the investor's tax basis.

Bond Ladders, Barbells, and Bullets

The use of **bond ladders** is a long-term strategy for diversifying and staggering maturity dates in a client's bond portfolio and, subsequently, for establishing a schedule for reinvesting the bond proceeds as they mature. This strategy provides two advantages.

- Due to a combination of long-term and short-term bonds in the portfolio, the laddered portfolio will provide higher yields than will a portfolio consisting entirely of short-term bonds.
- Because each bond matures at a different time, cash is more frequently made available to the investor at different maturity periods. This cash may be used to purchase another bond with a commensurate maturity period that will maintain the original structure of the bond portfolio and minimize the risk of increasing interest rates.

EXAMPLE An investor purchases $20,000 each of 10 different bonds, with maturities ranging from 1 to 10 years, for a total portfolio of $200,000. The shorter maturity bonds are less subject to price fluctuation (because of their shorter duration), which therefore reduces the overall portfolio interest rate risk.

The use of **bond barbells**, also known as the dumbbell strategy, is an active strategy for buying only short-term and long-term bond issues. The long-term end of the barbell allows the investor to lock in attractive long-term interest rates, whereas the short-term end ensures that the investor will have the opportunity to invest in other assets if the bond market declines in value. However, such a strategy also means that the original structure of the portfolio is not maintained because, as the short-term bonds mature, the proceeds need to be reinvested. In turn, this means that the portfolio requires active management by the portfolio manager.

The use of **bond bullets** is a strategy for having several bonds mature at the same time, thus minimizing interest rate risk. For example, assume that an investor wants all of his bonds to mature in 10 years. Therefore, using the bullet strategy, he buys two bonds immediately, two bonds two years from now, and two more bonds four years from now. As a result, the bonds purchased immediately have a maturity date of 10 years, the bonds purchased two years later have maturity dates of eight years, and the bonds purchased four years later have maturity dates of six years. This strategy may be an effective method in matching duration to the cash needs of the investor.

PRACTICE QUESTION

Choose the best answer for the question below.
The answer can be found at the end of this unit.

1. Which of the following statements regarding a bond ladder strategy is CORRECT?

A. A bond ladder strategy involves the purchase of very long-term and very short-term bonds.

B. A laddered portfolio of bonds will provide lower yields than a portfolio consisting entirely of short-term bonds.

C. A bond ladder strategy is generally more aggressive than a bond barbell strategy.

D. A bond ladder strategy is a relatively easy way to immunize a portfolio against interest rate risk.

C. BOND SWAPPING STRATEGIES

LO E.40.4 Evaluate the use of bond swaps.

Bond swapping is the process of selling one debt security (bond) and replacing it with another. The goal of the strategy is to increase the yield to maturity (YTM) on the bond portfolio, to save on income taxes, or to reduce the overall interest rate risk of the portfolio. The major types of bond swaps are presented below.

1. A **substitution swap** involves selling bonds with identical characteristics but different selling prices. This price difference is an arbitrage opportunity and will exist only shortly, until the market corrects the price inefficiency.
2. An **intermarket spread swap** involves the exchange of one type of bond (e.g., government bond) with another type of bond (e.g., corporate bond). This occurs when investors believe one type of bond is currently mispriced in relation to the other. The goal of this type of swap is to capitalize on a YTM disparity across bond markets.
3. A **rate anticipation swap** attempts to take advantage of expected changes in interest rates. For example, if rates are expected to increase, long-term bonds are swapped for short-term bonds. If rates are expected to decline, short-term bonds are swapped for bonds with long maturity dates.
4. In a **pure yield pickup swap**, a bond with a lower YTM is exchanged for a bond with a higher YTM. The new bond that replaces the old bond is either a longer-term bond or a lower-quality bond sufficient to generate a higher overall YTM.
5. A **tax swap** is motivated by current tax law. One such swap involves gaining from a capital loss by selling a previously purchased bond at a loss due to rising interest rates. For example, two years ago an investor bought a bond for $1,000. The bond currently trades for $800 in the secondary market. The investor may sell the bond for a $200 loss, reinvest the $800 proceeds, and hold the new bond to maturity. Assuming a 25% tax bracket, the investor would experience a tax savings of $50 ($200 × 0.25).

PRACTICE QUESTION

Choose the best answer for the question below.
The answer can be found at the end of this unit.

2. Which of the following statements about bond swaps is TRUE? (CFP® Certification Examination, released 11/94)

I. A substitution swap is designed to take advantage of a perceived yield differential between bonds that are similar with respect to coupons, ratings, maturities, and industry.

II. Rate anticipation swaps are based on forecasts of general interest rate changes.

III. The yield pickup swap is designed to change the cash flow of the portfolio by exchanging similar bonds that have different coupon rates.

IV. The tax swap is made in order to substitute capital gains for current yield.

A. I, II, and III
B. I and III
C. II and IV
D. IV only
E. I, II, III, and IV

D. TIMING OF INVESTMENT PURCHASES AND SALES

LO E.40.3 Explain and apply investment strategies such as market timing, indexing, buy-and-hold, and sector rotation.

Investment strategies also include the timing of buying and selling securities. Only active management investors or portfolio managers try to time purchases and sales, and, therefore, these individuals are sometimes called traders instead of long-term investors. In contrast to active management or active investors, many individuals practice passive management strategies, foremost among these being a buy-and-hold strategy.

Market Timing

Market timing is an attempt to predict the overall direction of the securities market and to take advantage of changes in the prices of those securities, whether those prices go up (going long) or down (selling short). In its most common form, investors or portfolio managers time their security purchases while staying fully or predominantly invested in the market. In essence, they are attempting to take advantage of market swings and trends.

Studies have shown that, by and large, market timing techniques do not work. If an investor is out of the market during only the five or six most profitable trading days, his dollar-weighted rate of return declines considerably. Therefore, an investor or portfolio manager who practices market timing should proceed carefully and realize that such a strategy, at least to date, has not been proven to be successful over the long term.

Buy and Hold

The **buy-and-hold** strategy is the conceptual opposite of market timing—that is, *buy and hold* generally means that no purchases or sales of an investor's existing portfolio will be done over a very long period of time (i.e., investment horizon). Buy and hold is a passive management strategy and is supported by the efficient market hypothesis (EMH) discussed earlier in this course.

The buy-and-hold strategy features three major advantages:

- The investor can minimize the transaction costs in the acquisition and trading of securities.
- The investor's income tax obligations (particularly income tax liabilities or tax due) may be managed more effectively.
- The strategy ensures that the investor will not be out of the market during an upturn in prices or its most profitable trading days.

Indexing

Indexing, or investing in index mutual funds or ETFs, is indicative of an investor who believes in passive portfolio management. The purpose of an indexed portfolio is not to beat the targeted index (e.g., S&P 500 Index) but merely to match its long-term performance, less any management fees and administrative costs. Accordingly, index funds tend to be distinguished by their low administrative costs and low turnover of existing assets.

A common way of constructing an indexed portfolio is simply to buy and hold the securities in the index in their appropriate weightings. This method is known as **replication** and is characterized by a low tracking error with the actual index that is targeted.

Sector Rotation

Sector rotation, an active portfolio management strategy, means emphasizing or overallocating certain economic sectors or industries in response to the next expected phase of the business cycle. The goal is to build a portfolio that will produce investment results that beat the overall market. This strategy requires investors to time the entry and the exit of specific sectors based on economic business cycles. For many investors, the ability to accurately identify and transition from one cycle to another may be difficult.

PRACTICE QUESTION

Choose the best answer for the question below.
The answer can be found at the end of this unit.

3. All of the following strategies are indicative of a passive portfolio management approach EXCEPT

A. buy and hold
B. indexing
C. market timing
D. replication

E. SHORT SELLING

LO E.40.7 Explain and apply short selling techniques.

Normally, investors purchase stock (go long) with the hope that the shares of stock will appreciate. However, investors can also make money when the price of the shares decline if they engage in a strategy known as **short selling**. Therefore, short selling allows investors to take advantage of falling stock prices. As such, individuals who engage in short selling are pessimistic (or bearish) about the future direction of prices. The strategy also allows investors to hedge investment risk. Short sellers are normally wealthy investors, hedge funds, large institutions, and day traders.

Selling a stock short involves four steps, as follows.

1. The investor uses a stockbroker to borrow stock from another investor's account. This requires the short seller to make a deposit, equal to the margin requirement (currently 50%) times the fair market value of the stock, to the broker. As an outgrowth of this requirement, the investor must also establish a margin account with the broker/dealer. This type of account allows the investor to borrow money from the brokerage firm.
2. The investor sells the borrowed stock in the open market.
3. The investor repurchases the stock in the open market.
4. Finally, the investor replaces, or covers, the borrowed stock.

The mechanics of a short sale are illustrated in the following graphic.

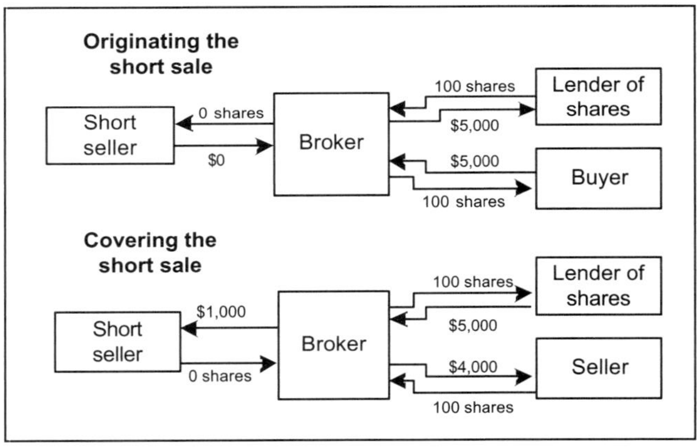

The end result of this technique is that the short seller will make money if he is able to repurchase the stock for less than the initial amount received on the sale of the stock (i.e., the price of the borrowed stock has declined in the interim). However, if the price of the borrowed stock increases, the short seller will lose money on the transaction. Also, if the company pays a dividend before the short sale is covered, the short seller is required to make a cash payment in lieu of the dividend to the investor whose stock was borrowed. Finally, investors have no particular time period to cover the short sale.

EXAMPLE Lauren short sells 200 shares of XYZ at $32 with a 50% initial margin. XYZ pays a dividend of $1 per share before she covers the short sale. She then buys back the stock for $30. What is her percent profit or loss?
Lauren's investment: 200 × $32 × 0.5 = $3,200

$6,400	Proceeds from short sale
(6,000)	Cost to repurchase shares
$400	Gain
(200)	Dividend payment
$200	Net profit

Net profit ÷ Investment = % Gain/Loss

$200 ÷ $3,200 = 6.25% Gain

For CFP® Exam purposes, you may be required to calculate the net dollar gain/loss or the percent gain/loss on a short sale.

PRACTICE QUESTIONS

Choose the best answer for each of the questions below.
Answers can be found at the end of this unit.

4. Robert wishes to short ABC stock. He places a market order to sell short 100 shares of ABC stock, and the order is filled at a price of $45 per share. If Robert later buys 100 shares of ABC stock at $40 per share, what is his gross profit, if any?
A. $0
B. $350
C. $450
D. $500

5. Which of the following investment strategies is the most risky for an investor?
A. Purchasing a put option
B. Short selling
C. Selling a covered call option
D. Purchasing a call option

F. MARGIN TRANSACTIONS

LO E.40.6 Explain the use of margin and when an investor would be subject to a margin call.

Margin accounts give investors the ability to use leverage within their investment accounts. In the financial world, **leverage** is defined as the financial advantage of an investment that controls property of greater value than the cash invested. More simply, leveraging is the use of borrowed money to achieve an individual's investment objectives.

When an investment is purchased on **margin**, one-half of the funds is deposited by the investor (known as the initial margin percentage, as established by Federal Reserve Regulation T), and the other half may be borrowed from the broker/dealer. However, some broker/dealers may require a higher initial margin percentage. The maintenance margin, which is usually set at 35%, is a second margin requirement put in place by the broker/dealer whereby the investor must add additional funds to the account to protect the broker/dealer from losses. Finally, the amount owed to the broker/dealer is known as the debit balance, and includes the original amount borrowed by the investor plus any accrued interest. The amount of equity that the investor has in the account is the current fair market value of the security purchased with the use of margin less the debit balance.

This formula is used to determine when a margin call will occur:

$$\text{margin call} = \frac{\text{debit balance}}{1 - \text{maintenance margin}}$$

Sometimes, this formula is also written as shown below:

$$\text{margin call} = \frac{1 - \text{initial margin percentage}}{1 - \text{maintenance margin}} \times \text{purchase price of stock}$$

EXAMPLE Harry pays $20,000 to purchase shares of XYZ Company, currently trading at $25 per share, using his margin account. Therefore, $20,000 is also borrowed from the broker/dealer. Harry can buy a total of 1,600 shares. At what point should Harry be concerned about receiving a margin call from the broker/dealer? The answer is when the stock price declines to $19.23.

$$\text{Margin call} = \frac{\$25 \times 0.50}{1 - 0.35} = \frac{\$12.50}{0.65} = \$19.23$$

Using the previous formulas, the number of dollars that must be deposited by an investor into a margin account may be calculated using the current trading price (not the original purchase price) of the margined stock.

EXAMPLE Continue with the previous example, but now assume that XYZ stock has dropped to $15 per share. How much money (dollar amount) is Harry now required to deposit to meet the margin call? The answer is $2.75 per share, or a total of $4,400 ($2.75 × 1,600 shares), calculated as follows.

Required Equity		Actual Equity	
Stock	$15.00	Stock	$15.00
× Equity %	× .35	– Loan amount	–12.50
Required equity	$5.25	Actual equity	$2.50

The required equity ($5.25) less the actual equity ($2.50) equals $2.75 per share.

Finally, margin accounts (or marginable securities) may be used as collateral by the broker/dealer for its own borrowing from a bank. If this is done, the bank will charge interest to the broker/dealer on the loan using a predetermined rate known as the call loan rate (also known as call money rate).

Holding Period Return with Use of Margin

The holding period return (HPR) computation may also be used in conjunction with the use of borrowed money by the investor. Intuitively, if an investor has borrowed money to make an investment, he has less *of his own* money at risk and, accordingly, his HPR should increase.

EXAMPLE Darrin bought 100 shares of XYZ stock at $100 per share on margin (a 50% initial margin percentage). The margin interest was 8% annually. After one year, Darrin sold all of his shares for $130 per share. XYZ stock paid no dividends during the one-year period. What was Darrin's HPR using margin? The answer is 52%, calculated in the following manner:

1. Ending value = 100 shares × $130/share = $13,000
2. Beginning value = 100 shares × $100 per share = $10,000
3. Cash flows:
   - Positive? No (no dividends)
   - Negative? Yes (margin interest = 8% × 50% × $10,000 = $400)
4. Darrin's investment (INV) = 50% × $10,000 = $5,000

Therefore,

$$HPR = \frac{\$13{,}000 - \$10{,}000 - \$400}{\$5{,}000} = \frac{\$2{,}600}{\$5{,}000} = 0.52 \times 100 = 52\%$$

In contrast, the HPR would have been only 30% if Darrin had not purchased this stock on margin:

$$HPR = \frac{\$13{,}000 - \$10{,}000}{\$10{,}000} = \frac{\$3{,}000}{\$10{,}000} = 0.30 \times 100 = 30\%$$

Therefore, Darrin has indeed leveraged, or increased, his percentage HPR through the use of margin. However, what if the value of XYZ stock had declined over the course of the year? In that case, the use of margin would also increase the potential percentage loss or downside risk.

PRACTICE QUESTIONS

Choose the best answer for each of the questions below. Answers can be found at the end of this unit.

6. Your client purchased 100 shares of FAQ stock at $60 per share with a 50% initial margin percentage and a 35% maintenance margin requirement. If the stock drops to $40 per share, how much money does your client need to deposit to meet the required equity amount in the margin account?

A. $400
B. $600
C. $615
D. $800

7. Abigail uses her margin account to purchase 300 shares of Monroe stock at $85 per share. The initial margin is 50% and the maintenance margin is 35%. Abigail's margin account charges 6% annual interest. Monroe stock pays the following dividends at the end of the first 2 years: $2.50 (Year 1) and $3.60 (Year 2). At the end of year 2, Abigail sells all of her stock for $100 per share. What is Abigail's holding period return?
   A. 24.85%
   B. 18.83%
   C. 37.65%
   D. 49.67%

8. Shelly purchased ABC stock on margin when it was selling for $60 per share. The initial margin was 60%, and the maintenance margin is 35%. At what price will Shelly receive a margin call?
   A. $30.00
   B. $32.31
   C. $36.92
   D. $46.15

G. ASSET ALLOCATION

LO E.37.5 Discuss asset allocation and model portfolios.

Asset allocation is the process of apportioning an investor's wealth among different countries and asset classes for investment purposes. Asset allocation is the main determinant of a portfolio's total return. Historically, these investment classes have consisted of cash and cash equivalents, equities (stock), and debt (bonds). However, recently (and more properly), the potential investment classes have been broadened to also include real estate, international investments, collectibles, and precious metals. Most financial planners who provide investment counseling use some type of **mean-variance optimization** software to determine an optimum portfolio or asset allocation based on a client's goals, risk tolerance, time horizon, tax situation, and economic forecasts. This tool is used to spread investment across different assets within a portfolio by assessing the trade-off between risk and return. The goal in using these software packages is to build an efficient portfolio for the client that maximizes the return and minimizes the risk.

The process of asset allocation is very important because academic studies have shown that approximately 90% of the variability of the long-term investment performance of assets is attributable to their allocation and weight within an investor's portfolio. Therefore, the objective in building any asset allocation model is to determine which investment classes will be used and in what percentage. This model will likely encompass any one or more of the investment strategies previously discussed in this unit, but the model should be built with the following considerations:

- An assumption of the client's level of investment risk and time horizon
- The client's past experience level with investments
- The client's expressed or determined required rate of return
- The tax status of the client

When constructing an asset allocation policy, four decisions should be made:

1. What *asset classes* should be considered for investment purposes?
2. What *weights* or *percentages* should be assigned to each of these asset classes?
3. What is the allowable *allocation range* based upon these weights?
4. What *specific securities* should be purchased for the portfolio?

In order to properly answer these questions, investors need to be specific as to the portfolio objective and risk and liquidity concerns. An investor's time horizon is also critical in the asset allocation decision. Those investors with a short-term time horizon, such as many retirees, will be most concerned about a significant loss of principal to their accumulated investments. This objective may lead them in the direction of a fixed-income investment strategy approach where debt instruments, such as bonds, will be the cornerstone of the portfolio. Conversely, those investors with a long-term time horizon, such as young professionals with many years until retirement or other major life event, will want the potential for a significant amount of capital appreciation. This objective may lead them to over balance their portfolio with equities. Each of these approaches lacks balance and shows a misunderstanding of the risks inherent in each general strategy.

Stocks encounter price volatility over time. If the client is not able to understand this and weather the subsequent discomfort that comes with, for example, a bear market, he may make a hasty investment decision counter to the satisfaction of his long-term investment goal. Similarly, bonds experience the erosion of purchasing power by inflation and, should an investor find that she is not able to maintain a desirable standard of living because of this fact, another ill-fated investment decision may occur. Accordingly, a proper understanding of time horizon issues can dramatically alter a client's risk tolerance, which is the ability to bear declines in the value of the investments. The financial planner's responsibility is to help clients understand the relationship between the time horizon and risk and properly evaluate the appropriate contribution to the asset allocation decision.

Model Portfolios

Perhaps the simplest solution for the investment advisor or portfolio manager in developing and implementing an asset allocation strategy is to adopt the use of a portfolio model. Such a model is often automatically provided by the sponsors of an investment product or family of products. Specifically, the investment advisor uses a questionnaire to determine the client's risk tolerance and, after answering a few additional standard questions provided by the model, inputs the answers and risk tolerance into a black box that, in turn, generates the appropriate allocation.

Sample Asset Allocations

Conservative risk tolerant investor:

- 40% bonds
- 30% money markets
- 20% large-cap equity
- 5% international equity
- 5% small-cap equity

This allocation is appropriate for an investor seeking higher yields and lower capital appreciation.

Moderate risk tolerant investor:

- 40% bonds
- 5% money markets
- 35% large-cap equity
- 15% international equity
- 5% small-cap equity

This allocation is appropriate for an investor seeking a balance between yield and capital appreciation.

High risk tolerant investor:

- 20% bonds
- 50% large-cap equity
- 20% international equity
- 10% small-cap equity

This allocation is appropriate for an investor seeking higher capital appreciation and lower yields. Note: these sample portfolios are not meant to be exact representations, but rather should serve as a guide to understanding the various types of investments that would appeal to a specific type of investor.

However, there are several limitations on the use of any of these models, including:

- the lack of specific customization to a client's particular financial goals, risk tolerance, time horizon, and current cash flow situation;
- the prevalence of a one size fits all mentality (e.g., when using a standardized model, the investment advisor may have no real appreciation of the specifics of the model's underlying assumptions, such as its expected returns, standard deviations, and correlation coefficients);
- the relevance of the asset class benchmark used by the model, tailored to the advisor's own investment style; and
- the lack of tax efficiency of some models whereby they either ignore or do not properly attribute the impact of income tax factors involved in the construction of an optimal asset allocation.

One of the goals of any financial planner in creating a properly constructed and diversified portfolio is tax efficiency. That is, while in most instances establishing a completely tax-free portfolio is imprudent (e.g., a portfolio consisting entirely of municipal bond funds), a realistic goal is to strive to maximize the amount of after-tax income possible from the portfolio.

PRACTICE QUESTIONS

Choose the best answer for each of the questions below.
Answers can be found at the end of this unit.

9. A portfolio consisting of 30% bonds, 20% growth stocks, 40% blue-chip conservative stocks, and 10% cash is most representative of which type of investment objective?

A. Growth and income
B. Current income
C. Aggressive growth
D. Capital preservation

10. Madeline, a financial adviser, is meeting with her clients, who are in their late 20s. They each wish to open a traditional IRA funded by a portfolio of mutual funds. After each of them complete an individual risk-return profile, Madeline determines that her clients are both moderate risk takers. This was partially determined by conversation and partially based on their answers to their respective risk tolerance questionnaires within their risk-return profiles. Madeline concludes that, based on all of the information gathered, both of them should be able to cope with the volatility in the equity and bond markets. Which of the following would be the most appropriate asset allocation for each of their individual portfolios within their respective IRAs?

A. Portfolio 1—40% Small-Cap Growth Fund, 30% International Stock Fund, 20% S&P 500 Index Fund
B. Portfolio 2—10% U.S. Government Securities Fund, 10% Utilities Fund, 30% Balanced Fund, 25% Small-Cap Growth Fund, 25% High-Yield Bond Fund
C. Portfolio 3—10% Small-Cap Growth Fund, 30% Corporate Bond Fund, 10% International Growth Fund, 50% S&P 500 Index Fund
D. Portfolio 4—25% Wilshire 5000 Index Fund, 25% High-Yield Bond Fund, 25% Asset Allocation Fund, 25% International Stock Fund

11. Patrick, age 57, has just retired from his job as a teacher. He is a widower and has three self-sufficient adult children. As part of his compensation plan, he has a cash balance retirement plan. He would like to transfer these assets to his broker and allocate the portfolio according to an income objective with low to moderate risk and a long-term time horizon. Which of the following portfolios should Patrick's financial advisor recommend?

A. Portfolio 1—65% Bond Index Fund, 20% S&P 500 Index Fund, 10% International Stock Fund, 5% Money Market Fund
B. Portfolio 2—40% High-Yield Bond Fund, 20% Municipal Bond Fund, 20% U.S. Government Securities Fund, 20% Small-Cap Growth Fund
C. Portfolio 3—80% S&P 500 Index, 10% International Bond Fund, 10% Money Market Fund
D. Portfolio 4—25% Bond Index Fund, 60% S&P 500 Index Fund, 10% International Stock Fund, 5% Money Market Fund

H. STRATEGIC ASSET ALLOCATION

LO E.37.3 Explain how investors use strategic asset allocation to meet their investment objectives.

The purpose of **strategic asset allocation** is to determine an appropriate allocation based on the long-term financial goals of the client. Accordingly, the risk tolerance of the client is assessed in conjunction with the current phase in the client's life cycle. For example, a client who is in the asset accumulation phase (i.e., younger, with or without children) will likely be able to tolerate more risk than a client who is in the gifting years (i.e., retired and focusing primarily on estate planning and asset distribution to heirs).

In strategic asset allocation, once the allocation is determined, it remains constant until (typically) some life-changing event occurs. Because the investment performance of the selected asset classes is different, **rebalancing** must take place to bring the portfolio in line with the strategic mix. Rebalancing is a process through which investment assets are redistributed between asset categories to achieve a new allocation model. Rebalancing may be done to bring the distribution of assets back into the original model (common if one category outperforms another), or it may be done to establish a new allocation model (perhaps upon entering a new stage in the life cycle). However, changing market conditions play only a very small role in determining the appropriate asset mix.

Life-cycle Section 401(k) plan mutual funds are an example of rebalancing that is done in the context of a strategic asset allocation orientation. In these types of funds, portfolio managers will vary the initial asset allocation based on the client's advancing age and/or associated risk tolerance (e.g., safety of principal becoming more important as the investor approaches retirement), but market conditions or timing does not play a part. The life-cycle adjustment that takes place is based on tried-and-true characteristics of investors proven over the years to generate the optimal risk-adjusted rate of return possible. An investor's life cycle consists of three phases: (1) asset accumulation, (2) conservation or protection, and (3) distribution or gifting. Each phase typically coincides with the investor's age, professional career, and retirement.

I. TACTICAL ASSET ALLOCATION

LO E.37.4 Discuss the objectives of tactical asset allocation as an investment strategy.

In contrast to the strategic approach, **tactical asset allocation** (TAA) continuously adjusts the asset allocation and class mix in an attempt to take advantage of changing market conditions and overall investor sentiment. In TAA, portfolio adjustments are driven solely by perceived changes in the market values of the asset classes, and very little consideration, if any, is given to the long-term financial goals of the client. In essence, TAA is a market timing approach to portfolio management that is intended to take advantage of perceived market inefficiencies (and opportunities for investor profit).

Inherently, TAA is characterized by a fundamentally contrarian approach to investing. As such, the portfolio manager is constantly buying an asset class that is currently out of favor with the majority of investors. In addition, transaction and turnover costs in reallocating these asset classes are much higher if the manager uses TAA instead of the more common strategic asset allocation approach.

Asset Allocation Selection

The type of asset allocation to use likely depends on the investor's or manager's portfolio management style. Certainly, an investor or manager who believes in *active portfolio management* (and that the market is inherently *inefficient*) will tend towards *tactical asset allocation.* Alternatively, an investor or manager who adopts more of a long-term *buy-and-hold* strategy (passive management style) will find *strategic asset allocation* to be preferable. Regardless, a thoughtful analysis of which asset allocation technique to adopt, and then adherence to this technique throughout the investor's time horizon, is critical because it constitutes the primary factor impacting long-term portfolio performance.

PRACTICE QUESTION

Choose the best answer for the question below.
The answer can be found at the end of this unit.

12. Which of the following statements regarding strategic and tactical asset allocation is(are) CORRECT?

I. Strategic asset allocation involves selecting the proper asset allocation based on the risk tolerance of the client and rebalancing to keep the portfolio within the parameters of the desired strategic mix.

II. Tactical asset allocation involves evaluating asset classes or industries with respect to their value and selling undervalued classes and purchasing overvalued classes.

A. I only
B. II only
C. Both I and II
D. Neither I nor II

J. CORE AND SATELLITE

LO E.40.11 Describe the core and satellite investment strategy.

The **core and satellite** investment strategy invests in both broad market indexes (core) and higher-risk alternatives (satellite). Core investments may include U.S. stocks, U.S. fixed-income, and developed international equities. Generally, these investments track a major market index such as the S&P 500, Russell 3000, and MSCI EAFE®. This part of the portfolio uses a passive investment philosophy to achieve market-based returns. Satellite investments may include REITs, emerging markets, and high-yield bonds. These investments attempt to achieve above-market returns through high risk and global exposure. Investors may choose to implement a core and satellite strategy through a portfolio of mutual funds. The goals of this strategy are to reduce portfolio risk through diversification, generate higher returns commensurate with required returns, minimize transaction costs, and manage taxes.

EXAMPLE Investor portfolio with an asset allocation consisting of 80% core investments and 20% satellite investments.

Sector	Core Percentage (80%)
U.S. equities	60%
International equities	10%
U.S. corporate bonds	30%

Sector	Satellite Percentage (20%)
Real estate	10%
Emerging market equity	25%
Emerging market debt	35%
High-yield bonds	20%
Commodities	10%

PRACTICE QUESTION

Choose the best answer for the question below.
The answer can be found at the end of this unit.

13. Henry, age 46, has $250,000 to invest in a long-term investment portfolio. He has come to his financial planner, Robbie, to ask for advice. He wants a diversified portfolio while simultaneously limiting risk, minimizing transaction costs, and managing taxes. Also, he desires a portfolio that is based on a passive management approach, but he would still like to include an active management component. Which of the following approaches would best suit Henry?

A. Index funds
B. Core and satellite
C. Commodities
D. Emerging markets

K. VALUE AND GROWTH INVESTING

LO E.40.10 Compare and contrast value and growth investing.

Value and growth investing are really just different sides of the same "investment coin." In this case, the investment coin is the price-to-earnings (P/E) ratio. **Value investing** is a strategy that tends to concentrate on the numerator (or price), while **growth investing** focuses on the denominator (or earnings). Specifically, value investing assumes the current P/E ratio is below its natural level and that an efficient market will soon recognize this situation and drive the stock price upward. In contrast, growth investors assume the P/E ratio will remain constant over the near term, and the stock price in an efficient market will increase as the forecasted earnings growth of the issuing company is realized. Such investors look for growth stocks, that is, stocks of companies that have a significant ability to develop products with a minimum of marketplace competition. These stocks usually have a superior rate of earnings growth (e.g., 15% per year or more), low dividend payouts, and an above-average price-to-earnings ratio. However, growth stocks are generally more volatile and, as a result, exhibit higher betas than other stocks. The value approach could be considered slow and steady, while the growth approach is more aggressive.

L. TYPES OF ORDERS

LO E.40.1 Differentiate between the types of orders investors use when either buying or selling securities.

The **market order**, which is the most popular and has the highest priority, is subject to the fluctuations and timeliness of the market. The **limit order** is used to sell or buy at a specific price, one that is better, than the market price at the time the order is placed. The price acts as a ceiling for purchases and a floor for sales. The **stop order** is used to protect investors from large losses. If the market price reaches a certain point, the stop order will turn into a market order. Likewise, this order is used to limit losses in connection with short sales. Also, the **stop limit order** is similar to a stop order except that it turns into a limit order when triggered. In a stop limit, both the stop order price and the limit order are specified.

A **good-till-canceled (GTC) order** is an order to buy or sell a security at a specific or limit price that lasts until the order is completed or cancelled. A GTC order will not be executed until the limit price has been reached, regardless of how many days or weeks it might take. Investors often use GTC orders to set a limit price that is far away from the current market price. Some brokerage firms may limit the time a GTC order can remain in effect and may charge more for executing this type of order.

PRACTICE QUESTION

Choose the best answer for the question below.
The answer can be found at the end of this unit.

14. Which of the following types of orders does NOT restrict the price at which an order is executed?

A. Limit
B. Stop
C. Market
D. Stop limit

M. STRATEGIES FOR CONCENTRATED PORTFOLIOS

LO E.40.9 Discuss the strategies investors use to manage a concentrated portfolio.

A common problem some clients face (particularly small business owners and executives with substantial compensation-based stock options) is that a significant portion of their wealth is concentrated in a single (usually, an employer) security. Clearly, this type of portfolio includes substantial unsystematic risk. As we have learned throughout this course, it is important to reduce or eliminate this risk as much as possible. The solution is, of course, to create a diversified portfolio for the businessowner or executive, but this is problematic because there may be a limited market for the securities owned by the owner or executive.

Several strategies may be implemented to manage a concentrated portfolio.

- *Sell the stock, if possible*. This may include an outright sale (typically to a family member), but a sale to an employee stock ownership plan, which is sometimes created just to provide a market for the stock, should be considered.
- *Gift the stock, if possible*. Again, transferring the stock or stock option to another (again, usually a family member), but this time for no consideration (a gift), should be considered. A gift tax may be imposed on this transfer; however, the donor/transferor will not be subject to income tax when gifting the securities.
- *Use a charitable remainder trust (CRT)*. When a CRT is established and assets are transferred to the trust, a charitable income tax deduction is created for the donor and may be used to offset compensation income. In addition to the charitable income tax deduction, the CRT can sell the securities without any income tax liability because it is a tax-exempt entity under law.
- *Use an exchange fund*. Many financial institutions sponsor exchange funds (not to be confused with *exchange-traded funds*) that permit investors with concentrated portfolios of publicly traded stock to contribute the stock to the fund. In exchange, the investor receives a proportional interest in the fund. A major benefit of this option is that an undiversified portfolio is thereby exchanged for a diversified portfolio without incurring immediate capital gains taxes.

PRACTICE QUESTION

Choose the best answer for the question below.
The answer can be found at the end of this unit.

15. Craig, age 63, is an executive with ABC corporation (a publicly-traded company). He wants to retire within 2 years. Over the years, he has accumulated a large position in his company's stock. He is concerned that his portfolio may not be diversified enough to withstand a substantial decline in ABC's stock price. He would like to retain control over the proceeds and create a diversified portfolio. He has come to you for advice on how to handle this situation. Based on this information, which is the best choice for Craig?

A. Gift the stock to a family member.
B. Sell the stock to a family member.
C. Use an exchange fund.
D. Sell the stock and transfer the proceeds to a charitable remainder trust.

103 UNIT 10 ANSWERS TO PRACTICE QUESTIONS

1. D. A bond ladder strategy is a relatively easy way to immunize a portfolio against interest rate risk. By holding many positions across the yield curve, the individual is diversified in the event that yields behave differently in one part of the curve than in another. The laddered portfolio will generally provide higher (not lower) yields than a portfolio consisting entirely of short-term bonds. Choice A describes the bond barbell strategy, not the bond ladder strategy.

2. A. Tax swaps generally take advantage of capital losses by selling bonds that have been devalued by rising interest rates.

3. C. Market timing is a type of active portfolio management.

4. D. Robert will make \$500 on the shares of ABC stock that he sells short, calculated as follows:
\$45.00 proceeds
– 40.00 cost
\$5.00 gain × 100 shares = \$500

5. B. Short selling involves the most risk to an investor because there is potentially no limit on the amount of loss. The loss to an investor when purchasing either a put or call option is limited to the amount of the premium paid for the option contract.

6. A. The client needs to deposit \$400, calculated as follows:

Value: \$40 × 100 shares	\$4,000
Loan amount: \$6,000 × .50	(3,000)
Actual equity	1,000
Required equity: \$4,000 × .35	(1,400)
Cash deposit needed	\$400

7. C. For HPR, we sum the cash flows and divide by the initial investment.
Profit on sale: \$100 – \$85 = \$15
Dividends: \$2.50 + \$3.60 = \$6.10
Margin account interest: 6% × 50% × \$85 × 2 (years) = \$5.10
HPR = (\$15 + \$6.10 – \$5.10) ÷ (50% × \$85) = 37.65%
or,
(\$30,000 – \$25,500 + \$750 + \$1,080 – \$1,530) ÷ \$12,750
\$4,800 ÷ \$12,750 = 37.65%

8. C. Margin call = debit balance ÷ (1 – maintenance margin) = (\$60 × 0.40) ÷ (1 – 0.35) = \$36.92.

9. A. A portfolio consisting of 30% bonds, 20% growth stocks, 40% blue-chip conservative stocks, and 10% cash is most representative of a growth and income investment objective.

10. C. Portfolio 3, comprised of 70% equities and 30% bonds, would be an appropriate allocation for a young couple with a moderate risk profile.

11. A. Portfolio 1 is the best choice for Patrick. Because he has recently retired, the portfolio should primarily provide income. In addition, his age necessitates a modest growth component to his portfolio. A portfolio consisting of 65% bonds, 30% stocks, and 5% money market is consistent with an income objective with low to moderate risk and a long-term time horizon.

12. A. Tactical asset allocation involves buying undervalued classes and selling overvalued classes.

13. B. The core and satellite approach is the best choice for Henry. Emerging markets and commodities may be used in the satellite portion of the portfolio. Index funds generally are used in a passive portfolio approach.

14. C. A market order does not reflect or restrict the price at which a security is excuted. A limit order limits the amount to be paid or received for securities. A limit order becomes a market order if the stock reaches or goes through the stop price. A stop limit order becomes a limit order if the stock hits or goes through the trigger price.

15. C. The best course of action for Craig is to use an exchange fund. This fund permits investors with concentrated portfolios to contribute the stock to the fund. In exchange, the investor receives a proportional interest in the fund. All of the other choices will require Craig to give up control of the proceeds.

103 UNIT 10 POST-STUDY CHECKLIST

- ☐ Can I explain how investors use strategic asset allocation to meet their investment objectives?
- ☐ Can I discuss the objectives of tactical asset allocation?
- ☐ Am I able to explain asset allocation and model portfolios?
- ☐ Can I describe the strategies investors use to manage a concentrated portfolio?
- ☐ Do I understand the importance of an investment policy statement as an integral part of the overall financial planning process?
- ☐ Can I explain and apply investment strategies such as market timing, indexing, buy-and-hold, and sector rotation?
- ☐ Am I able to discuss the various types of bond swaps and how they may be used by investors?
- ☐ Do I understand the types of formula investing such as dollar cost averaging; share averaging/averaging down; dividend reinvestment plans; and bond ladders, barbells, and bullets?
- ☐ Can I explain the use of margin and when an investor would be subject to a margin call?
- ☐ Can I explain the steps in short selling a security?
- ☐ Can I differentiate among the types of orders investors use when either buying or selling securities?
- ☐ Can I explain the core and satellite investment strategy?
- ☐ Do I know the difference between value and growth investing?

Am I able to define and understand the application of the following terms as they relate to investment planning?

- ☐ Asset allocation
- ☐ Averaging down
- ☐ Bond barbells
- ☐ Bond bullets
- ☐ Bond ladders
- ☐ Bond swapping
- ☐ Buy-and-hold
- ☐ Core and satellite
- ☐ Dividend reinvestment plans (DRIPs)
- ☐ Dollar cost averaging (DCA)
- ☐ Formula investing
- ☐ Good-till-canceled order
- ☐ Growth investing
- ☐ Indexing
- ☐ Intermarket spread swap
- ☐ Investment policy statement
- ☐ Leverage
- ☐ Limit order
- ☐ Margin
- ☐ Market order
- ☐ Market timing
- ☐ Mean-variance optimization
- ☐ Pure yield pickup swap
- ☐ Rate anticipation swap
- ☐ Rebalancing
- ☐ Replication
- ☐ Sector rotation
- ☐ Share averaging
- ☐ Short selling
- ☐ Stop limit order
- ☐ Stop order
- ☐ Strategic asset allocation
- ☐ Substitution swap
- ☐ Tactical asset allocation
- ☐ Tax swap
- ☐ Value investing

Case Study

Case studies are a principal part of the CFP® Certification Examination. The Allen case study below will allow you to become familiar with the presentation and layout of a case study. The questions and answers following this case study will give you a sampling of the Fundamentals and Ethical Considerations subject matter that may be tested on the exam.

The Allen case study will be presented throughout the 101 through 106 courses. Questions and answers presented in each course will focus on the particular subject matter of that course. After studying the Allen case in all six education courses, you should be well prepared for the 107 Financial Plan Development Course, a CFP Board requirement for all students matriculating in the education program after December 31, 2011.

These case study facts and the practice questions that follow will allow you to become familiar with case studies, which are found on the CFP® Exam. After completing this case study section, you will be required to complete the case study exam, which will present a different set of case study facts but will be of a similar format.

Case Study Approaches

Generally, there are two approaches you can use for case studies, the Case Facts Analysis Approach and the Question Review Approach.

Case Facts Analysis Approach

Read the case carefully and slowly, making sure that you pay attention to detail. Particularly note age, marital status, number of children and grandchildren, net worth, and income levels. These variables will give you a good idea regarding the key facts in the case and help you anticipate questions while you make notes. When a key topic is presented, make a mental or written note of that topic. When additional information is provided on that topic later in the case, a question regarding that topic usually appears unless the additional information negates the question.

Read each question and the answers provided. Answer the easy questions first, followed by the more complex questions. Calculation questions (e.g., probate estate, education funding, capital needs analysis, minimum distributions, and mortgage qualification) can be time consuming. Go back to them later.

Question Review Approach

Read the questions quickly. Make notes. Answer any questions that do not require reading the case, then read the case only looking for the answers to the questions asked.

Follow these steps:

1. Read the last line of the question.
2. Make notes.
3. Answer all questions that can be answered without reading the case. Record your answers.
4. Read the case to answer the questions that involve specific case facts. Record your answers.
5. Make sure all questions are answered.
6. Review the answers.

Note that this case is for practice purposes only. For your course 103 case study quiz, please download the case study facts available via your case study quiz launch page in your 103 course.

Michael and Marie Allen Case Study

Michael and Marie Allen have come to you, a financial planner, for help in developing a plan to accomplish their financial goals. You are a Series 7 general securities representative and hold insurance licenses for life and health insurance and variable contracts.

The Allens have been reading about various financial planning services and want to consider having a "fee-only" based arrangement with you. They ask if you are a "fee-only" planner and if you can work with them on that basis. They have great hope for their future; however, after having a conversation about investing with one of their neighbors, they have recently realized that they are not as financially comfortable as they would like to be at this point in their lives. Assume today is January 1, 2018.

Personal Background and Information

The Allens

Michael and Marie have been married for 12 years. They have two children, Max and Sam. Michael has a son, Alex, and a daughter, Abby, from a previous marriage.

Michael Allen (Age 45)

Michael is a vice president of Asher Bank and Trust. He has been employed there for 12 years and has an annual salary of $70,000.

Marie Allen (Age 40)

Until Sam was born, Marie was an architect with a local design firm. She has been uncertain when she would resume her career until recently when the top architecture firm in the city, Wright and Associates, approached her about joining the firm as a part-time independent contractor. Marie has a high level of skill using architectural design software, and Wright and Associates wants her to help with high-end design projects. Marie's annual earnings from the part-time work are expected to be at least $50,000. Marie is excited to accept the position because she feels she has the time with Sam now attending school full days.

Family

- Alex is 20 years old and is a junior at State University on a partial scholarship, 500 miles from Michael and Marie. When not boarding at school, he lives with his mother, Nicole. During the summers, Alex works at Asher Bank and Trust as an intern and lives with Michael and Marie. Nicole and Michael have agreed that Nicole may claim Alex as a dependent.
- Abby, 16 years old, lives in another state with her mother and attends public school. She has aspirations to study at The Juilliard School upon graduation and has applied for a scholarship. She is also Nicole's dependent for income tax purposes.
- Max is 10 years old and attends Woodridge Academy, a private school. He plays the trombone in the school band and attends band camp every summer. Max also plays on the school's basketball team.
- Samantha (Sam), 7 years old, is in second grade at Woodridge Academy. She meets with a private tutor once a week to get help with her reading skills.

- Carol, Michael's mother, died within the past month at the age of 70, and her estate is currently in probate. She had been in poor health and living with Michael and Marie the past two years and had been using her investments to meet her living expenses. Michael is the sole beneficiary and executor of Carol's estate.
- Grant and Rose, Marie's parents, are in good health and have agreed to pay for Max and Sam's private school tuition through the 8th grade. They are retired and travel year-round. Marie is their only child. Marie mentions to you that her parents want to know if there are any gift tax consequences for them paying the tuition for Max and Sam. They are also interested in making additional gifts for education, and Marie asks you what she should tell her parents.
- Nicole, Michael's ex-wife, who lives in another state, is an attorney for the Department of Justice. There is currently no child support agreement for Abby.

In addition to addressing their specific goals and concerns shared in your meetings, the Allens have asked you to comment and offer recommendations on any area of their current finances you feel has a weakness or vulnerability or presents an opportunity for improvement in reaching their goals.

Economic Information

The Allens expect medical inflation to be 5% annually and the annual general inflation rate to average 3% over both the short and long terms. The present average interest rate on their credit cards is approximately 16%. The risk-free rate is 3.25%, and the Allens' required rate of return on investments is 8%.

Current mortgage rates are 6% for 30-year fixed mortgages and 5.5% for 15-year fixed mortgages. Closing costs will approximate 3% of any mortgage refinanced and will be paid from separate funds. Michael and Marie feel this is an opportune time to refinance their home mortgage. Given their goals, they have asked you to evaluate available mortgage options and make a recommendation. Their credit score is good, but they are concerned about whether they will be able to meet some of the standard financial ratio tests required to qualify for a new mortgage.

Insurance Information

Health Insurance

The entire family is insured under Michael's company plan, which is a major medical plan with a $500 per person deductible, an 80/20 coinsurance clause, and a family annual stop-loss limit of $2,500. Michael's employer pays 100% of the health insurance premium.

Life Insurance

Michael has a group term life insurance policy with a face amount of $60,000 provided by his employer. Michael is not a highly compensated employee. The policy beneficiary is Marie. The premium of $9 per month is paid by his employer. The Section 79 table cost per $1,000 of protection is $0.15 for Michael's age.

Recently, one of their neighbors, who was the same age as Marie and had three very young children, died prematurely. After the Allens saw firsthand the financial stress of the surviving spouse, they decided to have you create a life insurance needs analysis for them. They want to know what type of information you need from them to help you prepare your life insurance recommendations.

Disability Insurance

Michael has a private disability income insurance policy with an own occupation definition of disability and a 30-day elimination period. Based on the policy's provisions, in the event Michael is totally disabled, he will receive a monthly benefit of $2,700 until his normal retirement age, defined as his retirement age under the Social Security Act on the date of his disability. The annual premium is $761 and is fully paid by Michael. Michael has asked you to explain the tax treatment of the disability insurance benefits in the event he is disabled.

Homeowners Insurance

The Allens have a HO-3 policy with dwelling extension and replacement cost on contents. The policy has a $1,000 deductible. The annual premium is $950.

Automobile Insurance

The Allens have automobile liability and bodily injury coverage of $100,000/$300,000/$100,000. They have both comprehensive coverage (other than collision) and collision. The deductibles are $250 (comprehensive) and $500 (collision). The annual premium is $900.

The Allens are not entirely happy with their auto and homeowners insurance carrier due to a dispute over hail damage last year. Michael has asked you what you think of their carrier and if you can get the Allens a better rate on their coverages.

Investment Information

The only investments the Allens have outside of the retirement plan are the ABC stock inherited by Marie from her grandmother in 2017 and the college fund certificates of deposit.

The Allens have had little investment experience but consider themselves to have a moderate risk tolerance (7 on a scale of 10), given their ages and long-term goals.

ABC stock has paid a steady dividend of $3.50 per share. The dividend is expected to grow at a constant rate of 5% per year into the foreseeable future. Given the Allens' required rate of return, they have asked you to determine if the stock is overpriced or underpriced in the secondary market.

The Allens are concerned that ABC stock may substantially decline in price in the near future. They want to know which investment strategies would best protect their position in ABC over the next 60 days. Also, they have asked you to determine the tax that would be incurred if they choose to sell the stock at the current FMV.

Income Tax Considerations

Michael and Marie tell you that they are in the 15% federal income tax bracket. They pay $1,320 annually in state and local income taxes. The Allens want to know the income tax implications of Marie returning to work as an independent contractor. The majority of Marie's work will be done at home, and the Allens are currently remodeling a guest bedroom as office space for Marie. Marie has asked if there are any tax benefits associated with maintaining a home office.

The Allens have also asked you if there are any income tax consequences related to the life insurance and health insurance for which Michael's employer pays the premiums.

Retirement Information

Michael wants to retire at age 62 with income equal to 80% of his preretirement income. He expects to receive Social Security benefits of $24,000 (in today's dollars) for himself and $12,000 for Marie (in today's dollars) at full retirement age 67. The Allens are aware that Social Security retirement benefits are reduced if claimed prior to their full retirement age, but they have asked you to determine the approximate benefit if Michael retires at age 62. With Marie returning to work, she may earn a higher benefit on her own work record.

The bank offers a Section 401(k) plan in which Michael is an active participant. The bank matches contributions dollar for dollar up to 3% of Michael's salary. Michael currently defers 3% of his salary.

The Allens want to know the amount of required capital, after considering Social Security, to support their retirement goal.

Marie wants to know what type of retirement plan would allow her to contribute the most for retirement on a tax-favored basis if her work with Wright and Associates generates sufficient income.

Education Information

Max is 10 years old and currently attending fifth grade at Woodridge Academy, which he will attend through high school. Michael and Marie have $2,500 in CDs that they contribute to once a year ($500 each year) for Max. This account will be used for college and is in Max's name.

Samantha (Sam) is 7 years old. She is in second grade at Woodridge Academy and will attend the academy through high school. Michael and Marie have $1,000 in CDs to which they contribute once a year ($500 each year) for Sam. This account will be used for college and is in Sam's name.

Michael and Marie invested in CDs for Max and Sam's college educations; the CDs are owned by Michael and Marie. The rate of return on this college fund is 2%, and the current balance is $15,000. Michael and Marie would also like to be able to send their children to school for five years instead of the traditional four years. The extra year could be used to pursue a graduate degree.

The current cost of college (including room, board, tuition, and books) is $15,000 per year per child. They expect their children to start college at the age of 18. The Allens expect an educational CPI of 5%.

To this point, the Allens have had limited resources to save for college for the children. They intend to assist Alex and Abby the best they can out of current cash flows and want to know the best way to do so from a tax perspective and what other college funding resources may be available. Additionally, they would like to know the amount of annual savings required to provide for college for Max and Sam. The Allens are open to your ideas regarding any investment alternatives they should consider for their existing college savings currently invested in certificates of deposit.

Gifts, Estates, Trusts, and Will Information

Michael's will leaves everything to Marie conditioned on a six-month survivorship clause, otherwise, equally in separate trusts for the four children.

Marie does not have a will. The Allens want to know the next step to take to begin basic estate planning and what areas are critical to include in the plan at this time.

Michael has questions regarding several assets in Carol's estate:

- A nonqualified variable annuity consisting of an initial investment of $50,000 made in 1995. The current value of the annuity is $126,000, and Michael is the sole primary beneficiary. If Michael chooses to take the entire $126,000 in a lump-sum distribution to help refinance the mortgage, what would be the tax consequence?
- A universal life insurance policy with a face amount of $100,000. The policy had a cash surrender value of $18,000, and Carol had paid total premiums of $15,000. Carol had elected death benefit option B at the time the policy was issued. Michael wants to know the amount he will receive from the policy after taxes.

- A nonqualified fixed annuity in which she had invested a total of $40,000. This contract was purchased in 1997 and has a current value of $93,000. Michael is the sole beneficiary. He decided to take the life income option on this portion of his inheritance to help out with the entertainment section of the budget. Michael's life expectancy is 35 years, and he is to receive $500 per month for the rest of his life. He has asked how much of this monthly distribution is taxable.
- A Roth IRA with an account balance of $50,000 into which contributions of $30,000 had been made over the past 10 years. Michael would like to make this account part of their retirement savings and has asked about his options regarding this account and the respective income tax treatment of those options.
- A mutual fund valued at $30,000 at the time of Carol's death. Carol invested $10,000 initially in the mutual fund, and the fund had generated $5,000 in dividends and capital gains (all reinvested in the fund) over her 10-year holding period. Michael is considering liquidating the fund once ownership is established in his name and wants to know the tax consequences of this transaction.
- Michael also has asked you to brief him on the general responsibilities he has as executor of his mother's estate.

STATEMENT OF CASH FLOWS Michael and Marie Allen For the Year 2018			
INFLOWS			
Salary and Schedule C Income			
Salary—Michael	$70,000		
Schedule C Income—Marie	50,000		
Total Salary and Schedule C Income		**$120,000**	
Investment income			
Interest (taxable)	$900		
Dividends	150		
Total investment income		**$1,050**	
TOTAL INFLOWS			**$121,050**
OUTFLOWS			
Savings			
Reinvestment interest/dividends	$1,050		
Section 401(k) plan elective contribution	2,100		
College fund CDs	1,000		
Total savings		**$4,150**	
Ordinary living expenses			
Food	$6,000		
Clothing	3,600		
Child care	600		
Entertainment	1,814		
Utilities	3,600		
Auto maintenance	2,000		
Church contributions	3,500		
Total ordinary living expenses		**$21,114**	

Other payments			
Credit card payments[1]	$960		
Mortgage payments[2]	21,954		
Boat loan[3]	3,040		
Total payments		**$25,954**	
Insurance premiums			
Automobile	$900		
Disability	761		
Homeowners	950		
Total insurance premiums		**$2,611**	
Tuition and education expenses		**$1,000**	
Taxes			
Federal FICA and withholding	$22,855		
State and city income tax	1,320		
Property tax (principal residence)	1,000		
Total Taxes		**$25,175**	
TOTAL OUTFLOWS			**$80,004**
NET CASH FLOW (SURPLUS)			**$41,046**

[1] Credit card payments: Principal $345; Interest $615
[2] Mortgage payments: Principal $1,234; Interest $20,720
[3] Boat loan payments: Principal $1,493; Interest $1,547

STATEMENT OF FINANCIAL POSITION
Michael and Marie Allen
January 1, 2018

ASSETS[1]		
Liquid assets		
JT Checking account	$1,500	
JT Savings account	1,000	
Total liquid assets		$2,500
Investments		
S2 ABC stock (100 shares)[2]	$13,000	
JT Certificates of deposit (college fund)	15,000	
S1 Section 401(k) vested plan balance	43,000	
Total investments		$71,000
JT Personal real estate – residence[3]		$250,000
Other personal use assets		
JT Automobiles	$15,000	
JT Boat	20,000	
JT Jewelry	13,500	
JT Furniture/household	60,000	
Total other personal use assets		$108,500
TOTAL ASSETS		**$432,000**
LIABILITIES[4] AND NET WORTH		
Current liabilities		
JT Credit cards		$4,000
Long-term liabilities		
JT Mortgage on residence[5]	197,888	
JT Boat loan	13,559	
Total long-term liabilities		$211,447
TOTAL LIABILITIES		**$215,447**
ALLEN FAMILY NET WORTH		**$216,553**
TOTAL LIABILITIES AND NET WORTH		**$432,000**

S1 – Michael Allen; S2 – Marie Allen; JT – jointly owned by Michael and Marie Allen

Other notes to the Statement of Financial Position:

1 Assets are stated at fair market value.

2 The ABC stock was inherited from Marie's grandmother on November 15, 2017. Her grandmother originally paid $20,000 for it on October 31, 2017. The fair market value at her grandmother's death was $12,000.

3 The replacement value of the Allen's home is $225,000.

4 Liabilities are stated at principal only.

5 Note that some statements of financial position may show the current year's mortgage liability as a current liability. However, the total liability may also be listed as a long-term liability, as done in this case.

Case Study Practice Questions

1. Given the following historical return information for ABC stock:

Year	Annual Rate of Return
1	12%
2	18%
3	–10%
4	–14%
5	23%

Calculate the standard deviation for this series of returns.

A. 5.18%
B. 5.80%
C. 16.77%
D. 25.82%

2. The Allens are considering purchasing an AAA rated 10-year bond with a coupon rate of 7.75% paid semiannually. The bond is currently trading for $987.50 in the secondary market. What are both the current yield (CY) and the yield to maturity (YTM) of this bond?

A. CY = 7.85%; YTM = 7.93%
B. CY = 7.75%; YTM = 8.26%
C. CY = 3.88%; YTM = 8.54%
D. CY = 7.85%; YTM = 3.97%

3. Michael's Section 401(k) plan has experienced returns over the last 5 years of –10%, 15.55%, –5.87%, 12.75%, and 14.85%. Calculate both the arithmetic and geometric means for this series of returns.

A. Arithmetic mean = 5.45%; geometric mean = 4.85%
B. Arithmetic mean = 6.91%; geometric mean = 8.57%
C. Arithmetic mean = 4.85%; geometric mean = 5.34%
D. Arithmetic mean = 11.80%; geometric mean = 26.71%

4. Assume the Allens may acquire 100 shares of ABC stock with a current market price of $130 per share. If ABC stock subsequently undergoes a 2-for-1 stock split, how many shares of ABC stock will they own at what new market price per share?

A. 200 shares @ $65 per share
B. 50 shares @ $260 per share
C. 400 shares @ $32.50 per share
D. 200 shares @ $195 per share

5. Michael is considering repositioning his Section 401(k) plan assets into the asset allocation portfolio. Over the past year, the portfolio produced a 14.50% return with a beta of 1.15. The risk-free rate is 3.25%, and the overall market returned 12.65%. Based on this information, calculate Jensen's alpha and determine if the fund manager added any value to the portfolio.

A. Alpha = 0.44%; the fund manager underperformed the market by 2.81%
B. Alpha = 1.15%; the fund manager outperformed the market by 1.15%
C. Alpha = –0.29%; the fund manager underperformed the market by 0.29%
D. Alpha = 0.44%; the fund manager outperformed the market by 0.44%

6. ABC stock has a current market price of $130 and has paid a steady annual dividend of $3.50 per share. The dividend is expected to grow at a constant rate of 5% per year into the foreseeable future. If the Allens have a required rate of return of 8%, calculate the intrinsic value of the stock using the constant growth dividend discount model and determine if the stock is overpriced or underpriced in the secondary market.
   A. $122.50; underpriced
   B. $116.67; overpriced
   C. $122.50; overpriced
   D. $140.40; underpriced

7. ABC stock is subject to all of the following risks EXCEPT
   A. default risk
   B. market risk
   C. business risk
   D. financial risk

8. The Allens are considering purchasing LAC stock based on a stock tip from their brother-in-law, Jack. Jack has provided them with the following information:

   Current dividend: $2.50
   Expected dividend growth rate for years 1 and 2: 8%
   Expected dividend growth rate for years 3+: 10%

   Based on the information provided, what is the intrinsic value of LAC stock if the Allens have a required rate of return for this investment of 14%?
   A. $41.67
   B. $66.37
   C. $67.50
   D. $123.59

9. The Allens are concerned that ABC stock may substantially decline in price in the near future. Which of the following option strategies would best protect the Allens' position in ABC stock? (Assume they own 100 shares currently valued at $130 per share and all options will expire within 60 days.)
   A. Sell one call option with an exercise price of $150 for $0.50 per share
   B. Sell one put option with an exercise price of $120 for $2.95 per share
   C. Buy one put option with an exercise price of $120 for $3.00 per share
   D. Buy one call option with an exercise price of $100 for $38.25 per share

10. Based on the desire for Michael to retire at age 62, the Allens should consider preparing a comprehensive investment strategy. Which of the following steps should be included in the investment planning process?
    1. Determine the appropriate level of risk and return based on their risk tolerance and required return.
    2. Match the appropriate investment vehicles to meet their needs and objectives.
    3. Prepare a complete and thorough investment policy statement detailing their financial goals and objectives.
    4. Review and examine their tax situation and personal financial statements.

    A. 3 only
    B. 2 and 4
    C. 1, 2, and 4
    D. 1, 2, 3, and 4

Case Study Practice Questions Answers

1. **C.** The standard deviation for this historical series of return for ABC stock is 16.77%.

   Using the HP 10bII/HP 10bII+

Keystrokes	Display
[■] [C ALL]	0.0000
12 [Σ+]	1.0000
18 [Σ+]	2.0000
10 [+/–][Σ+]	3.0000
14 [+/–][Σ+]	4.0000
23 [Σ+]	5.0000
[■] [Sx, Sy]	16.769, or 16.77%

2. **A.** The current yield (CY) for the bond equals 7.85%, calculated as follows: CY = ($1,000 × 7.75%) ÷ $987.50 = 7.85%. The yield to maturity (YTM) calculation: PV = –987.50; FV = 1,000; PMT = 38.75 (1,000 × 7.75% ÷ 2); n = 20 (10 × 2); solve for i = 3.9667 × 2 = 7.9334, or 7.93%.

3. **A.** Arithmetic mean: [(–0.10 + 0.155 – 0.0587 + 0.1275 + 0.1485) ÷ 5] = 0.0545, or 5.45%. Geometric mean: PV = –1; FV = (1 – 0.10)(1 + 0.155)(1 – 0.0587)(1 + 0.1275)(1 + 0.1485) = 1.2671; n = 5; solve for i = 4.85, or 4.85%.

4. **A.** In a 2-for-1 stock split, the number of shares double, so the Allens will own 200 (100 × 2) shares of ABC stock. The total value of their stock holding will not change; however, the stock price will be reduced by one-half. Therefore, the new market price of ABC stock will be $65 ($130 ÷ 2) per share.

5. **D.** Jensen's alpha for this portfolio is 0.44%, calculated as follows: 14.50% – [3.25% + (12.65% – 3.25%) 1.15] = 0.44%. A positive alpha indicates the portfolio manager outperformed the market on a risk-adjusted basis.

6. **C.** Using the constant growth dividend discount model, the intrinsic value of ABC stock is $122.50, calculated as follows: ($3.50 × 1.05%) ÷ (8% – 5%) = 3.6750 ÷ 0.03 = $122.50. When the intrinsic value of the stock is less than the current market price, the stock is deemed to be overpriced in the secondary market.

7. **A.** Common stock is subject to a variety of risks including, but not limited to, business risk, financial risk, and market risk. However, common stock is not subject to default risk. Default risk is the potential inability of a debt issuer to make timely interest and principal repayments.

8. **B.** Using the multistage growth dividend discount model, calculate LAC stock's intrinsic value:

Step 1: Compute the value of each future dividend until the growth rate stabilizes (Years 1–2).

D_1 = \$2.50 × 1.08 = \$2.70
D_2 = \$2.70 × 1.08 = \$2.92

Step 2: Use the constant growth dividend discount model to compute the remaining intrinsic value of the stock at the beginning of the year when the dividend growth rate stabilizes (Year 3).

D_3 = \$2.92 × 1.10 = \$3.21

V = \$3.21 ÷ (0.14 – 0.10) = \$80.25

Step 3: Use the uneven cash flow method to solve for the net present (intrinsic) value of the stock.

CF_0 = \$0
CF_1 = \$2.70
CF_2 = \$2.92 + \$80.25
I/YR = 14%
Solve for NPV = \$66.37

The intrinsic value of the stock is \$66.37.

9. **C.** If the Allens are bearish, they will either sell a call or buy a put. In this particular case, the Allens should purchase one put option with an exercise price of \$120 for \$3 per share. The total cost of the put option, excluding transaction costs, is \$300 (\$3 × 100). Each put option contract gives the holder the right to sell 100 shares of the underlying stock at the exercise price within a specified time frame.

10. **D.** Their financial plan should include all of these steps. Investment planning requires examining the client's financial situation to determine if the client's goals and objectives can be met while simultaneously meeting any investment needs and requirements. In order to do an effective job of investment counseling, the advisor should examine and review the client's financial goals and time horizon, risk tolerance and risk exposure, tax situation, liquidity and marketability needs, and personal financial statements.

Index

Notes

Notes

Notes

Notes

Notes

Notes

Notes

Notes

Notes

Notes

Notes

Notes

Notes

Notes